Agit-prop to Theatre Workshop

Political playscripts 1930–50

Agit-prop *to* Theatre Workshop

edited by **Howard Goorney** *and* **Ewan MacColl**

MANCHESTER UNIVERSITY PRESS

Published by Manchester University Press,
Oxford Road, Manchester, M13 9PL, UK
and
51 Washington Street, Dover, NH 03802, USA

British Library Cataloguing in Publication Data
Agit-prop to Theatre Workshop: political playscripts 1930–50.
  1. English drama—20th century
  I. Goorney, Howard   II. MacColl, Ewan
  822'912'08   PR1272

Library of Congress Cataloging in Publication Data
applied for

ISBN 0–7190–1762–9 *hardback*

**PERFORMING RIGHTS in all these plays are fully reserved,
and application should be made, before rehearsals begin, to
Manchester University Press, Oxford Road, Manchester M13 9PL**

Photoset in Linotron Plantin with Syntax
by Northern Phototypesetting Co., Bolton

Printed in Great Britain
at the Alden Press, Oxford

Contents

List of illustrations

Preface

Little has been written about the Workers' Theatre Movement of the thirties. My original intention was to help fill the gap by collecting and editing material used by left-wing theatre groups in the Manchester area during that period. I soon discovered that very little had survived the passing of the years. My own involvement from 1938 onwards enabled me to piece together a complete script of *Last Edition* – a living newspaper produced in 1940, and Joan Littlewood was able to come up with her own handwritten script of *John Bullion*. These, plus the American Laboratory Theatre's *Newsboy* and some mass declamations from the late thirties were the only complete scripts available. It was understandable that no written record of the early agit-prop sketches could be traced. They dealt with day-to-day political issues and were by their very nature ephemeral – long-forgotten notes on bits of paper, if written down at all. However, it was disappointing to find that typed scripts from the late thirties had not been kept by those involved, including myself. It became necessary for me to alter my original conception, and I hope I have succeeded in turning my initial disappointment to advantage. Ewan MacColl's early plays written for Theatre Workshop in the 1940's had a direct link in theatrical style with the pre-war agit-prop sketches and living newspapers and he was willing to take on the task of tracing this development. His involvement with the political groups in Manchester and Salford from the late twenties has enabled him to present a personal first-hand account over a much longer period than I would have been able to do.

Lack of space faced us with the choice of including either *Last Edition* or *The Other Animals*. As it happened, Ewan had reservations about the former. Looking at it over forty years on he felt that it contained, as well as much exciting theatre, 'long tedious passages of indigested flab'.

However, it did represent a big step forward from the early agit-prop and it translated into actual production many of the ideas and theatre concepts of the preceding years. It was therefore decided to include extracts from the script.

Last Edition stands as a political statement of its own day, but it is a sad comment on our time that the theme of the three post-war plays – unemployment, the threat of The Bomb, and the use of political torture – are as relevant today as when they were written forty years ago.

Johnny Noble, *Uranium 235*, and *The Other Animals* have an 'epic' quality appropriate to their themes – a form of theatre with great potential which socialist theatre groups in this country have, on the whole, failed to explore. Of course no group in Britain has the resources to emulate the Epic theatre of Piscator in pre-war Germany, with his use of slide projections, moving film, animated cartoons and a double treadmill stage, and this may be not altogether a bad thing. Too much technology can swamp the actor – it can also go wrong, and often did, as Piscator himself admits. However, Theatre Workshop, ploughing a lone furrow and with no subsidy, was able to tour these plays extensively, so their essential requirements in terms of lighting and sound-equipment should be well within the resources of the larger and more established groups. *Johnny Noble* and *Uranium 235* are adaptable to any size of stage area and were played in a great variety of venues, from tiny stages in the Lake District to some of the biggest theatres in Sweden. *The Other Animals*, on the other hand, does require full stage facilities and enough space to accommodate the area of the cage.

But socialist theatre can take many forms. We are beginning to see, as political tensions increase, agit-prop groups again taking to the streets in protest against the injustices in our society and the threat of nuclear holocaust, giving a new meaning to the term 'non-violent direct action'. The Narrator in *Johnny Noble* speaks in the 1940s of '. . . days that linger in the memory like a bad taste in the mouth. Come back with us a dozen years or so. . . . Here is a man of those years, a man without hope, without work, a man burdened with time.'

Only now there is no need to go back. The wheel has come full circle. . . .

Introduction

The evolution of a revolutionary theatre style

manifesto

THE THEATRE must face up to the problems of its time; it cannot ignore the poverty and human suffering which increases every day. It cannot, with sincerity, close its eyes to the disasters of its time. Means Test suicides, wars, fascism and the million sordid accidents reported in the daily press. If the theatre of to-day would reach the heights achieved four thousand years ago in Greece and four hundred years ago in Elizabethan England it must face up to such problems. To those who say that such affairs are not the concern of the theatre or that the theatre should confine itself to treading in the paths of ' beauty ' and ' dignity ', we would say "Read Shakespeare, Marlowe, Webster, Sophocles, Aeschylus, Aristophanes, Calderon, Moliere, Lope-de-Vega, Schiller and the rest." The Theatre Union says that in facing up to the problems of our time and by intensifying our efforts to get at the essence of reality, we are also attempting to solve our own theatrical problems both technical and ideological. By doing this we are ensuring the future of the theatre, a future which will not be born in the genteel atmosphere of retirement and seclusion, but rather in the clash and turmoil of the battles between the oppressors and the oppressed.

theatre union

THE THEATRE OF THE PEOPLE

Each new development in the theatre, however slight that development may be, makes it necessary to evaluate and re-evaluate the immediate past, a process often beset with difficulties. The remote past presents fewer problems since, so to speak, it offers a bird's-eye view of history and allows us to achieve a semblance of objectivity. The point is admirably demonstrated by television where a programme dealing with ancient Egypt or the descent of man presents few pitfalls. When it comes to passing judgement on the ancient world even the most opiniated pundit contrives to appear like Solomon, all cool deliberation and wisdom. With so few facts to deal with, banalities can be made to resonate like eternal truths. The immediate past has to be approached with a good deal more circumspection, for the road which leads to it is cluttered with an embarrassing array of facts, some of which may be mutually exclusive. The problem is to know which to select in order to give a 'balanced report'.

This 'report' does not constitute a history of Theatre Workshop: Howard Goorney's *The Theatre Workshop Story* has already provided us with the main outline of that history. It is an attempt to bring into focus certain of Theatre Workshop's stylistic ideas, to show how they originated and how they influenced the company's development. It is, above all, a personal statement by one who was closely associated with those developments and who was, to some extent, responsible for some of the ideas.

Theatre Workshop was formed in 1945 and, to all intents and purposes, ceased to exist in 1973. In the course of those years it underwent a series of transformations. It would be incorrect to regard its history as a single unbroken line of development or even as a smooth cycle of development and decay. Up until the early fifties, however, Theatre Workshop can be seen to have been fairly consistent in its efforts to create a revolutionary working-class theatre. If that aim was not specifically formulated in the theatre's earliest days, it certainly existed as a less than nebulous idea from the beginning. That beginning is, as far as the editors of this book are concerned, the period which opens the decade of the thirties.

Increasingly, sociologists and historians are preoccupied with the thirties; film-makers and dramatists in search of exotic backgrounds recreate the period in the terms of a *Bonnie and Clyde*, costume departments of television companies ransack their wardrobes for plus-fours and celluloid collars while the cobbled streets of northern mill towns become advertisers' clichés.

It was, in fact, a decade in which enormous changes in the way of living were affecting millions of working people. It was also a period in which many of the ideas and practices of the nineteenth century managed to find a foothold. Indeed the new and the old were to be found existing side by side in comfortable symbiosis. Techniques of mass-production, the conveyor-belt and the assembly-line were being introduced into carefully selected industries but, at the same time, most working-class families took it for granted that at least one son would learn a trade and become a craftsman. Monopoly capitalism had arrived with gigantic enterprises like Imperial Chemical Industries but, if you lived in a city like Manchester, Leeds or Liverpool, the chances were that your milk would be delivered to you by a local farmer or farm-hand riding a horse-drawn float and serving the milk from a churn. Your corner-shop still sold bread which had been baked on the premises and factory-processed cheese was still regarded as an exotic culinary invention.

Children's games and pastimes reflected perfectly the Janus-like visage of the time. They were, on the whole, little changed from the games which had been played down the centuries, though cigarette-cards, those attractive symbols of commercial competition, had been added to the games repertoire and young girls made swings from straw ropes salvaged from orange-boxes and thrown over the arms of lamp-posts, universal symbols of the age of cast iron. These, and the decorating of flagstones with coloured chalks, were innovations effortlessly assimilated into the lives of the post-war generation of children. Perhaps the most significant symbol of the times was the 'steely', the steel ball-bearing which had become an emperor in the game of marbles. For the rest, teenage youths still played chuck-stones on any available piece of waste ground and girls played elabo-rate ball-bouncing games or, in the days leading up to May the first, would go from house to house carrying a broomstick maypole hung with coloured paper streamers, singing a song in honour of the season. Sometimes on rainy days a group of children would put on a concert in a neighbour's house where, on payment of a piece of broken pottery or a shard of coloured glass, one could hear songs and watch improvised dances and imitations of Charlie Chaplin.

If all this sounds somewhat idyllic then it is time to remind the reader that the past is not unlike one of those king-size sandwiches in which an occasional delicious morsel is concealed in great gobbets of plastic filling. The fact is that the streets through which those little girls carried their broomstick maypoles were mean streets, foul places and whether they were in Manchester, Glasgow, Leeds, Liverpool or Salford no child should have been condemned to grow up in them. Most of them had been built to house the hordes of dispossessed cottagers driven from their homes by successive poor-law acts in the nineteenth century. They were slum-built monuments to the rapacity and inhumanity of those who built them. Those who lived in them had long been familiar with poverty, war, strikes, lockouts, betrayals and defeats. Now they were beginning to experience unemployment on a scale hitherto unknown.

The betrayal and collapse of the general strike in 1926 did incalculable harm to the working-class movement and the demoralization which followed in its wake was still evident at the beginning of the thirties. The Labour Party which still regarded itself as the party of the working class tended to confine its activities to electioneering and skirmishes with the extreme Left. Its lack of a theoretical base had left it unprepared for the savage blows directed against the working class in the course of the deepening economic crisis. The Communist Party, though much more in touch with events, was a very small organisation and was outlawed by both the Labour Party and the T.U.C. The Socialist Party of Great Britain (S.P.G.B.) and the Social Democratic Federation (S.D.F.), each with a handful of members, managed to make themselves heard from time to time as did the Anarchists and Syndicalists, although most of the militant Left tended to regard them as curious survivals from an earlier age. A common meeting ground for members of all the Left organisations as well as for rationalists and freethinkers were the Sunday afternoon debates organised by the Clarion Clubs. These generally took place in a local restaurant and would often attract eighty or a hundred men and a sprinkling of women who would listen and support one or the other of the speakers debating evolutionary theory or Edward Clod's *History of Creation*, or *Colonization and Christianity* or Marx's *Civil War in France*.

And as the seasons came and went, the queues outside the Labour exchanges grew longer and longer, a coalition government was formed, the means test was introduced, the navy mutinied at Invergordon and the hunger-marches began. Those who lived through those years often recall them with a sigh. Ah, the good old days! And yet they didn't exactly offer the average worker a rich full life. For the three million unemployed they were days of despair. For an unemployed youth living in Salford in 1930 the options were, to say the least, limited. Nevertheless the days had to be got through somehow; presupposing that you signed on at the 'broo' at, say, 9 a.m., you still had some fourteen or fifteen hours to dispose of. A number of alternative activities were open to you:

You could call at the library and read the newspapers or you could study there, provided that you knew how to study.

Weather permitting you could go to the public park and lie on the sour grass or sleep on a park-bench. If your friends were unemployed too, then you could do these things together.

From ten o'clock in the morning you could, on payment of a modest threepence, find refuge in the darkness of one of the new super-cinemas.

In the evening, another threepence would get you into 'the Jig', a notorious dance hall situated at the Oldfield Road end of Liverpool Street.

Almost directly opposite there was Hyndman Hall, also known as The Workers' Arts Club. There, threepence would get you a game of billiards or snooker on the solitary table which occupied most of the ground-floor bar-room.

If it was a Saturday or Thursday evening you could spend a 'bob' on a 'hop' (a shilling on a dance) in the first-floor public room or, if it was the second Saturday in the month you could attend a dance-cum-social there.

You could, of course, go up to the top-floor gym where you could stand in as a sparring-partner for some budding fighter without paying anything at all.

If you were totally without money and lacked the inclination to punch and be punched then you could stand at the end of the bar on the ground floor and listen to the pensioned-off warriors arguing the pros and cons of Volney's *Ruins of Empires* or Tom Paine's *Rights of Man*.

These debates were, at times, as entertaining and dramatic as any theatrical presentation. The debaters, rarely numbering more than eight or ten men, would sit in a rough semicircle midway between the billiard-table and the bar. The central figure of the group, the pivot as it were, was Jimmy Tillbrook, a huge mountain of a man who would sit there in his specially built windsor chair like a monarch surrounded by vassal kings. From time to time he would clear his throat and the discussion would cease for a moment so that his heavy breathing and the click of billiard-balls would dominate the silence as he prepared to pass judgement on this or that opinion. He carried a small volume of Proudhon's *Philosopy of Poverty* from which he would, at times, read aloud in a low rumbling voice. From another pocket he would some-times laboriously extract a slim copy of Kant's *Critique of Pure Reason* which he would hold up in front of his companions while he slowly stared each one of them down. When he felt that they were sufficiently intimidated he would lower his book and, tapping gently upon its cover with a forefinger the size of an overfilled pork sausage, he would make his pronouncement. The smallest of his gestures was loaded with drama, the slow turn of that enormous head with its cascade of chins, the lifting of the hand holding the pint of Tetley's mild-and-bitter, the deliberate exploration of his pockets leading to the majestic flourish of his voluminous silk handkerchief were all actions which gave the impression of having been rehearsed to the point of perfection. I cannot believe that I was the only spectator there who experienced an almost overwhelming compulsion to applaud.

This is not to say that the Workers' Arts Club discussions were one-man performances. They were not. There were other fine performers; Jock Smiley, for example, an unemployed iron-moulder from Falkirk who amused himself and others by baiting Jack Williams, a mercurial Welshman who worked as a maintenance engineer at a local cotton mill and who was given to quoting the *Rubaiyát of Omar Khayyám* and selected passages from Shakespeare's tragedies. Smiley, who had been a youthful disciple of the Scottish Marxist, John MacLean, suspected Williams of holding orthodox Labour Party views. Orthodoxy was, in Smiley's opinion, the worst kind of heresy and he felt obliged to belabour Williams with quotations from Marx and Engels and with some of Burns' satirical poems. In full flight he was a formidable opponent. Though physically small he had an enormous voice and his knowledge of Shakespeare was prodigious. Ridicule was his métier, it became him and he could use it as a rapier or as a bludgeon. There was something horribly fascinating about the way he would use lengthy passages from the bard to reduce Williams before finishing him off with one of the high-kilted pieces from Burns' *Merry Muses*. Jack Williams' face would flame with embarrassment while Smiley's would become chalk white as passion drained the blood from his features. He was dying from tuberculosis and there were times when his fulminations would be interrupted by a fierce bout of coughing. Afterwards he would glare round at the circle defying anyone to comment or show sympathy.

For anyone with a sense of drama these sessions were absolutely invaluable; for a fourteen-year-old hopeful on the threshold of a fifty-year love-affair with the theatre they were unforgettable experiences. Not exactly show business perhaps, but infinitely more important to my education than either of the two examples of legitimate theatre I had seen. The first of these was a production of *Monsieur Beaucaire*, a dreary play by Booth Tarkington and Mrs E. G. Sutherland. I saw it, along with three or four hundred other schoolchildren, when I was eight or nine years of age. I can still remember the tremendous thrill of sitting in that theatre and waiting for the play to begin. I can remember, too, the boredom which enveloped me like a thick, stultifying fog as the play progressed. The antipathy I feel for a great deal of formal theatre was, I think, born at that moment. A few months later I saw my second straight play, a melodrama entitled *The Face at the Window*. The Victoria in Lower Broughton, where it was presented, was a converted cinema which occasionally re-converted and presented short seasons of 'live' theatre. In addition to these two shows I had been taken several times by my parents to the Salford Hippodrome where I had seen some of the most notable comics of the English stage. It was the variety theatre which really made the most profound impression on me; the live music, the wandering limelights, the incredibly beautiful chorus girls, the grotesquely made-up comics and the dashing acrobats – these were indeed the stuff that dreams are made on!

Visits to the theatre, however, were few and far between: they were exceptional experiences. Much more common were the regular per-formances of street-singers, jugglers, bones-players, fiddlers, trumpeters, step-dancers, escapologists, barrel-organ grinders and Punch-and-Judy men. During the summer months in particular there was a constant procession of these street-entertainers. Their contri-bution to my theatre background was considerable. Would it be too much to suggest that they formed part of the fabric of working-class culture?

Another vital thread in this fabric were films. This was the era of the growth of Hollywood, the era of the first international stars, the age of the comedians, the celluloid sweethearts and the tough guys. As the lines of unemployed grew longer and longer, so the gigantic baroque palaces of Hollywood's new art form grew more and more sumptuous and the lines of high-kicking chorus girls more and more desirable. The Hollywood film of the late twenties and early thirties was the staple diet of the vast army of unemployed and I would venture to suggest that it provided the main art fare for the entire working class. It was certainly one of the most important artistic influences in my life up until late 1929. In the autumn of that year the Deansgate cinema ran a season of Russian films. This was long before the art-cinema concept first appeared and it must have been a financial flop for I remember going there for several weeks and sitting in splendid isola-tion as the great epics of Pudovkin, Eisenstein and Dovzhenko unrolled on the screen. It was, I think, Eisenstein's *October* and Pudovkin's *End of St Petersburg* which started me on the road I was to travel for the next twenty years. When, in 1930, the Salford Workers'

Film Society was formed, I was among its foundation members. It was, I believe, on the Labour Party's list of proscribed (communist) organisations and every Sunday morning, in a small flea-pit on Oldfield Road, it presented the cream of the world's best films. There, in the space of the next few months, I saw *Storm over Asia*, *The New Babylon*, Pabst's *Kamaradschaft*, Dziga Vertov's *Man with the Movie Camera*, Aaron Room's *Bed and Sofa* and *The Ghost that Never Returns*, Fritz Lang's *Metropolis* and Dovzhenko's *Earth*. The opportunity of seeing films of such stature compensated for some of the deprivation experienced by an ill-educated adolescent who faced the bleak prospect of trying to earn a living in the arid desert of 1929.

I was fourteen and had left school knowing how to read and write and how to 'do' simple arithmetic. At the same time I was what is called 'well read'. From the time I was eight or nine years old I had been reading the second-hand books which my father bought off the second-hand book-barrows at Pendleton market as he returned from the foundry on a Saturday morning. The books, which never cost more than a couple of coppers, were bought as presents for me and through them I became acquainted with Darwin's *Voyage of the Beagle*, Jack London's *People of the Abyss* and *Martin Eden*, *The Arabian Nights*, *Barnaby Rudge*, *The Golden Ass* of Lucius Apuleius, *Candide* and volume three of Molière's *Collected Plays*. Not typical children's books! But then my father wasn't exactly typical either. He was one of those working-class militants who believed that books were weapons in the armoury of the class-struggle and though he, himself, was not a great reader, he was determined that I should be given the opportunity of becoming one.

Between 1929 and the beginning of 1931 I moved from one dead-end job to another and finally joined the great army of permanently unemployed. It was at this point that my real education began. Three times a week I would stand in the queue outside the Albion Street labour exchange and, after signing-on, beat a path to the local reference library where I was determined to read my way through the stacks. As a plan it left a lot to be desired and I soon abandoned it for the more practical one of using the library for 'serious' reading and borrowing novels and plays to read at home. Shortly after embarking on this project I came across a volume of Gogol's short stories and I remember sitting and weeping at the tale of Akaki Akakyevitch's lost overcoat. That night I took home a copy of *Dead Souls* and in the next few days read everything that Gogol had written. I ready Gorky in the same way, beginning with two short novellas, *The Orloff Couple* and *Malva*. This habit of reading an author's entire output is one which has stayed with me all my life.

My daytime efforts to read Berkeley on *The Principles of Human Knowledge* or Hobbes' *Leviathan* or *The Apologia* of Socrates were not always crowned with success: I fell asleep frequently and would often grow weary of turning the pages of the dictionary as I hunted up the meaning of this or that word. I persevered, however, and occasionally managed to grasp the meaning of some of the ideas hidden in the tortured prose. I was too self-indulgent to be a real scholar and I used to bribe myself with the promise of a half-hour's relaxation with a book of poems as payment for reading another five pages of John Stuart Mill. In this way I became familiar with the works of Chaucer, William Dunbar, D. H. Lawrence, Ezra Pound, Swinburne, Mayakovsky and many others. I owe a lifetime's affection for Alexander Blok's poem *The Twelve* to the tedium generated by Ricardo's *Theory of Rent*.

But how did an unemployed youth with no educational background know which books to choose? Well, it wasn't so difficult. That initial encounter with Gogol had led me to a *History of Russian Literature* and from there I had gone on to read Pushkin, Lermontov, Griboyedov, Chekhov and Gorky. A reference to Balzac in one of Jack London's novels had introduced me to *The Splendours and Miseries of Courtesans* and after that it was inevitable that I should read all fifty-two volumes of *The Human Comedy*. A friend who was working as a rubber-stamp moulder in a small sweat-shop above Manchester's largest second-hand bookseller's began his education by browsing among the stacks of second-hand books during his lunch-hour break. He it was who introduced me to James Joyce, *The Good Soldier Schweik* and to a cheap remaindered copy of *The Satyricon* of Petronius Arbiter. Through him too I discovered Thomas Mann, Sherwood Anderson, Alfred Doblin, Jacob Wasserman, Robert Briffault and Theodore Plivier.

Looking back it seems that I was constantly encountering people whose main aim in life was to encourage me to read. My knowledge of the world's literature was, of course, eclectic and as far as drama was concerned I knew very little outside the works of Pushkin, Griboyedov, Chekhov, Gogol, Aristophanes, Wedekind, Kaiser, Eugene O'Neill and Büchner. A strange assemblage! Of Shakespeare's works I had read only *Macbeth* and *Troilus and Cressida* and Ben Jonson was not even a name to me. I was to reach the age of twenty-four before I was to plunge into the great sea of Elizabethan and Jacobean drama.

I was about fifteen when I joined a socialist drama group called the Clarion Players. My introduction to them was through a young man who lodged with us at the time. He was an unemployed waterproof worker and a member of the tiny communist organisation in our district. I remember him as a man who had learned to live, almost exclusively, on cheese-and-onion sandwiches and whose blue serge suit shone with the lustre of polished pewter. He was a fastidious little man who, six days a week, stood naked in our backyard while he scrubbed himself under a cold hose; on the seventh day he visited the public baths whence he returned boiled scarlet. He owned a hand-cranked portable gramophone – his only luxury – and on this he would play his Parlophone recordings of *I Pagliacci* and selections from Wagner's *Nibelungenlied*. Without much effort I was able to commit both works to memory and amused my friends by singing all the different parts in 'cod' voices. Our lodger must have heard one of these ridiculous renditions for he offered to introduce me to some of his friends, who, he thought, would be able to make use of my talents as a mimic.

His friends were the Clarion Players, all of whom were much older than I was and much better informed about everything except being dirt poor. Not that they were much better off than I was, though most of them had jobs of one kind or another. My first meeting with them left me feeling thoroughly intimidated. The young couple who appeared to be the leading spirits of the group were so self-possessed and so loquacious that I was overwhelmed with a sense of inferiority. Their conversation was larded with the names of writers, most of whom I had never heard of; they tossed them into the conversation with a fine abandon and the more they talked, the more tongue-tied I became. I have a feeling that they were under the impression that I was in some way retarded, not exactly an idiot but not quite all there either. My somewhat grotesque costume may have contributed to their impression; I was wearing a shockingly green sports jacket which had been given to my mother by a lady who employed her as a charwoman. It had been tailored for a giant and enveloped me to mid-calf giving me the appearance of a monstrous aphid. Indeed some time later I wore it for rehearsals of Čapek's *Insect Play*. Everything about that evening conspired against me; even the house in which the meeting took place intimidated me. It seemed enormous. It was, in fact, a house which had seen better days but which had now been absorbed into the surrounding slum. Up until that time I had never been in any dwelling larger than the two-up and two-down in which I lived.

The eight or ten members of the group were engaged in rehearsing *The Ragged-Trousered Philanthropist*. It was all very informal and not, in any way, like the rehearsals I had seen in the films of Hollywood musicals. I was deeply disappointed and regarded the elderly producer with a good deal of disfavour. After what seemed to me to have been a complete shambles the rehearsal ended and coffee was served (the first I had ever tasted!). There followed a discussion in the course of which I heard, for the first time, the names of Ibsen and George Bernard Shaw.

The following week I was given a small part in Upton Sinclair's *Singing Jailbirds*. The rehearsals of this not very good play followed the same pattern as the one I had seen the previous week. I found myself becoming more and more censorious and more impatient. In more prosperous times I might have had the opportunity of being apprenticed to a carpenter or a plasterer or a machine-tool maker but with three million on the dole who could look foward to anything? So perhaps my impatience arose out of the need to master a skill, any kind of skill. Alas! I don't remember a single Clarion Players' rehearsal being anything other than a slovenly performed charade. The fact that I was young and somewhat timorous in the presence of people who knew about Ibsen and Toller and Shaw meant that my criticism never got beyond the grumbling stage. In any case, what did I know about production or running a group?

At some point during my early association with the group we affiliated with the Workers' Theatre Movement and from that time on we ceased to refer to ourselves as the Clarion Players. I cannot remember how long I remained a member of the group, a year perhaps or maybe a little longer. Certainly long enough to take part in a production of *The Ragged-Trousered Philanthropist*. I don't think we ever actually staged the full production though we did present odd scenes from it at dances and socials.

After the *Philanthropist* we began work on Čapek's *Insect Play* but later abandoned it in favour of Toller's *Machine Wreckers*. This too was never actually staged though a Sunday afternoon reading of it was give to a small audience. Toller was the producer's favourite dramatist and it was inevitable that we should rehearse scenes from his most ambitious expressionistic play, *Masses and Man*. For a fifteen-year-old romantic this was very exciting stuff indeed. We never got further than rehearsing two or three of the group choruses but that was enough to convince me of the powerful dramatic effect of mass declamation. Among the other interesting plays read during my stay with the group, I remember Galsworthy's *Strife*, Shaw's *Heartbreak House* and Hauptmann's *The Weavers*. We also staged a political revue written by two members of the group and consisting, for the most part, of Gilbert and Sullivan parodies.

Quite the most interesting and successful show in the group's repertoire was *Still Talking*, a collectively written piece which had been produced prior to my joining the group. All the other items in the group's repertoire were ones which postulated a formal relationship between audience and actors. Even when they were performed in situations where normal theatre facilities were lacking, where there was no special lighting or special décor or costumes, where the players frequently read their lines from a typescript, even then that special theatre relationship was taken for granted. The French window, the Tudor fireplace or the wall lined with simulated books may have been missing but both audience and players recognised that it was meant to be there and, in their imaginations, it still was there. It was there because the author had conceived it as a necessary part of his or her play. *Still Talking*, on the other hand, had been conceived as an open-ended happening at a political meeting. Its presentation required no stage since the entire interior of the hall where it was being performed became a stage. The lack of props, costumes, décor and special lighting effects was not due to a lack of funds or to the inadequacies of the acting area: they were an intrinsic part of the dramatic situation. No signal was given to alert the audience that a play was about to begin. All that happened was that two people, looking like any other two people in the hall, suddenly confronted the audience. One of them called for order and then proceeded to introduce the other as a Labour or Tory politician. The supposed politician then launched into a speech dealing with whatever political or economic issues were most topical. At fixed points in the speech actors planted in the audience would heckle the speaker and then enact small scenes illustrating points raised in the speech. The form was so elastic that almost anything could happen without destroying the structure of the play. It was a fascinating experiment and had we explored it further it might well have led us to discover the road to a truly popular revolutionary theatre form.

Still Talking was only performed on four or five occasions but as far as we were concerned it was a completely successful show. In that success, however, lay the seeds of the Clarion Players' destruction, for the group was now almost evenly divided between those who believed that *Still Talking* was a signpost pointing to the group's future and those who felt that such an approach would result in a theatre where there would be no room for writers other than those who could draft political speeches and pamphlets. The actors would become political orators and all those with a genuine love of theatre would be alienated.

To create such a theatre would, they argued, imply the repudiation of all that had been created in the past by Shakespeare, Ibsen, Shaw and so on. The political faction countered by saying that by pursuing a strong political line, the theatre would be returning to its origins. After all, was not the morality play essentially a political tract?

Exactly, countered the theatre-first faction, a return to feudalism! And so the arguments and counter-arguments thundered over innumerable cups of weak coffee. In the end, the inevitable happened; the theatre-first people abandoned the group leaving the political faction to run things as best they could.

The move to establish a more politically involved theatre wasn't confined to Manchester. In London too there was a healthy Workers' Theatre Movement with several flourishing groups and from them we began to receive a fairly regular supply of sketches written in the agit-prop style. The first of these was a short piece called *R.I.P.* (*Rent, Interest and Profit*), a satirical sketch dealing with the mechanics of capitalist exploitation. It was clever, witty with the kind of political humour that had delighted Elizabethan audiences, the kind of thing, in short, that college-educated comics would be performing on television forty years later. In the space of seven or eight minutes an audience was presented with a schematized picture of a political problem, the specific function of the class forces involved and finally, the solution of the problem. Seven or eight minutes of knockabout comedy, some simplified Marxist analyses, two songs and a mass declamation! Crude? Perhaps, but not without its own rough style. For those of us who had been struggling through the wordy undergrowth of formal drama, these sketches were tremendously exciting.

In October 1931 the first of the mass-unemployed demonstrations which were to sweep the country during the next few months took place in Salford. The following day another enormous demonstration was held on the Liverpool Street gasworks' croft and there, from the back of a horse-drawn coal lorry, three of us enacted a sketch dealing with the means test. It was our first open-air performance and one of our most successful. The occasion was marked with baton-charges by mounted police. I wrote a song about it, a parody of Billy Boy, and it was performed as a duet at a number of unemployed rallies.

As the economic crisis, with its attendant political upheavals, developed and became world-wide we, the radical wing of the group, were possessed by a terrible sense of urgency, a need to create a political theatre which would help to change the world where we found ourselves constantly in danger of drowning. In the months which followed that first open-air performance we took to the streets,

or rather to the public parks, city squares and factory gates, performing at anti-war rallies, unemployed demonstrations, political meetings and, occasionally, at the entrance to the Manchester City football
ground.

Though our repertoire had changed radically, our approach to
rehearsals and production generally was unaltered. The level of
presentation was still slapdash; furthermore the slovenliness of production tended to be more obvious in the agit-prop sketches than it
had been in the naturalistic plays. Rehearsals were still regarded by
some of the older group members as social occasions; the rest of us
found the slackness and lack of discipline almost unbearable. Some of
the problems undoubtedly arose out of the fact that the group was
almost equally divided between younger members who were unemployed and older ones most of whom had jobs. The unemployed had
time at their disposal and wanted to make use of it by improving their
work on the sketches. The employed, on the other hand, were reluc-
tant to give up any more of their already limited free time. The result
was another split; seven unemployed members decided to form an
agit-prop group which would concentrate on problems of political
immediacy such as unemployment and the gathering storm in the
cotton-textile industry. The new group adopted the name Red Megaphones and I, who knew little or nothing about production, became
its producer and scriptwriter. The oldest member of the new group
was seventeen, the youngest, fifteen. There were four men and three
women. Our rehearsal room was a disused cellar in the Salford
Workers' Arts Club; it was cold, dark, dirty and it smelled bad. We
rehearsed by candlelight.

For our first production we chose a sketch called *Meerut* written by
the North-West London Hammer and Sickle Group. It was a simple
but extremely effective piece of theatre. Its form was mass declamation, its theme the savage prison sentences given to the leaders of
the Indian rail-strike at Meerut. It could be performed by four, five or
six actors of either sex. Its 'set' consisted of wooden poles carried by
the actors, three of whom would stand with poles held vertically in
front of them while the other performers knelt down with their poles
held at the horizontal. In this fashion the front of a cage or prison-cell
was created. There followed a group declamation lasting five or six
minutes at the end of which each of the players would extend a hand
through the bars and call for a show of international solidarity with the
Meerut prisoners. The small cast, the marvellously portable 'set' and
the brevity of the sketch made it a perfect item for a street-drama
group. At the time, it was quite the most exciting bit of theatre I had

ever seen and, looking back over the fifty years that have slipped by since then, I find it still has the power to move and excite me.

From a production point of view *Meerut* presented few problems, even to a beginner such as I was. All that was necessary was to get the cast to speak together like a choir and move together like a platoon of soldiers. So, bawling and shouting like any sergeant-major and generally behaving in a way that no producer should ever behave, I drilled my small cast. It took six sessions of two or three hours each, spread over a fortnight, and then we were ready for the streets.

Our first performance of *Meerut* took place outside the dock gates on Trafford Road, Salford. Our audience numbered about twenty people, six Lascar seamen and the rest dockers. It was time for the morning shift and about half the audience soon left so as to get to the pens where they would stand in the hope of being awarded a day's work. Of those who stayed one or two shouted words of encouragement, one gave a loud raspberry and another dismissed us as 'a bunch of snotty-nosed kids'. One or two applauded at the end of the performance, the others departed without showing either approval or disapproval. Chastened, we moved to the entrance to Howarth's mill and hung around the gates waiting for the lunch-time exodus. Two girls in the group had been weavers and they were recognised by some of their erstwhile mates. As a result, our reception there was an improvement on the docks and we were able to finish our performance before the police arrived. From there we repaired to the corner of Regent Road and Oldfield Road where we were heckled by a postman on a bicycle. We ignored him but he sparked off hecklers in the small crowd and when it looked as if opposing factions were about to start a riot, we left in a hurry.

Looking back, it seems to me that we were, on the whole, received with a distinct lack of enthusiasm by most of the men and women of our own class. Often they would pass us by with heads averted so as not to be involved, occasionally one or two would stop to jeer, others met us with blank apathy and this was harder to take than the abuse. Only a small minority seemed to agree with the things we were saying and with our way of saying them. We consoled ourselves by saying that audiences would improve when we ourselves improved with hard work and rehearsal. We lacked many qualities but humility was not among them. Week-ends were our best times, for then we could be assured of being seen by shoppers in the market-places and week-end bathers at the public baths. The stone steps that were an architectural feature of Manchester and Salford's public baths soon became our favourite venues for performances. For one thing, there were generally queues there on a Saturday morning and, for another, they provided us with a point of vantage where we could be seen and from which we could easily spot 'the law'.

Our most sympathetic audiences were those drawn from the ranks of the unemployed, particularly those organised in the National Unemployed Workers' Movement (N.U.W.M.). From being a small and weak offshoot of the Communist Party, the N.U.W.M. had grown in the space of a few months into an enormous movement numbering tens of thousands. At their meetings, demonstrations and hunger-marches we could always rely on a sympathetic hearing and had it not been for them I doubt whether the Red Megaphones would have surivived. But now a new struggle was developing and the cotton towns round Lancashire and Cheshire began to rumble with talk of strikes and further massive lay-offs.

The cotton industry which had made Lancashire famous was now ailing and the textile barons were withdrawing their capital from towns such as Preston and Burnley and reinvesting it in Tokyo and Hong Kong. Here at home the speed-up and other forms of 'rationalisation' were making the lot of the cotton operatives more and more difficult; their anger and frustration had been building up for years and when the employers announced their intention of introducing the eight-looms system the anger reached boiling-point. The manufacture of cotton textiles was one of our oldest industries and, perhaps because of this, it was difficult to organise its labour force. The main reason for this lay in the fact that from the earliest days unionisation had been on a craft basis. Since there were scores of different processes involved in the manufacture of cotton goods, it followed that there were also scores of different unions. Weavers, ring-spinners, mule-spinners, big piecers, little piecers, back-tenters, combers and others all had their separate organisations. Some of them had tens of thousands of members, some had only a few hundred and one or two counted their membership in tens. The situation was further complicated by the industry having grown up on the basis of regional specialisation. This meant that a town famed for its weaving could have a neighbour six miles to the North of it which specialized in spinning while four miles to the South-East was another town whose workers were mostly employed as finishers. Consequently when it came to adopting industrial action such as a strike, the decision had to be taken by each of the independent unions in turn, which meant virtually by each town and sometimes by each mill.

The two weavers in the Red Megaphones insisted, quite properly, that our duty, as a workers' theatre, was to support the striking cotton workers. Our first attempt at a cotton script was a crude affair even by our standards but we brightened it up by writing new words to a couple of pop tunes and including them. It was mostly mass declamation enlivened by rhythmic movements based on the working actions of a weaver and a mule-spinner. Shortly before the strike some of us had seen a German dance group called, I think, the Bodenweiser. We had watched them, from the 'gods' at the Salford Hippodrome, perform a piece called the Dance of the Machines. It had fascinated us and for quite a long time afterwards its influence could be seen in everything we did. Consequently when we performed our eight-looms sketch outside the Pendleton mill of Elkanah Armitage we were taking our first tentative steps in the field of modern dance.

As the strike gathered momentum we became more and more involved. We were out on the streets almost every night of the week performing, or trying to perform since the police harassed us continuously. Those areas like Earby, Burnley, Nelson and Colne which had been among the first of the towns to come out on strike were soon feeling the pinch, and union funds, which were small, soon gave out. Now was the time for workers throughout Britain to show their solidarity with the strikers. The response to the union's appeal for help was magnificent. Food convoys began to roll in from Glasgow, Tonypandy, Hull, Whitechapel, Newcastle-upon-Tyne, Sunderland and Sheffield. We added the collection of food to our performance routine and after each performance of our eight-looms sketch we went from door to door with an old hand-cart we had acquired and collected food for the strikers. The more active we became the more the police hounded us and scarcely a week went by without one of us being arrested and fined for obstruction, creating a public nuisance or contravening any one of the thousand and one restrictions and by-laws that are there to safeguard the status quo.

The strike dragged on and we found ourselves going further afield at week-ends, to places as far away as Todmorden, Blackburn, Burnley and Great Harwood. More often, however, we would take a threepenny or fourpenny tram or bus ride to a nearby town and play two or three shows there. Where there were three or four towns adjacent to each other we would play all of them in a single afternoon. A typical itinerary would be Ashton-under-Lyne – a show in the market-place and, after a couple of quick appearances in the main shopping area, off to Dukinfield where the pattern would be repeated. If we succeeded in raising a few coppers in the collection we would then take a tram to Hyde where we would repeat the routine again, finishing up in Stockport or Failsworth. The following week we might

play Oldham, Rochdale and Bury. During the week we generally
confined ourselves to performances in Manchester, Salford and, occasionally, in Eccles, Monton, Pendlebury and Swinton.

At this stage I don't believe that any of us regarded ourselves as
artists or, indeed, as being in any way involved with art. We saw
ourselves as guerrillas using the theatre as a weapon against the
capitalist system. That system had made it perfectly clear that the
authorities regarded us as production units which could be used, then
thrown away. As far as they were concerned we were zeroes, born to
lose. So what the hell had we to do with art, or art with us? On the
other hand one needed a skill in order to survive and nobody was
going to help you to acquire that skill. You must do it yourself or go
under. Now the theatre was the kind of artefact that we could deal
with; one could pick up ways of dealing with it just as one could pick
up ways of dealing with a lathe or a milling-machine. And that's what
we were doing; picking up ways of dealing with a new tool. We knew
about tools, about how to fashion them and how to make them work.
So we were going to make this new tool work for us. But art . . .!

It was an agit-prop script which contained a passage of writing by
Maxim Gorky that first made me aware of the fact that I might be
involved in something which could be described as art. The quotation
went something like this: 'There is no art in the world today worthy of
its name beside the art created by the working-class in the course of its
struggle. We are the ones who build this art. By means of it we are
working for the great causes of labour, destroying the chains of
slavery.' It may strike the reader as incongruous that a small group of
unemployed teenagers, wearing bib-and-brace overalls and khaki
shirts, should stand on the steps of a decaying bath-house and bawl
out such sentiments. And yet there is something quite remarkable too
in the fact that these young, under-privileged rejects of a nineteenth-
century slum should have been able to preserve such hope, such
shining belief, such glorious optimism in a world which offered them
nothing but the scrap-heap.

We are, we said, the propertyless theatre of a propertyless class so to
hell with art, let's get on with the job, and the immediate job was to
collect food, clothing and cash for the besieged strikers. It also meant
performing for the strikers themselves and reminding them that they
were not alone. It meant, too, explaining the strike to other groups of
workers who were not, themselves, directly involved in it. That was
the immediate task. The long-term objective was to forge an efficient
weapon which could be used to bring about fundamental changes in
society. All of us agreed that society needed changing and all of us

subscribed to the Marxist theory that such changes could only be brought about by the working class. In the half-century which has passed since that time, nothing has happened to make me alter that point of view.

On the few occasions that I visited the commercial theatre during those years I don't remember seeing anything that wasn't a completely unconvincing sham – badly acted, badly written and badly produced. Obviously one's view of society is determined by one's angle of vision; if one lives under the foot of society one tends to see the entire body as a pair of dwarf-like legs and two enormous, flabby buttocks. I was conscious of all these things but at the same time I remained absolutely convinced that the theatre, in the right hands, could be a symbol of truth, passion and beauty. I am not suggesting that the Red Megaphones were 'the right hands' or that our productions were any more convincing or that they were better written or better acted. In one respect, however, they were infinitely superior: there was no shamming in them, all of us believed passionately in what we were doing and what we were saying and real, unadulterated passion is a rare thing to find, on the stage or anywhere else.

It was this passion which drove us on in the face of constant harassment by police, the jeers and taunts of workers whom we claimed to represent, and the physical attacks by Blackshirts and others. Anyone who believes that street theatre can win an audience more easily than other kinds of theatre has more imagination than experience. Only on rare occasions did we succeed in attracting more than a handful of people to stop whatever they were doing and listen to us. Such rare occasions were unemployed demonstrations or gatherings of strikers. Our most memorable shows were connected with these events. One of them took place in Wigan market-place on the day of the local strike ballot. The entire town was tense with barely concealed excitement and we were met, with a good deal of enthusiasm, by a crowd of three or four hundred women. Small groups of unemployed miners were stationed on the perimeter of the crowd and were there to act as a defence force if necessary. An empty coal-cart had been positioned in the centre of the square and this was to be our platform.

We had scarcely started on our first sketch when we were interrupted by a police sergeant who told us to clear off. Several miners, however, surrounded the platform and, ignoring the policeman, told us to carry on. After a few moments the sergeant went away and returned shortly afterwards with an inspector and several uniformed constables. This time the crowd closed ranks and prevented them from approaching the platform. After a brief argument with a very angry group of women the police withdrew, whereupon a young miner climbed an ornamental lamp-standard and raised our banner on it to the cheers of the crowd. In the course of the next ninety minutes we ran through every item in our repertoire and then, at the insistence of the crowd, repeated it all over again.

Burnley, Lancashire, was the scene of another memorable performance. A very critical point in the eight-looms strike had been reached and, a few days earlier in Earby and Nelson, pitched battles between police and strikers had been fought. On the day of our performance tens of thousands of strikers from the mill towns of Lancashire and Cheshire had poured into Burnley to welcome the food convoys which were due to arrive. We performed our eight-looms sketch from the top of one of these giant pantechnicons, looking out over the sea of faces which filled Burnley's main square and all the roads leading into it. A thrilling experience!

When, eventually, the strikers were defeated we returned to our street-corner performances with occasional shows at anti-war demonstrations or at meetings organised by one or other of the various anti-fascist groups. But times and the political situation were changing rapidly. Unemployment and the demoralising poverty which is part of it were now an established part of our life. The mass demonstrations of hundreds of thousands of unemployed men and women which had highlighted the winter months of 1931–2 had now given way to a different kind of struggle. The emphasis which all through the twenties and the beginning of the thirties had been on economic issues was now shifting to political events, the national and the international were becoming one. Dmitrov, hero of the Reichstag fire trial, speaking at an international anti-fascist congress, gave voice to the hopes and fears of many people when he brought his oration to a close with the words: 'We are entering a period of wars and revolutions.'

In the course of the eight-looms strike the Red Megaphones had been visited by two young German refugees who, until the Nazis came to power, had been actors in a famous German agit-prop group. They were now working as organisers for the International Union of Revolutionary Theatres and were members of a committee which was organising an international Olympiad of Workers' Theatres. Salford was one of the whistle-stops on their international fact-finding tour. They arrived on the week-end of the big meeting and travelled with us to Burnley. They appear to have been impressed by our performance or perhaps they felt that our enthusiasm should be rewarded, for from that time on we were bombarded through the post with scripts and magazines from exiled German theatre groups, from Russia, Czechoslovakia and the United States. One of these scripts, *Wer ist der Dummste*, had been performed by a group led by the distinguished theatre workers Inge and Gustav von Wangenheim. It was an experiment in the kind of theatre that we ourselves had dreamed of creating and were quite incapable of performing. It brought to a head all the discontent with our standards and repertoire which had been building up over several months. Our repertoire now consisted of *Meerut, Rent, Interest and Profit, The Spirit of Invergordon, Their Theatre and Ours, The Fight against the Eight-Looms, The Archbishop's Prayer* and *Suppress, Oppress and Depress*. We also had a number of parodies of popular songs and could recite several revolutionary poems.

As a repertoire it left a lot to be desired. The sketches appeared to have been written to a formula which called for loud voices rather than acting ability on the part of the performers. In almost all of them there were some good lines and occasional flashes of real wit. The satire was sometimes crude but it was often very effective indeed though sometimes embedded in stodgy journalese or obscured by horseplay. The message was usually delivered at the top of the human voice in the form of slogans hurled by actors standing head on to the audience. What little movement there was tended to be limited to minor changes in position and absurd capering and this wasn't entirely due to the limited stage area. The fact is we were dealing with literary tracts not very dissimilar in tone and style to those denunciatory broadsides which eighteenth-century pamphleteers were in the habit of hurling at their enemies. The audience was never allowed to forget itself and at the end of each sketch a group of six or more young people would swing towards the onlookers and, with its maximum collective voice, exhort them to do this or do that. We were not asking them, we were commanding them and, not unnaturally, some of them resented us.

Our criticism of our way of working and of our repertoire became increasingly vocal throughout 1933 and when we decided to embark on the production of a piece called *Newsboy* there was a general sigh of relief. This short play had been sent to us by the New York Laboratory Theatre who had taken a poem by V. J. Jerome and made it into a very exciting short drama. It had many features in common with agit-prop theatre and was certainly no less political. But whereas our agit-prop sketches had been largely static, too obviously didactic and over-dependent on caricature, *Newsboy* was full of action and made use of 'real' characters, fairly run-of-the-mill characters but characters none-the-less. The format was simplicity itself: a bare stage lit by a centre-spot in which a newsboy dances and sells newspapers. As he dances he shouts the headlines of the world's news. From time to time he slips out of the light and his place is taken by two, and sometimes three, actors who perform short scenes in which an item of news is 'acted out'. Beyond the rim of the light various representatives of the outside world pass and go about their business. The slogans were still there but they arose naturally out of the play and were not imposed upon it.

The production of *Newsboy* raised problems that we had not had to face before. The central character had to be able to dance! The short scenes demanded actors. It was one thing to learn, parrot-fashion, a mass declamation and one could be drilled into carrying out a series of simple group manoeuvres. But to act! Furthermore, *Newsboy* called for the use of stage lighting, and stage lighting meant an indoor venue. Now we knew nothing about dance, little about acting, less about stage lighting and there was also the matter of length. *Newsboy* was meant to run for fifteen minutes which meant that we needed another seventy-five minutes to make a reasonably full performance. For a group of penniless young people without much knowledge of the theatre, these were enormous problems. The solution of the dance problem came about as the result of a chance meeting. Signing on at the labour exchange I ran into a childhood acquaintance who on leaving school had gone into the building trade and was now a steel-erector. He was one of a large Catholic family, all of whom possessed names which, in our district, were regarded as somewhat high-flown. His parents were actors in a fit-up company and they christened their children with names borrowed from whatever plays they happened to be playing in at the time. My friend's birth had coincided with a tour of *The Fortunes of Gerard, Richard the Third* and *Antony and Cleopatra*, hence his name – Gerard Richard Antony Davies. Good names, all of them but not particularly appropriate: they sounded too soft. It wasn't merely that he was a steel-erector, he actually looked as if he had been fashioned in a Bessemer furnace. When I told him about our problems he offered immediately to play the part of the newsboy and he turned out to be a natural-born dancer. His voice too was admirably suited to the part; working outdoors and being forced to make himself heard above the clang of steel girders and the rattle of jack-hammers had given him a voice that could have been heard above a salvo of bombs. He stayed in the group for three or four years, until his job took him to distant parts.

The lighting problems were solved by Alf Armitt, a seventeen-year-old vertical-lathe operator who had once run with the Percy Street mob, one of Salford's most feared juvenile street gangs. He had been a foundation member of the Red Megaphones and was active in the Labour League of Youth. While reading up on lighting in the Manchester Reference Library he came upon a reference to Adolph Appia, the Swiss stage-director and a revolutionary theorist on the nature and function of light in the theatre. Somehow Alf managed to lay his hands on a rough translation of one of Appia's books and from that time on we were all Appia disciples. Alf Armitt's researches didn't only provide us with a theoretical base for what was to be an important element in our work. It also gave us three spotlights which he had made out of ten-pound barrel-type biscuit-tins fitted with 500-watt lamps 'borrowed' from the floodlighting equipment used to illuminate the Salford greyhound-racing track. This was our first foray into the world of theatre lighting: no dimmers, no floods, no switchboard, just three converted biscuit-tins and an off/on wall switch. Later Alf was to demonstrate his ingenuity by building us a switchboard.

The problem of finding enough material to fill an entire evening was solved by making *Newsboy* the centrepiece of a variety show which included a mass declamation calling for the release of Ernst Thaelmann, the German Communist leader who was a prisoner of the Nazis, an agit-prop anti-war sketch, a group of songs of Eisler and Brecht and a surrealistic poem by the American, Funarov. The programme was presented at the Round House, Ancoats, in February or March 1934.

It was during the rehearsals of this show that we were joined by Joan Littlewood. She had come to Manchester to take part in a B.B.C. feature programme and had been taken on by the director of the Rusholme Repertory Theatre to act as A.S.M. and play small roles. Her job occupied most of her evenings but the little free time she managed to get was spent helping us and she was even able to take part in the recitation of the Funarov poem *The Fire Sermon* at the Round House.

In the weeks that followed we took the show to a number of small halls in the Manchester area and added Shelley's *Mask of Anarchy* and Louis Aragon's poem *The Red Front* to the other items.

The comparative success of this first indoor performance and the fact that we no longer were faced with the constant threat of being moved on or arrested produced temporary feelings of euphoria in the group. Shortly before the Round House performance we had reorganised the group and we were now calling ourselves the Theatre of Action, a title which, I believe, we had borrowed from the New York group. Now we were beginning to look around for ideas and models which would help us to arrive at a clearer picture of the kind of theatre we wanted to create. Though we were hostile to the commercial theatre and generally spoke of it with contempt, we really knew very little about it. Most of us had seen three or four plays and a few of us had read quite a lot of plays as well as various critiques and histories of theatre. It was upon these that our opposition was based. We were not, at this stage, opposed to the classical repertoire, the techniques employed or what one might call the machinery of theatre. Our hostility was towards the kind of plays that were being presented in the theatre, towards the kind of people depicted in those plays, to the triviality of the themes and to the kind of audience being catered for. In short our hostility was towards certain products of the theatre and not to the theatre itself. Joan was the only one among us who felt differently about it; four years at R.A.D.A. and the opportunity to see the London theatre at work, followed by her current experience in one of Britain's leading repertory theatres, had convinced her that the theatre was sick in all its parts. It wasn't long before the rest of us were to be converted to Joan's point of view.

Six or seven months after the formation of the Theatre of Action, Ernst Toller, the refugee German dramatist, came to Manchester to supervise a production of his play *Draw the Fires* at the repertory theatre. The play deals with the mutiny of the German fleet in the Kiel canal in 1918. A good deal of its action takes place in the stokehold of the flagship *Von Tirpitz*. Stokers and trimmers, stripped to the waist, shovel coal into the furnaces throughout a complete scene and, indeed, the high point of the drama occurs when the stokers throw down their shovels and refuse to carry on working. The actors, more familiar with a cigarette-case than with shovels, appeared to be incapable of delivering lines and heaving coal at the same time. The disdain with which they regarded these simple tools was scarcely in accord with the surroundings. Actors, at the time, were recruited almost exclusively from the middle classes and they regarded themselves as gentlemen, and it was right and proper that they should have a gentleman's contempt for work and for those who did it. Given a French window or a Tudor fireplace and they would have felt perfectly at home but the stokehold was definitely not their milieu. Toller, alarmed at the prospect of seeing his high drama converted to farce, asked Joan whether there were any actors in the vicinity who didn't appear to be chronic invalids. Joan told him about Theatre of Action and that evening she brought him to our rehearsal. He watched us for ten minutes and then left after telling us to be at the theatre at ten o'clock the following morning.

The awe we felt at being backstage in a 'real' theatre didn't last long. The leading man, an angry boy from one of Britain's lesser public-schools, hated us on sight and most of the company followed his example. It wasn't that they felt, in any way, threatened by us and it wasn't the mild contempt that many professionals feel towards amateurs. They positively hated us and didn't attempt to hide their hatred. Maybe it was because we brought an unwelcome sniff of the real world into their make-believe existence, the world of unemployment, dirt and deprivation. They were contemptuous of the way we spoke and some of them pretended not to understand us when we asked questions. The leading lady held a handkerchief to her nose every time one of us stood near her. For the first hour or two we were suitably humble until we realised just how physically inept they were. We were tempted to show that we too could show a lack of generosity equal to theirs but they looked so weak and ineffectual that we felt sorry for them. One or two of our members felt that we were wasting our time and suggested that we pulled out of the show before we got more involved. The majority, however, voted to stay so as to learn as much as possible about the craft, if not the art, of theatre. During the fortnight's run of the show we were disabused of any illusions we may have had; the general attitude of the rep company to work, the flip dismissal of any serious ideas, the slipshod attitude to rehearsal and the shoddy tricks used as a substitute for acting shocked us profoundly and when we left we had a very clear picture of the kind of theatre we didn't want.

From the beginning Joan's relationship with the repertory company had been an uneasy one and now her employers regarded her as our sponsor; the atmosphere was, to say the least, brittle and it wasn't long before it reached breaking-point. Her resignation was received with relief by the managing committee of the repertory theatre and Joan and I settled down to a period of study and experiment. The bulk of our studying was done at the Manchester Central Reference Library where, for several hours each day, we sat and read everything we could lay our hands on which had any bearing on the theatre: plays, analyses, critical surveys, biographies of dramatists, technical manuals on lighting, lavishly illustrated folios on décor and obsolete essays by forgotten French and German writers.

In the summer of 1934 we attended a Workers' Theatre Movement conference in London where in the course of a speech by a rising West End actor and producer were were advised to abandon the agit-prop technique and 'embrace the techniques of the established theatre'. This advice had already been taken to heart by two of the London groups, and that evening we sat through one of their productions, a mediocre piece called *Hammer*. It was a typical example of the well-made play; typical in the sense that the dialogue was artificial, the plot mechanical and the characters a series of stereotypes. The production was straight, uninspired 'rep' stuff and the acting a typical amateur copy of fashionable west-end posturing. We were appalled and left London raging against the producer and those who had allowed him to 'capture the left theatre'.

Back in Manchester we discussed our experience with the other members of the group who shrugged their shoulders and said: 'What else can you expect from Londoners? No guts! Decadent lot! Not like us Northerners!' And if that suggests that we were typical north-country bigots then it is no less than the truth, for we wrote London off and for the next few years had scarcely any contact with it at all.

We did not, however, feel cut off in any way from the mainstream of socially committed experimental theatre. We were still in touch with groups in the United States and the Soviet Union and with the various groups of exiled German theatre workers. In addition we were avid readers of the theatrical press and magazines like *New Theatre* and *Theatre Arts Monthly* kept us informed about what was happening on the other side of the Atlantic. For European stimulus there was always Leon Moussinac's *New Movement in the Theatre*, a veritable treasure-trove of concepts and ideas. It was through Moussinac's book that we had our first real introduction to Myerhold's theatre and to some extent, at any rate, his ideas were to dominate much of our next production, *John Bullion*. This had started life as *Hammer*, the rather dreary play we had seen in London on the night of the Workers' Theatre Movement conference. The script was quite as bad as the production had been but we were desperately in need of something to produce so we set about adapting it to our needs. For a start, we reduced the number of characters, then cut out all of them and introduced new ones in their place. This necessitated a change of dialogue which, in turn, resulted in several scenes being shortened and then cut out. This called for further changes in the dialogue which, in turn, meant more cuts. We finally cut out all the dialogue and substituted for it catch-phrases spoken by a chorus of typists. The décor, which in the London production had included a naturalistic office with desk, filing-cabinets, chairs, hatstand, doors, windows, etc., now became a bare platform with a raised wooden plane standing along the back wall along which various figures representing the outside world passed. Downstage there were three skeletoid wooden stools, six, seven and eight feet high. Seated on them and attached to them by chains were three young women, clones of the script's original secretary. Their faces and bodies were painted white and they wore black panties and bras. The main character, John Bullion, was made-up to look like a grotesque clown and had a stomach padded to Falstaffian proportions covered by a waistcoat fashioned from a Union Jack. The production was a kind of ménage-à-trois of styles borrowed from agit-prop, constructivism and expressionism. These three elements were to play important roles in many of our productions over the next few years.

Early in 1935 we embarked on a production of *Waiting for Lefty* which had recently opened in New York and was playing there to enthusiastic audiences. Odett's play was an ideal one for us: it was not too long but long enough to fill a substantial part of an evening, it dealt with a significant area of class-struggle and it did so in a way that was direct and uncompromising. Its theme was one which would appeal to almost any working-class audience and its dialogue would be easily comprehended by people whose main theatrical fare was Hollywood films. Like that earlier piece of the Clarion Players, *Still Talking*, *Waiting for Lefty* contained many agit-prop elements in its make-up. Both plays made use of the public-meeting framework and, consequently, neither needed much in the way of décor and props. Both made use of the auditorium as an acting area and both used the device of the political oration interrupted by short dramatic vignettes. The slogans were still there but they were no longer used as a homiletic epilogue to the main action.

We opened with *Waiting for Lefty* and a supporting programme at the Milton Hall, Deansgate, and, after playing successfully there for three nights, moved to the Houldsworth Hall for a further five nights. Later we presented it at the Hyde Socialist Sunday School and in Haslingden, north-east Lancashire. It was, I believe, in this period that we began to envisage our future ideal theatre as one which toured working-class areas exclusively.

Between the productions of *Newsboy* and *Waiting for Lefty* the group had grown considerably and now numbered some twenty-three members. Furthermore we now had premises, a studio loaned to us by a friendly painter. The organisational structure of the theatre, however, had scarcely changed at all from the days of the Red Megaphones. Rehearsals were called by Joan or me, plays were directed by both of us or by whichever one of us was free at the time. Scripts which arrived through the post were read by us and it was left to us to decide whether they should be produced. There was no secretary, no treasurer (no money either), no technicians, no stage-designer, no wardrobe, no stage-management – just a small collective of would-be political actors. It had worked well enough with a small group of individuals each one of whom related to each other in much the same way that children who are members of the same street gang relate.

But more than working methods had changed. The social composition of the group had changed too and among the new members there were several professional people including two solicitors, a university lecturer and an art-school teacher. Almost all of them were more experienced in the business of running an organisation than were any of the half-dozen adolescents who had graduated through the Red Megaphones. Our way of dealing with our various tasks was very simple: if a job needed doing then whoever was free did it, and that was that! Anarchic? Possibly. Certainly some of our new recruits were shocked to the core by our way of doing things and it wasn't long before we had a management committee and two or three sub-committees. Things progressed smoothly for several weeks after their formation and then the management committee decided that matters concerning production, casting of roles, choice of plays, could no longer be left in the hands of 'a couple of prima donnas'; a production committee was needed. Joan and I treated the suggestion with scorn whereupon an 'extraordinary general meeting' was called in the course of which we were transformed into counter-revolutionaries, Trotskyists, social-fascists, mere formalists and enemies of the working class. It is ironical that those who were most vociferous in their condemnation of us became, in the course of the next decade, pillars of the establishment and solidly reactionary to a man and woman. At the time Joan and I were badly shaken by these events, particularly when, at a pre-arranged point in the meeting, a motion to expel us was proposed and seconded. In the voting which followed, the results were twelve in favour and twelve against. The chairman cast his vote in favour but by now we were sickened by the entire business. We left in disgust.

The attacks on us had left us feeling demoralised and for the next two or three weeks we seriously considered giving up all thought of working in the theatre. Our despair was dissipated by a letter which came from Moscow offering us scholarships to the Academy of Theatre and Cinema. Our spirits soared. Soon we would be studying at first hand the work of Myerhold, Vakhtangov, Stanislavski and Oplopkhov. We would be listening to Pudovkin and Eisenstein lecturing and would be able to watch them at work! Friends who had walked out in protest at the last Theatre of Action meeting, held a farewell party for us and, at a whip-round raised twelve pounds towards our travel expenses.

We arrived in London in November 1935, applied for visas at the Soviet Embassy and settled down to wait. While we were waiting we organised a training class for people who wanted to study our kind of theatre and, on our free nights, gave lectures to anyone who was prepared to listen. I still find myself blushing with embarrassment when I remember the kind of lectures I gave: long, incoherent disquisitions larded with quotations from Aristotle, Diderot, Goethe, Gordon Craig, Richter, Appia and Stanislavski and inapposite references to Moussinac's monumental tome. During one such lecture at the Slade School, I was so overcome with confusion that I couldn't continue. Fortunately Joan was at hand and was able to fill the breach. Her voice could charm birds out of the trees and if her references to Cimabue, Giorgione and Piero della Francesca baffled the listeners, their ears were charmed by her beautiful cadences.

We succeeded in persuading eight or nine trusting souls to become members of our acting school. Two of them were unemployed railway workers from Battersea, one worked as a labourer in the Morgan Crucible works; another, his sister, was a filing-clerk at Nine Elms, one was an art student, one was an unemployed youth from Wandsworth and the names and faces of the rest escape my memory. The instruction consisted mostly of movement classes which were run by Joan who had, at R.A.D.A. taken a movement course which appears to have been based on the Laban method. We also made a few tentative attempts at teaching voice production but abandoned them almost immediately. My teaching role was to lecture on the history of theatre and to conduct classes in Stanislavski's theory of acting. It really was a case of the blind leading the blind.

The fact that we couldn't afford money for premises made life difficult so we decided to live communally and thus solve the problem of living-accommodation and school premises at the same time. So we moved into a rather grand establishment on the west side of Clapham Common. We rattled around in it for a couple of months and then, our meagre travel fund exhausted, found we couldn't pay the rent. Once again our salvation came via the postman. The letter he brought didn't come from Moscow. Our visa application had probably been lost in the frozen waste of the embassy's bureaucracy and we were reconciled to the idea that it might never arrive. Indeed we made a virtue out of necessity and were comforting ourselves by saying that we hadn't really wanted to go to a foreign country to become part of somebody else's theatre. The real need was here in Britain, here where all the conditions existed for the creation of a new theatre, a theatre of the

British working class. So when the Manchester branch of the Peace Pledge Union invited us to produce Hans Schlumberg's *Miracle at Verdun* for them, we were overjoyed. Two days later we were back in Manchester.

The Peace Pledge Union and the Quakers, who were collaborating in this venture, had substantial resources at their disposal, or at least they seemed substantial to us. To begin with, they had an organisation and a secretarial staff who could organise rehearsal schedules, type scripts, deal with correspondents, produce posters and leaflets, arrange newspaper interviews and so on. The Friends' Meeting House, owned by the Quakers, was right in the centre of the city which meant we would have rehearsal premises which would be conveniently situated for just about everybody. This was important for a production which called for a score or more actors. *Miracle at Verdun* hasn't only got an enormous cast but one which includes Africans, French, Germans, Italians, Americans, Russians, Indians, Chinese, Swedes and Turks. Through their membership in the university and technical colleges, the Peace Pledge Union and the Quakers would be able to provide us with students from all the above countries. The big problem was to find a rehearsal room large enough to accommodate so many actors. We solved the problem by rehearsing all the small scenes at the Friends' Meeting House while the mass scenes were reserved for the final week and rehearsed in a large empty warehouse at the corner of Deansgate and Victoria Street.

From the time that Joan had joined the Theatre of Action we had worked together as a production team, often both working on the same unit at the same time. If there were occasional disagreements, they were unimportant. We discussed our ideas so often and at such length that either of us was capable of carrying out the other's wishes. *Miracle at Verdun* called for a different way of working for it had an inordinate number of scenes. So many scenes in fact that we began to doubt whether we had enough time to rehearse them all before the opening date. We solved this problem by sharing out the scenes between us and running simultaneous rehearsals in adjacent rooms. A kind of production-line approach! Not one to be recommended as a general principle though it worked well enough on this particular occasion.

Miracle at Verdun was a rather clumsily constructed play. Its author had not been able to make up his mind about whether he was writing an expressionistic drama or a naturalistic one. He had finally decided to write both and the result, while not entirely satisfactory, had made it a simple matter to divide the play up in the way I have described and when it opened its two-week run at the Lesser Free Trade Hall the critics were enthusiastic. We were less so. We had no reservations about the theme or message of the play but we felt that it was excessively wordy and soft-centred in the main confrontation scene. The fact is that we had a profound distrust of naturalistic theatre and every time we came to grips with it, we failed.

From an organisational point of view *Miracle at Verdun* was a very important stage in the development of our theatre. Not only did it win us a far bigger audience than we'd ever had before but it left us with a skeleton organisation which we could build on. It had, in addition, made it possible for us to reach the student population, it had put us in contact with amateur drama groups throughout the Manchester district and had won us support from a number of painters, sculptors, printers and journalists. A few days after the play's final performance, we called a meeting of all those who had taken part in it and there it was decided to form a new group. The aims of Theatre Union, as this new group was called, are summed up in this manifesto:

> We live in times of great social upheaval; faced with an ever-increasing danger of war and fascism, the democratic people of the world have been forced into action. Their struggle for peace and progress manifests itself in many forms and not the least important of these is the drama.
>
> Theatre Union is Manchester's contribution to the forces of democracy. It has set itself the task of establishing a complete theatre unit consisting of producers, actors, writers, artists and technicians, which will present to the widest possible public, and particularly to that section of the public which has been starved theatrically, plays of social significance. Where the censorship of the period makes it impossible for such productions to be open to the general public they will be given for private audiences of Theatre Union members. All that is most vital in the repertoire of the world's theatre will find expression on the stage of Theatre Union.
>
> It has been said that every society has the theatre it deserves; if that is so, then Manchester, one of the greatest industrial and commercial centres in the world deserves only the best. It is for the people of Manchester to see that Theatre Union's goal is attained. Theatre Union intends that its productions will be made accessible to the broadest possible mass of people in the Manchester district, and consequently it appeals to all Trade Unions and to all parties engaged in the struggle for peace and progress to become affiliated immediately.

This manifesto was still hot from the press when Spain was plunged into civil war. Like many people we were horrified at the turn events were taking and at a meeting of the newly formed Theatre Union, it was decided that we should mount a production which would have the dual function of drawing public attention to the struggle of the

Spanish people against Fascism and raising funds for medical aid. Lope de Vega's *Fuente Ovejuna* (*The Sheep-well*) was the play we chose to produce. It was our first excursion in the field of classical drama, the beginning of a road that was to lead to Marlowe's *Edward the Second*, Marston's *Dutch Courtesan, Arden of Faversham, Volpone* and *Macbeth*.

In every respect *Fuente Ovejuna* was the ideal play for the time. Its theme, the revolt of a village community against a ruthless and bloody dictator, was a reflection in microcosm of what was actually taking place in Spain. A colourful play with lots of action and a superb climax, it has a fairly big cast and like *Miracle at Verdun*, there are a number of crowd scenes. But whereas *Miracle* had been a rather static play, relying on a series of tableaus, *Fuente* had a tremendous amount of real action. In *Miracle* most of the roles were lay-figures who delivered speeches; there was no real conversation, instead there was oration. In *Fuente*, on the other hand, the characters were men and women who laughed and wept and cried out in pain and made jokes. Even the crowd was made up of characters who fought and danced and rioted like a crowd of football enthusiasts expressing their devotion to Manchester United. In our agit-prop days we had made great use of songs but had abandoned the practice when we left the streets. In *Fuente* we set Lope's lyrics to the tunes of stirring republican battle songs and used them as a continuous thread throughout the production.

The static nature of *Miracle at Verdun* had called for décor which underlined the play's lack of real physical conflict. The production of *Fuente Ovejuna*, on the other hand, demanded the maximum area of uncluttered stage where the crowds could move and give vent to their violent feelings. The single setting which our newly formed artists' group created for us consisted of a circular drinking-well situated upstage of centre with a large sculpted figure of a rampant sheep towering above it. This and a backcloth of ruffled hessian painted and dyed in autumnal colours of russet, brown and gold provided a wonderfully effective background for Lope's masterpiece.

In addition to extending our stylistic vocabulary, the production of *Fuente Ovejuna* gave us an enormous amount of confidence and won us wider support than we had ever enjoyed before. It occupies a very important place in our calendar of events for not only was it the first time that a play by Spain's most important dramatist had been performed in Britain, it was also the first time that we had dared to step outside the territory of agit-prop-cum-expressionistic theatre.

As the Spanish Civil War dragged on we found ourselves becoming more and more involved with it and soon we were staging pageants and specially written dramatic episodes for public meetings and demonstrations. Indeed, some of the dramatic interludes staged at Medical-Aid for Spain rallies rank among our most successful experiments. In them we carried the agit-prop form to new heights. The group declamations, occasional songs, the tableau-like groupings of the actors had, in our street-theatre days, suffered from sloppy presentation, a lack of nuance; we were either too casual in our approach or too rigidly regimented. We were still dealing with the same basic elements of group declamation, songs and group action but these had become refined, polished and imbued with that special luminescence which a large audience generates. Furthermore we were now using whole batteries of spotlights and they were adding their own kind of excitement. The four or five overworked voices of the Red Megaphones attempting to make themselves heard above traffic and the noise of the streets had now become a choir of fifteen or twenty mixed voices backed by a small band of instrumentalists. The text of the group declamation, which in the past had generally consisted of rather turgid prose, was now the work of Hugh MacDiarmid who could handle words like a Chinese juggler keeping twelve plates in the air with his feet.

There was a new ingredient too, the personal statement or statements made by members of the audience. These were planned and rehearsed interpolations made by two or three individuals seated in different parts of the auditorium and interviewed by us before the actual event. They would be asked several questions about themselves and their answers would then be whittled down to a few short sentences lasting anything from thirty to forty-five seconds. This is the kind of thing:

> My name is Arthur D. I'm a face worker at Agecroft Colliery, Pendleton. I'm on short time, a three-day week. I support the Spanish people's struggle because their fight and my fight is the same.

or:

> My name is Mary Parkinson. I'm thirty-four years old and I'm a back-tenter in Worral's Mill, Salford. I'm married with two children, Norah aged fourteen and Eddie aged twelve. My husband's a brass-moulder but he's out of work. Been idle for two years. I think it's terrible what's happening in Spain, the way our Government's helping the fascists.

At pre-arranged points in the script, these speakers would stand up, spotlights would pick them out and they would say their piece. Their statements would be sandwiched between republican songs sung by the choir or, on some occasions, by Paul Robeson and the whole thing would be given shape by a framework composed of passages from Hugh MacDiarmid's magnificent poem on the Spanish Civil War, *The Flaming Poetaster*. The effect produced by juxtaposing the flat Lancashire accents of housewives and unemployed workers against the soaring voices of the choir, the rich velvety base-baritone of Paul Robeson, or the stinging hail of MacDiarmid's poetry, was riveting. The use of such contrasts was to become an integral feature of many of our productions in the years ahead, particularly in plays like *Johnny Noble* and *Uranium 235*. It was also destined to become a notable feature of the post-war radio-ballads, those B.B.C. documentaries in which the form and spirit of folk-music and recorded actuality strive to become a single entity.

Following the production of *Fuente Ovejuna* we staged, in fairly quick succession, two plays dealing with war and peace, very different from each other in style and content. The first of these was *The Good Soldier Schweik*. Both Joan and I had read Hasek's novel some years before and had fallen in love with it, and when we heard that Piscator had produced a stage version of it in Germany we were determined that we would give it its first British production. We acquired a copy of the script without too much trouble but, unfortunately, it was in German and neither of us could read it. However by using the English translation of the novel and a German dictionary we succeeded in making a reasonable English adaptation.

In his production Piscator had made use of back-projection and life-sized marionettes. We rejected the marionettes but embraced the idea of back-projection with enthusiasm. Our unending discussions and planning for the ultimate theatre had made us receptive to new technical developments and innovations which might lend extra dimensions to the theatre. So we set about investigating the possibility of borrowing or acquiring in some way the special equipment required. The results of our investigations were not encouraging. German refugee actors spoke disparagingly of equipment which kept breaking down and which, when it did work, made so much noise that the actors couldn't be heard. Replies to enquiries were even more discouraging, the cost of hiring was prohibitive – more than we spent on an entire production; furthermore one needed a stage with great depth in order to give the projector an 'adequate throw'. To clinch matters, there was only one such projector in the country and the owners were not prepared to hire it without a team of operating technicians. We decided that we would dispense with back-projection. The following day there appeared in one of the evening papers an item dealing, in some detail, with our unsuccessful quest. That same evening four young men turned up at our rehearsal, engineering research scientists from Metropolitan-Vickers. They wanted details concerning our specific needs. We told them and they went away. Three days before the dress rehearsal they turned up again, this time in a Ford truck with our back-projector which they had built! It worked beautifully, much better than Piscator's, said our German friends.

Schweik fell naturally into our style of production. It contained so many of the basic elements of agit-prop technique. It possessed characters, true! But those characters leaned heavily towards caricature. Its episodic structure was firmly in the agit-prop tradition as was its anabasis. Even the expressionistic side of agit-prop was present, in the form of comic dance-interludes. In the second of our anti-war plays there were few such influences.

I had discovered Aristophanes a few years earlier in a second-hand bookshop in Leeds. It was my first contact with the classical theatre of Greece and what better introduction could there be for an adolescent youth? The pub-crawling episode in *Schweik* had taught us to respect the knockabout-comedy routines of the variety stage; our presentation of the drunken perambulations of Schweik and Woditchka owed a great deal to the various comic turns we had seen at the Salford Hippodrome. Now *Lysistrata's* chorus of old men were being given the same treatment, and it worked splendidly! And wasn't the Magistrate a figure straight out of burlesque? Then there was the singing and dancing which occupied a fair slice of Aristophanes' text: surely that wasn't too far removed from the style of the musicals which were coming out of Hollywood! Unfortunately we lacked the resources which would have allowed us to present *Lysistrata* as a musical. We did the next best thing and produced it as a spirited romp with lots of bawdy jokes and amusing horseplay. It laid the foundations for a more radical reworking of the text in which soldiers' scenes were interpolated between scenes of striking women and where recondite references to obsolete religious practices were cut out in favour of lines and short sequences borrowed from *The Acharnians*, *The Thesmophoriazusae* and *The Peace*.

Lysistrata opened at the Lesser Free Trade Hall at the time Chamberlain and Daladier were preparing to hand Czechoslovakia over to Hitler and the excitement of our play was lost in the rising tide of fear and confusion which accompanied that episode. We were consumed with a terrible sense of urgency and felt we could no longer afford the luxury of producing plays which didn't make an immediate and specific political statement about the danger confronting us all. The oblique parallels of *Schweik* and *Fuente* were all very well but the world was racing headlong towards disaster and we had passed the point where events could be influenced by a reference to the Peloponnesian War or even to that other war which had given birth to Schweik. It's not enough, we said, to have plays which make a generalised exposure of the nature of Capitalism, they must have specific objectives and they must be about events which are taking place now. It wasn't a matter of having less art and more politics but of having more clearly stated politics and more powerful art. The better the politics, we reasoned, the better the art and the nearer we would be to achieving our goal of a truly popular theatre.

Our next pre-war production was to make use of all our newly developed talents. We had often toyed with the idea of producing a living newspaper. The Russians had pioneered the form during the building of the Turksib railway when travelling-theatre groups, faced with audiences of illiterates, had presented shows dealing with the day-to-day politics of the project. The American Federal Theatre had adopted the idea and in 1936 produced *Triple A Ploughed Under* and its most successful living newspaper *One Third of a Nation* had just closed after playing for 237 performances, something of a record for a left theatre at the time. We felt that the time had arrived for us to see what we could do with the form.

The task of collecting newspaper items dealing with the events leading up to the Munich pact and its appalling aftermath was undertaken by the entire company. Everything we had learned about theatre and politics in the years of work was now to be put to use – the mass-declamatory form, the satirical comedy style of agit-prop, the dance-drama of *Newsboy*, the simulated public meetings of *Still Talking* and *Waiting for Lefty*, the constructivism of *John Bullion*, the expressionism of *Miracle at Verdun*, the burlesque comedy of *Lysistrata*, the juxtaposition of song and actuality from the Spanish Civil War pageants and the fast-moving episodic style of *The Good Soldier Schweik*.

From the agit-prop period onwards, we had adopted a somewhat eclectic approach to stage-design. *Newsboy* and the sketches accompanying it had been presented on a bare stage with simple spotlighting marking off the acting areas. *Waiting for Lefty* had also used a bare stage with some action in the auditorium and with two kitchen chairs and a small table for the inset scenes. *Miracle at Verdun* had used a formalised set for the graveyard scenes and some rather nondescript furniture for the League of Nations sequence. *John Bullion* had been unashamedly constructivist. *Fuente Ovejuna* had been architectonic-cum-impressionist and *Schweik* had been played in portable revers-ible screens. *Last Edition* represented a complete break with formal theatre staging. When it opened at the Lesser Free Trade Hall, it was on a stage which, in addition to the central platform or stage proper, had two further platforms running the full length of each side of the auditorium so that that the audience was enclosed on three sides. There were scenes during which all three stages were in use at the same time; other scenes used only one or two of the stages. Following spots were used for each of the two side-platforms and the overall effect was not unlike a fast-moving variety show, the kind of theatre, that is, with which most of us were familiar. The similarity was reinforced by an added use of song and dance. One or two of the episodes were reworked versions of ideas which had been used in the early days of Theatre of Action when we had neither enough actors nor sufficient resources to carry them out properly. In some instances we combined ideas from *Newsboy* with scenes which had been inspired by early Hollywood musicals like *42nd Street* and *Fox Movie-tone Follies of 1932*.

The theme of unemployment ran like a thread through *Last Edi-tion*. It was a subject about which we were well informed. Some of us, indeed, were experts on the subject and there was scarcely an actor in the group who hadn't been on the dole at some time or another. For many of us the most potent symbols of the thirties were the unem-ployed hunger-marches. In the confines of a formal stage structure the presentation of a hunger-march would have involved all kinds of problems; with our three connected stages it became a very simple matter. The hunger-march episodes in *Last Edition* were an amalgam of ideas drawn from agit-prop sketches, *Schweik* and *Waiting for Lefty*.

Among the most effective scenes in the production were those dealing with the Gresford pit disaster. Gresford was one of those mass killings which were a periodic feature of the privately owned coal industry. The annual toll of deaths due to rock-falls, explosions and pneumoconiosis was, apparently, acceptable to the public, provided that only one or two corpses at a time were added to the list. But 265 dead in one fell swoop! Even the Tories couldn't talk that away. We presented the episode in two parts, first as an 'open' scene with simultaneous action on all three stages with writing and acting strongly influenced by the crowd scenes from *Fuente Ovejuna*, and secondly, in marked contrast, as a trial scene with dialogue taken from verbatim accounts which appeared in newspapers at the time of the disaster. The people depicted on the stage are real people.

Specific political events and the individuals associated with them were dealt with in a variety of ways. One of the most interesting was what we called 'acting-out' episodes. These were scenes within scenes in which actors were called upon to step out of a role they were playing in order to assume a completely different role. This parenthetical device had been used frequently in agit-prop sketches such as *Rent, Interest and Profit* and *Their Theatre and Ours* and was used effectively in several Theatre Workshop post-war productions. An example is the 'Politics of Democracy' section printed below.

The staged recitation of poems like *The Fire Sermon*, Shelley's *Mask of Anarchy* and Aragon's *The Red Front* had been a regular feature of the early Theatre of Action shows. In *Aid for Spain* pageants we had made use of MacDiarmid's exhortatory poem on the Spanish Civil War and now we were using it again in *Last Edition* as a link between the several small scenes which made up the civil-war sequence.

The second part of that sequence, the departure of the four International Brigaders, made use of a device which had been a favourite with radio producers ever since Archie Harding had first used it in his brilliant B.B.C. documentary *'Crisis in Spain'*. The device was a simple one: an uncharacterised voice would repeat a phrase at intervals or would read out a list of names or a group of statistics or a catalogue of dates. Inset between the names, or places or dates there would be a naturalistic scene. The juxtaposition of flat statement against dramatic interludes produced a special kind of excitement. It was not unlike the effect of incremental repetition in a traditional ballad. We tended to over-use the device for we were still as poor as church mice and it was a cheap alternative to a change of décor. On the whole it worked well, though there was the odd occasion when it gave the wrong emphasis to a scene by making it unnecessarily portentous.

The Launcelot–Sigismund scene which came prancing at the heels of the Spanish Civil War episode was rooted in the idiom of Christmas pantomime. Indeed, the parodying of popular types of show-biz was an important ingredient of almost all our early shows. The burlesque of the Hollywood gangster film was one we were particularly attached to. It had featured in one of our earliest agit-prop sketches, *Their Theatre and Ours* and we used it in *Last Edition* (as in the Munich Pact episode printed below) and again in *Uranium 235*.

It will be obvious from the above that we tended to use the term 'Living Newspaper' rather loosely. Part documentary and part revue,

Last Edition was, stylistically, an anthology of everything we had ever done in the theatre. While some of it was very exciting, much of it was either ridiculously overwritten or hopelessly pedestrian and tedious. There were episodes when it must have seemed to the audience that the narrator's voice would never stop churning out statistics, items of news and the threadbare clichés which pass for wisdom in the mouths of politicians.

After five performances *Last Edition* was stopped by the police. Joan and I were arrested and fined for behaviour likely to lead to a breach of the peace, and though the company managed to survive for several months longer, the war finally put an end to its activities.

There had never been any doubt in our minds that we would reassemble after the war and continue with our work. When we did so only five of the original Theatre Union company were present. We met in a small rented warehouse near Manchester's Central station and, over a period of several weeks, discussed plans for a new theatre. We were fairly clear in our minds as to the kind of theatre we intended to build; our discussions were mainly about practical issues like finance, finding premises, drawing up training programmes, allocating jobs and responsibilities and deciding on a suitable opening programme. Most of us, I think, still believed that our aims could only be achieved by playing to working-class audiences. All the great theatres of the past, we argued, had been popular theatres and we cited Aeschylus, Sophocles, Aristophanes, Marlowe, Shakespeare, Jonson, Calderón, Lope de Vega, the Commedia dell'arte, Molière, etc. Furthermore, we said, all the great theatres had, in one way or another, been experimental theatres. Think of the way Marlowe's mighty line had streaked across the literary firmament scarcely twenty-five years after the limping cadences of *Gorbuduc* had first sounded in the Inner Temple. And hadn't Shakespeare teased and manipulated the language till it fitted the hands of the age like magic gloves? And how quickly Jonson was off the mark, eager to dissect the new merchant class at the moment of its birth and, in the process, fashioning brilliant new satires out of the old moralities. In Italy the troupes of the Gelosi and I Comici Confidenti had taken the characters from the ancient rituals and had sent them cavorting through sixteenth- and seventeenth-century Europe. Molière had taken those same characters and had worked with them to create a brilliant dramatic literature.

Not that experiment in itself was enough to create popular theatre; nineteenth- and twentieth-century theatrical experiments had proved that. The numerous attempts to change the physical relationship of actors and audience were among the most important of those experiments. The proscenium arch had, in some cases, been banished; apron stages, thrust stages, and central stages had been adopted. Opponents of the illusionist type of theatre had removed everything which might conceal technical aids such as light and sound sources or engineering devices. In some extreme cases actors had been replaced with life-sized puppets and even with cut-out abstract shapes. Less adventurous innovators had settled for a theatre of synthesis where acting, dancing, singing, music, sculpture, painting and architecture would come together in a meaningful fusion.

As far as we were concerned experiment was merely a part of our social and political commitment; it was a tool which would make the theatre more capable of dealing with the reality of the world we were living in. Our emphasis on a working-class audience was part of that reality. We were not concerned with philanthropic gestures or with demonstrating that our hearts were in the right place. We *needed* a working-class audience in order to survive; without it there could be no real development, the theatre could never be anything more than a charming toy. How in the world could one possibly build a great theatre unless one identified with and drew sustenance from the people who, in our society, produce wealth – the working class? Of course, it was also a reality that working people had stayed away from the theatre in large numbers ever since the Elizabethan age or, at least, since Jacobean times. Indeed there were large areas of Britain where no theatre existed at all. Scores of provincial theatres had been converted to cinemas in the years following the First World War and it's doubtful whether more than a handful of folk regretted it. For most working people the basic form of entertainment was the Hollywood film. It might be argued that the films current at the time were in no way superior to the plays produced by provincial theatres. Were they not just as escapist, just as lacking in real ideas as the worst kind of repertory play? The answer must be no. Furthermore, the making of a film demanded a degree of technical expertise which few theatres could match. As an art form film belonged to the age of the internal-combustion engine and the assembly-line, the age of speed and through the use of montages, rapid cross-cutting and speeding up of the projected visual images, it could reflect that speed. It could produce a quick succession of short scenes in a way that was beyond the resources of all but the most splendidly equipped theatres.

More important was the fact that film actors and actresses like James Cagney, Edward G. Robinson, Spencer Tracy, Jean Harlow, Sylvia Sydney were frequently called upon to act working-class roles and could do so convincingly. They were certainly more like the audiences who watched them than were the average hero and heroine of the English stage play of the period or, for that matter, than the top-hatted-and-tailed heroes of many British films. My memory of English films of the early thirties is of endless inane caperings of actors got up to look like butlers disguised as Claude Hulbert or Jack Buchanan and of leading ladies who delivered their lines like well-brought-up children intent on pleasing nanny. Small wonder that we were emotionally prepared for the acculturative invasion of the Hollywood talkie with its tough guys and its wisecracks.

In our theatre, we said, an actor will be able to walk into a steel foundry and pass as a puddler, our actresses will be able to stand at a loom and look like any other Lancashire mill-girl. Perhaps we were a little over-ambitious but the company which we assembled didn't look like a group of actors and they spoke in the accents of Glasgow, Tyneside, Huddersfield, Chichester, Leeds, Salford and South London. This new company we called Theatre Workshop since we intended that it should be both a production unit and a training school where new approaches to acting could be tried out. Our actors would be able to handle their bodies with the same degree of skill and control that was generally regarded as the special domain of ballet-dancers and professional athletes. We were going to find ways of developing our voices so that we could handle the most exacting kind of roles. As for acting proper, we would combine Stanislavski's method of 'living the role' with the improvisational techniques of the Italian Comedy. And for a repertoire – we would create a tailor-made one for ourselves, a repertory consisting of plays which would match at every stage the talents of the company and would extend those talents with each new production. We would, at the same time, carry the lessons learned in *Newsboy*, *Last Edition* and the agit-prop theatre to new heights.

I don't think any of us doubted that we could and would realise our objectives. How else can one explain a dozen young men and women abandoning their various livelihoods in order to become strolling players? We knew, of course, that the work would be hard but we had worked hard in the years before the war and we had done so while doing all kinds of other jobs, jobs which had virtually subsidised our theatre activities. Now we were going to give all our energy and all our attention to building a theatre and, furthermore, we were going to be paid for our work. That, at least, was the theory.

It was taken for granted that Joan would be the producer in the new company and that I should take on the job of Art Director, a title which embraced various functions including being the company dramatist, dramaturg, teacher and songwriter. One of my first tasks was to write material for an opening production. During the period in which the company was being assembled we discussed frequently and at great length the kind of show needed to launch our venture success-fully. What was needed was a show in which entertainment and a statement of aims would be combined. It was important to make our political position clear while at the same time underlining our specific theatrical approach. Our introduction to the public should be in a show which, we felt, would lend itself to the kind of production ideas which had made *Last Edition* such an exciting experience. It should also give full scope to our views about the way actors should use their bodies, and make it possible for sound and light to make their full emotional impact. What we really needed was to create a form which was infinitely flexible, which would make it possible for us to move backwards and forwards in time and space as, say, with a film, and which could accommodate improvisations.

I wrote a double bill of two plays, each lasting about an hour. The first of them was an adaptation of Molière's *Flying Doctor*, a very free adaptation owing more to the Marx Brothers and the Commedia dell'arte than to Molière. It also included a scene taken straight from Rabelais's *Gargantua and Pantagruel* ('How a great scholar of England would have argued against Pantagruel and was overcome by Pan-urge'). In the period between the demise of Theatre Union and the birth of Theatre Workshop, some of us had been studying the history of the Commedia dell'arte and actors like the Andreinis and the Biancholellis had become saints in our calendar. And now we were about to pay homage to them! The other half of the bill was a ballad-opera called *Johnny Noble*.

An offer of premises in Kendal, Westmorland, had been accepted with enthusiasm and we packed and crated our gear ready for the great day when we would be told that our sponsors had completed their arrangements for our reception. The arrangements were never com-pleted, indeed they never got off the ground. In retrospect I doubt whether the sponsorship offer was ever meant seriously. When it finally dawned on us that we had spent several weeks waiting for premises that didn't exist we were in despair. All our plans had been made with Kendal in mind; it had become a kind of Mecca, a promised land where marvellous things could happen. To hell with sponsors, we said, let's go! So early in June 1945 we arrived in Kendal, booked a room in the Conservative Club there and proceeded to rehearse *Johnny Noble* and *The Flying Doctor*.

The launching of these two short plays took place at the Girls' High

School, Kendal, in August 1945. In their different ways they were both typical examples of the early Theatre Workshop style. *The Flying Doctor* was our first attempt at interpreting the ideas of the Commedia dell'arte, or rather what we imagined those ideas to be. The classic roles of Sganarelle, Gorgibus, Doctor Palaprat, Lucille and the rest were played as broad caricatures in the way that we imagined the Gelosi had played Scapino, Dottore, Pantalone and il Inamorata. Movement training which had gone hand-in-hand with rehearsals was now being put to full use, for the production was full of stylised movement, sometimes graceful, sometimes grotesque; indeed the entire production had been as carefully choreographed as any ballet. Costumes for the show owed much of their inspiration and flair to Callot's superb engravings. The set was a small miracle of ingenuity, consisting of a small, manually operated revolving stage. Its surface was made of thin wooden board which made it light enough to be handled with ease. To prevent creaking, the underside was strutted and wired in the manner of an old-fashioned aeroplane wing. The disc was divided into two halves by a cut-out door and window, one side of which represented the street while the other represented a house interior. It was a beautiful set, economic, light and airy; one felt that, at any moment, it might take off and fly.

It would have been difficult to find a more complete contrast than *Johnny Noble*. This hour-long saga of a young, deep-sea fisherman's life in the thirties and forties was played in black drapes without the use of any props or stage furniture. The elaborate use of light and sound provided a setting which was wonderfully versatile; at one moment the stage would represent a working-class street and, a moment later, it would be the deck of a battleship or the execution yard of a Nazi prison. No quick changes of screens or platforms, just an added spot or flood or the sound of a factory siren cross-fading with the cry of gulls. In *The Flying Doctor* the movement style had been consistent throughout; in *Johnny Noble* the actors were called upon to change from modern dance to naturalistic movement and back again without any break in the action of the play. A typical sequence has Johnny, the central character, sitting on a box during a night-watch aboard ship, a short contemplative scene which is shattered by alarum bells signalling the approach of enemy planes. Immediately Johnny becomes a member of the gunnery squad and then, as the bombs begin to crash down, becomes part of the gun's mechanism. A tremendously exciting moment of theatre lasting some three or four minutes, then the stage is a street again with children playing hop-scotch, neighbours gossiping and a young woman returning home from work.

In our press handouts we sometimes referred to *Johnny Noble* as 'a simple tale of thwarted love'. Thwarted love was certainly part of the story but the simplicity was achieved by using all our technical resources. New portable switchboards had been built and parallel-beamed lamps specially created so that it could be lit properly. A sound unit consisting of six turntables with speakers and amplifier had been built and there were times when David Scase and his assistant sound-operators were using all six turntables at once. In addition to recorded sounds of factory noises, ships' engines, aeroplanes, artillery and bombs, we also used passages of recorded instrumental music; the contrast between this and the *a capella* singing of the narrators was a sure way of altering the perspective of a scene.

Perhaps our most valuable resource was the fact that we were beginning to function like a real ensemble; the movement training, voice production, acting theory and classes dealing with the history of theatre were combining to weld us into a group with common aims and a common vision of the future. There was also the fact that we were able to draw, to some extent, upon our past work, for *Johnny Noble* was a lineal descendant of *Last Edition* and could trace its ancestry back through *Newsboy* to the Red Megaphones. It wasn't merely a case of having stylistic links with the past, there were actual incidents and scenes in *Johnny Noble* which had first surfaced in *Last Edition*. They had been refined and stripped of all that was superfluous in much the same way that the text of a traditional ballad is stripped down by passing through the mouths of generations of singers. As a production both *Johnny Noble* and *The Flying Doctor* reflected fairly accurately most of our ideas about theatre at that time. After the Kendal opening we toured our double bill through the surrounding district for the next two months. Both productions were kept in the company repertoire for the next five years and played throughout Britain, Norway, Sweden, West Germany and Czechoslovakia.

In the weeks following our first tour we added another short play to our repertoire, Lorca's magnificently erotic *Don Perlimplin's Love for Belisa in her Garden*. We were rehearsing it when the Smythe Report was published. This official account of the events leading up to the creation of the first atom bombs and the destruction of Hiroshima and Nagasaki made horrifying and fascinating reading. Two of the members of the group had been trained as scientists and they were of the opinion that 'The Bomb' was an ideal subject for a play. When I was urged to begin writing it, my immediate reaction was to treat the suggestion as a bad joke. My knowledge of scientific matters was, to say the least, rudimentary; I had once sat in a class with forty other boys and watched a strip of litmus-paper change colour. That was the full extent of my scientific training. It didn't, I felt, equip me to write a play dealing with atomic physics. My two scientist friends, however, were persuasive and they undertook to put me through a crash-course in physics and the history of science. By the time the company was ready to embark on its second tour I had completed the first phase of my scientific education and had begun the actual writing of the script.

I continued to write throughout the tour, mostly in dressing-rooms and rehearsal premises. Occasionally I would have to leave off writing a scene to go on stage and sing the Narrator in *Johnny Noble* or play a zany in *The Flying Doctor*. In December 1945 we were playing at the David Lewis Theatre in Liverpool and it was there that Joan began to rehearse the as yet unfinished *Uranium 235*. We continued to tour through January and early February 1946 and by that time we had reached the point where Joan's production had caught up with me and there was usually someone standing at my elbow waiting to grab the pages from me as soon as they were written.

Uranium 235 was first performed at the Newcastle People's Theatre on 18 February 1946. It ran for just sixty-five minutes and consisted of a short opening sequence similar to the one used later in the two-hour version, and most of the scenes which later formed Part II of the play's final version. Only the gangster-cum-atomic-ballet scene was missing. By our somewhat modest standards it was a great success. As part of a double bill, however, it raised all kinds of problems. Like *Johnny Noble*, *Uranium 235* was played in black drapes but the lighting-rig was different in each show. What suited *Johnny Noble*, *The Flying Doctor* and *Don Perlimplin* didn't suit *Uranium 235* so it was decided that I should extend it to full length so that no changes in the lighting-rig would be necessary once the light settings had been made. Fortunately, by then I had completed my course in the history of science and it was no hardship to sit down and write about Copernicus, Giordano Bruno, Democritus, Mendeleyev and the rest.

The first of the two-hour versions of *Uranium 235* was staged at the Community Theatre, Blackburn, on 22 April 1946. A revised opening and a new ending was written for a production at the Riley Smith Hall, Leeds University, on 23 September and the atomic-ballet sequence was added two or three weeks later.

In Uranium 235 we had again returned to the agit-prop style of theatre and had dug deep into its rich deposits of theatrical ideas. We had, so to speak, struck gold and had come up with sufficient raw material to fashion the kind of play needed to deal with the complex world of politics and atomic physics. *Johnny Noble* had made use of singing, dancing and acting and had succeeded in combining them into a cohesive style; we had, in the words of a newspaper critic, 'evolved a kind of working-class dance drama'. Apart from the final ten minutes of the show when the two roaring boys enter, the style of production had been fairly consistent throughout. In *Uranium 235*, however, a whole variety of styles were used; indeed the clash of different idioms was a vitally important feature of the over-all style.

How does one describe such a piece? An episodic play? A documentary? A historical pageant? A twentieth-century morality play? Almost any of these descriptions would be pertinent, but not completely so. In some ways it resembled the playing of a good jazz ensemble in which, after the theme has been stated, solo instruments take turns in exploring the theme's chordal structure, each one restating the theme in a different way. In *Uranium 235*, however, an actor was expected to be a trombone at one moment and a guitar the next and then to be a trumpet and a piano playing counter-melodies. They were faced with a series of rapidly changing scenes in which they were called upon to dance, sing, act, to speak in unison and to parody themselves doing all these things. A brief breakdown of the play illustrates the extent to which we were indebted to our earlier work in Theatre Union, Theatre of Action and the Red Megaphones.

The play opens with the Firewatcher's monologue, a blank-verse parody of the Watchman's soliloquy in Aeschylus' *Agamemnon*. There follows a short exchange between the Scientist and a 'planted' member of the audience (the Politician and the Heckler from *Still Talking*).

The expressionistic jazz-dance scene which follows is borrowed from the opening scene of *Last Edition* which was based on an idea in *Newsboy*.

There follows a short naturalistic episode in which actors play themselves engaging in an argument with the Scientist. This device for stripping away unnecessary layers of argument was used frequently in agit-prop sketches as was the double acting-out technique of the Greek scene in which parody and burlesque are used to expose false historical romanticism and its nineteenth-century theatrical reflection.

The Microphone Voice reeling off the list of wars and battles fought during the Greek and Roman eras was borrowed from radio-documentary technique and had been used extensively in *Last Edition*.

When the depersonalised Microphone Voice abandons the narration, it is taken up by an actor who talks directly to the audience as he changes his costume. This use of actor-as-narrator was a prominent feature of *Last Edition*.

Abandoning his narrator role, the actor leads us into a scene composed of three vignettes which mirror that early scene in which the Scientist tries to make himself heard above the frenzied chatter of a group of dancers. In the first of these vignettes a spirited fool's jig becomes a lynch-mob and culminates with the burning of a witch. In the second, a group of alchemists performs a slow formalised dance to the chorus of stichomythic gobbledegook, an episode with all the deliberation of a slow-motion film about gymnastics, and contrasting sharply with the scene which preceded it. The last of these historical vignettes has Giordano Bruno and Paracelsus caught up in a band of dancing revellers in which Death sets the pace. Bruno is finally burned at the stake. Elaborate costumes, the clever use of light and shadow and the richly orchestrated music gave these scenes a Goya-like texture and helped to underline the apparent lack of artifice in the actors scene which followed close on their heels.

Once again the passing of historical time was dealt with by actors playing themselves and talking directly to the audience, preparation for the impact of the nineteenth century and John Dalton's atomic theory!

The Dalton scene is played in a style borrowed from *Still Talking* and *Waiting for Lefty*; our audience is transformed into a nineteenth-century audience – members of the Manchester Literary and Philosophical Society. The political orator of *Still Talking* (the corrupt trade-union leader of *Waiting for Lefty*) has become the non-political, uncorrupted John Dalton. He is flanked by two committee members who mime sitting at a non-existent table, an idea borrowed from the Chinese theatre and filtered through Oplopkhov. Only the hecklers of those early productions have remained unchanged.

The final episode of the first part of *Uranium 235* deals with the Royal Society's reception of Mendeleyev's theory of the atomic table. We based it on an idea which had been used in *John Bullion* where the three gibberish-speaking secretaries collapse and melt like wax dummies.

For most of Part II of *Uranium* the stage is dominated by the Puppet Master, his Secretary and his servant Death, three characters whose expressionistic ancestry is obvious. They hold a series of auditions in the course of which we meet some of the leading figures in the history of atomic science.

The first of these auditionees is a duo – Marie and Pierre Curie. They describe their discovery of radium in rhymed verse as they dance a spirited waltz. Finally Pierre is ushered off by Death and Marie is left to complete the account in unrhymed verse to the rhythm of a slow waltz. She too is finally taken off by Death.

There followed a circus-act in which J. J. Thomson, discoverer of the electron, introduces us to his lion-taming act. After him comes Albert Einstein and his two cronies Nils Bohr and Max Planck. They are presented as knockabout comedians who claim to be ballet impresarios who prove their claim by staging their atomic ballet. This simple but effectively choreographed modern dance dealt with the step-by-step discovery of atomic fission. Fission having taken place, the dancers take over the stage and re-enact the fission process in a scene which is a burlesque of the Hollywood gangster movie of the thirties. A somewhat similar type of burlesque has been used in *Last Edition*.

This was the last of the scenes to deal with the purely scientific aspects of nuclear matters. The three short scenes which followed dealt with the social and political background of the events and had their stylistic roots in *Newsboy* and *Last Edition*. The drilling scientists which followed them was pure agit-prop, possibly the most effective example of agit-prop theatre we had ever staged.

The closing scenes of *Uranium 235* deal with the social and political consequences of the discovery of atomic fission. In terms of style they are a kind of simplified diagram of the whole play for they move easily through the expressionism of the modern morality play into the kind of political confrontation which is one of the main features of agit-prop theatre. The scene which actually ended the play was constantly being revised in order to keep pace with the constantly changing political situation.

At some point between Theatre Workshop's first presentation of *Uranium 235* in 1946 and its final performance at the Comedy Theatre in 1952 I wrote *The Other Animals*, a piece in which, for the last time, I attempted to bring together the various disparate elements which had combined to add up to a style.

At first glance it appears to have little in common with *John Bullion*, *Last Edition* or *Uranium 235* and yet, on reflection, one has to acknowledge that there is a family likeness. All of them, for instance, are political and all of them share the same kind of episodic structure, though in *The Other Animals* the episodes do not have the same sharp outline of those in *Last Edition* and *Uranium 235*. Again, all of them require the stage to simultaneously accommodate different times and places without a change of décor. They all call upon their actors to sing and dance as well as act, they all attempt to combine two or more contrasted theatrical idioms and they all incline towards expressionism.

And there the similarity ends. The central theme of *The Other Animals* differs radically from the rest of the plays discussed here. In them specific political events are dealt with and the actions which lead to those events. *The Other Animals*, on the other hand, is not so much concerned with specific political events as with the effects of the impact of political concepts on the inner life of a human being. In terms of real time, the play deals with the last two hours in the life of a condemned political prisoner, Robert Hanau. Prolonged ill-treatment and torture have reduced him to the point where he can no longer distinguish between fantasy and reality; his captors have become less real to him than the phantoms he conjures up in his delirium. The cage he occupies is real enough but no more real than the cage he has erected in his mind, the bars of which are fears, loyalties, beliefs, obligations and the need to maintain an identity. By betraying his comrades he could escape from the cage provided by his enemies; only through self-betrayal could he escape from that other cage.

In each of the plays from *John Bullion* to *Uranium 235* we were concerned to create a series of dramatic metaphors about the political struggles of a society. *The Other Animals* is a single extended metaphor of a man's struggle to create order out of chaos. It was rehearsed in a disused garage on Wilmslow Road, Manchester, and opened at the Library Theatre there on 5 July 1948. It was Theatre Workshop's last serious experiment in the theatre of expressionism.

A ballet with words

John Bullion

by James H. Miller *and* Joan Littlewood

CAST

BIRTHRIGHT, Sir Weldon, an armament's boss
WINMORE, Lord, an aristocratic coupon-clipper
DEAFEN'EM, Mister, a big noise in the Press
FORTUNE, Mister, a large piece of Finance Capital
DANCY PYE, Reverend, a fashionable creeper
BANKS, Miss, a used-up secretary

Four typists, three newsboys, three mannequins, three crippled ex-servicemen, two munition workers, one junior director and one electrician.

A hyper-pathetic voice, an ultra-unpleasant voice, a sanctimonious voice, a BBC announcer's voice and an echo of Pye's voice.

Chorus of children and crowd of workers.

NOTES

The set is constructivist, being designed to facilitate the movement of the actors rather than to represent anything. Curtains are dispensed with and the transitions from one movement to another are achieved by using documented sound sequences. The stage is divided into three levels or planes these being 1. a five-foot level which runs from left to right upstage, which is used for purposes of dramatic generalisation. 2. a level consisting of two sections, the meeting point of the sections being up centre just below the first level; they are placed at an angle of 90 degrees from each other (i.e. each section at an angle of 45 degrees from the first level). The height of the planes at this point is 2 feet. From here they slope down to stage level. These planes are used for stylised dance movements. The ordinary stage level completes the list.

LIGHTING

The lighting should be as rhythmic as possible and must be perfectly timed. The blackouts do not conclude an episode – they are part of the development of the play and therefore need careful rehearsal.

FIRST MOVEMENT. Basic set, no additional furniture.
SECOND MOVEMENT. Basic set plus 2 skeleton desks set down right and down left.
THIRD MOVEMENT. Basic set.
FOURTH MOVEMENT. Basic set plus 3 directors' stools down left and desk down right.
FIFTH MOVEMENT. Same as 4th plus skeleton pulpit set in angle of two sloping planes.
SIXTH MOVEMENT. Basic set plus desk down right.

[THE FIRST MOVEMENT] The auditorium lights are blacked out and the faint reverberation of a native drum is heard accompanied by the low chanting of repetition melody by a chorus. A green spotlight begins to creep over the stage and discovers a native witch-doctor squatting centre stage. He is wearing a black mask painted with white streaks and his body is swaying to the low chanting of the chorus. The rhythm intensifies and the witch-doctor rises to his feet and begins to build up a frenzied war-dance. The tempo and volume increase and, at peak, a second figure enters dressed in evening clothes and tall hat, a huge grotesque caricature of a man. He too wears a mask, the features being the same as the witch-doctor's, the colour, different, being white with black streaks. He dismisses the witch-doctor with a contemptuous hand movement and begins to execute a weird dance symbolising the modern war for profits. At the peak of the dance there is a blackout,

[THE SECOND MOVEMENT] Which lasts for ten seconds. During the blackout two desks are brought on and placed down right and down left. During this movement typing is heard offstage keeping time to the rhythm of the mime. Lights flash up, stylised typist discovered poised in an insouciant attitude on desk down left. 1 – 2 – 3 – Typist takes imaginary powder-puff (1,) flicks it (2,) powders her nose (3). 1 – 2 – Miss Banks enters (1,) takes one step and looks shocked (2,). 3 – 4 – Typist shrugs shoulders (3,) plants hands on hips (4). 1 – 2 – 3 – 4 – Miss Banks takes four determined and offended steps which land her down centre. On (4) she turns and faces the typist grimly.

I / used / to be / his sec - re - tri. /

> These words are spoken by a hyper-pathetic voice coming from offstage. Miss Banks makes four movements expressing the sense of the phrase. The voice offstage repeats 'I used to be his secretary' in the same rhythm. This time the typist responds with four movements, then: 1 – 2 – 3 – 4 – Miss Banks moves to desk right, puts down imaginary papers. 1 – 2 – Miss Banks turns (1,) sniffs (2). 3 – 4 – Typist flourishes puff (3,) makes contemptuous hand movement (4).

He'll turn / you over // to the junior / director. /

> This is spoken by an ultra-unpleasant voice coming from offstage. Miss Banks acts it in four vicious movements.

He'll turn / you over // to the Junior / Director. /

> Repeated by ultra-unpleasant voice on a slightly higher note. Miss Banks and typist freeze. The backplane is faded up to reveal a replica of Birthright (right), and the Junior Director (left). On 'he'll turn / you over' Birthright makes a scornful movement of throwing something over. On 'to the Junior / Director' the Junior Director comes to life: (to the) looks down his nose at Miss Banks, (Junior), cocks his thumb down disparagingly (Director).

He'll turn / you over // to the Junior / Director. /

Good Morning Sir!!!
Good Morning Sir!!

Good Morning Sir!

> *The lights on the back plane fade down on 'he'll turn you over'. The 'good morning sirs' are spoken, each on a higher note, finishing up simultaneously with 'director'. Miss Banks and the typist react to the 'good morning sirs.'*

And so / the day / of toil / begins. /

> *This is spoken by a sanctimonious voice offstage, cue 'Junior Director'. Simultaneously Birthright enters and makes four lascivious movements towards typist. On 'begins' he embraces her and there is a blackout.*

[THE THIRD MOVEMENT] During the blackout the typing from behind the previous movement is carried on. The two desks are cleared and the lights flash up to reveal, in roseate lighting, the four Directors Birthright, Deafen'em, Winmore and Fortune standing on the right sloping plane, Birthright downstage, and the four stylised typists on the left sloping plane. Miss Banks stands centre stage. Prokofiev's 'Chout ballet' commences and the movement begins.

1 – The whole cast stands, fixedly emphasising the various characteristics of the groups.

Miss Banks reacts to all the moves. Birthright remains frozen until 10. The four Directors remain frozen until (6).

2 – The typists poise fingers and point right toes. 3 – The typists place hands on hips. 4 – The typists bend their heads left, sway their hips. 5 – The typists smile coyly, make suggestive flirting movement.

The four typists remain frozen until (10).

6 – Deafen'em, Winmore, Fortune come to life and stare at typists pop-eyed. 7 – Three Directors wink, satisfied, begin to raise their left hands. 8 – Three Directors point their left thumbs at typists, grinning. 9 – Three Directors nudge man on right of them with right elbows. 10 – All four Directors nod heads approvingly, typists exaggerate the invitation of their gestures.

The music breaks into a satirical dance, the Directors and the typists begin to move down the sloping planes and round to meet centre stage. The Directors gambol fatly, throwing their feet up in front of them and behind them. The typists move sexually, first with their hands on their hips then, moving their arms more loosely and expressively. As they meet, centre, they turn and move upstage, still keeping the rhythm of the dance. One after another the typists turn daintily to face the audience. On a rising phrase in the music the typists retreat coyly to the left. The Directors summon them back imperiously, they fly across the stage like butterflies and there is an embrace. Miss Banks has retreated before the dancers and now stands up centre.

A deep motor-horn, sounding once in the rhythm of a telephone bell, is heard above the music. Birthright thrusts his typist away and pirouettes to an imaginary desk down right. The typist falls, like an overturned tailor's dummy on to Miss Banks.

Three other motor-horns, telephone bells are heard one after another and first

Deafen'em, then Winmore, then Fortune pirouette to their imagined stools down left. The typists, thrown aside, have fallen one on top of the other in a flattened diagonal. The music grows louder; to it is added the sound of recurrent motor-horns and sirens and Newsboys' shouts. As the sounds reach peak three newsboys dash across the back plane from right to left shouting topical newspaper slogans (e.g. 'Anglo-German Naval Agreement Reached'). As the newsboys exit, blackout.

[THE FOURTH MOVEMENT] The sounds are sustained during the blackout. Birthright's desk (down right) and the three directors' stools (left centre) are brought on during the blackout. Miss Banks goes off. The lights fade up and the sounds fade down to leave sound of a typewriter which continues behind Fortune's speech. Birthright is seated at his desk, the other three on their stools; as the lights fade up there is the sound of one isolated telephone motor-horn. On this Fortune speaks into an imaginary telephone.

Fortune. Hello Birthright! So Vickers' armament shares are booming, eh? I've just heard from Deafen'em that the price is up to 63. (*Cross-fade typing with sound of machine-gun fire.*) I want another ten thousand if you can get them.

As Fortune begins speaking the four typists slowly come to life and move downstage to their Director. Three of them sit by the stools and mechanically begin typing. Birthright's typist stands by his side and on the cross-fade he gives her a handful of papers, she moves up the right sloping plane; in the rhythm of the machine-gun fire, at the top she chalks ten thousand in huge figures on a blackboard above the upstage plane; she then moves down to stand left of Birthright again.

Winmore. (*Cutting in quickly on Fortune*) Ai say, hello! hello darling boy, is that you? No. Is it *really*? What! Oh yes. Yes quaite! No! Not really! Oh! My dear, it's too utterly incredible. Ai say, old thing (*Cross-fade machine-gun fire with typing.*) Archie's just told me Vickers' are doing frightfully well. No, really! Well, I was just sort of wondering if you could chuck me over a few thousand, say ten thousand. (*Cross-fade typing with machine-gun fire.*) Do sort of try and wangle it for me, darling boy.

Again the typist moves up the plane and down again.

Deafen'em. (*Cutting in quickly on Winmore*) Hallo! Hallo! Welly? Deafen'em of the 'Daily Excess' speaking. Listen! (*Cross-fade machine-gun fire with typing.*) I've got the latest news hot from Geneva; the great International Peace Conference has broken down for the thirteenth and *last* time. What's that? Your representative brought back the news forty-eight hours ago? No. Oh, I get you. So that accounts for the boom in Vickers. (*Cross-fade typing with machine-gun fire.*) Any rise in the prices since this morning? No! Get me ten thousand right away!

Machine-gun fire held behind the following sequence.

Birthright. One thousand, two thousand.

Birthright
Deafen'em. (*Together*) Booming. (*Add sounds of heavy artillery.*)

Deafen'em. Three thousand, four thousand. (*On a higher note*).

Birthright.
Deafen'em.
Winmore. (*Together, loudly*) BOOMING. (*Up heavy artillery.*)

Winmore. Five tharsand, six tharsand. (*Very high note.*)

Birthright.
Deafen'em.
Winmore.
Fortune. (*Together, louder still*) BOOMING (*Hold heavy artillery.*)

Birthright.
Deafen'em. (*Together, very quickly*) Seven thousand, eight thousand.

Winmore.
Fortune. (*Together, very quickly*) Nine thousand, ten thousand.

All. Booming, booming, booming etc. (*Increasing in speed and volume.*)

> *On 'Eight thousand' the three typists slowly begin to rise to their feet as if impelled. The 'Booming' chorus goes faster and faster and the typists begin to move towards the right in a straight line; they move stiffly, mechanically. To the chorus, sounds of general warfare are added. As the effects reach peak, three mannequins in bathing costumes and hideous gas masks enter right on the upstage plane. The effects drop, 'Booming' is now only hissed, the typists freeze and the sound of children singing*

> > *All things bright and beautiful,*
> > *All creatures great and small,*
> > *All things wise and wonderful,*
> > *The Lord God made them all.' –*

> *is heard off stage. As the mannequins exeunt left the sounds of warfare quickly swell up and drown the children's voices. There is a sudden blackout and silence.*

[THE FIFTH MOVEMENT] During the silent blackout there is a loud crash and the electrician is heard swearing. He then comes stumbling on to the stage with a torch or flash-lamp. The whole of this speech must be made to sound spontaneous.

Electrician. It's alright everybody, it's alright. Stay there, _____ (*Using the name of the actor who is playing Birthright*). I say, don't move at the back there! We'll be going on in a minute. Excuse me, everybody, but I'm the electrician of this damn show. I've just fallen across a chap, in the wings here! Let me see, what does he call himself? (*Produces a card from his waistcoat pocket.*) The Reverend Dancy Pye; he wants to spout to you about 'Peace'. That alright with you, _____ (*Using the name of the actor who is playing Birthright*)? Right! Ring up the curtain!

The lights flash up. Pye has carried his pulpit on during the blackout and placed it up centre. The Directors have turned their backs on the audience and are seated as if in church. The four typists are kneeling in front of the pulpit. Pye prepares to speak, when the electrician nearly pushes him over by shoving his hand on Pye's shoulder and vaulting on the left sloping plane. (This should momentarily destroy the equilibrium of the set and break down the superficial reality of Pye, turning him into a mere property.) The electrician then chalks a huge cross over the 10,000s on the blackboard; he strolls off along the back plane, whistling, and Pye's second attempt at speech is crushed by a tremendous clatter, as the electrician jumps off the plane into the wings. Again Pye makes elaborate preparations for beginning his sermon but as he opens his mouth sounds of applause and of an orchestra tuning up are heard. He pauses, bows, then as the sounds die away he begins to speak. (The lighting at the beginning of his speech is dim and religious).

Pye. *(In an exaggeratedly sanctimonious voice)* This morning, my dear brethren in Jesus Christ, I am going to address you all on the subject of Peace. Peace the sanctified, Peace the divine.

The parts of Pye's speech set to a narrower measure to the left of the page require an entire change of personality, voice and gesture on the part of the actor. He changes from his heroic, sanctimonious self and twists in servile fashion round the side of the pulpit. The voice which drones on behind his 'business-man' voice, (set to the right) is a caricature of his pulpit manner. It is done by **His Double** *standing behind the back plane (if possible) who should sound almost like a gramophone running down. There should be a change of lighting on the changes of speech, the dim religious lighting for the pulpit speeches and the ordinary stage lighting for the mixed speeches. The typists kneel piously during the sermon parts, but chatter and twist their heads during the business bits.*

What! Birthright, Winmore, Deafen'em, Fortune, you here? Well, well, well!

His Double. *(See above)*
Peace the sanctified,
Peace the divine.
Peace the sanctified,
Peace the divine . . .
(Repeat to end of speech.)

Birthright opens his mouth and emits a long-drawn-out mocking sound, like the sound of a saxophone.

I – er – trust your armament activities have been successful lately. Ah, but need I ask, need I ask? Your talents as a business man are too well known, my dear Sir Weldon, God be praised that we still have men of such ability to enrich the commerce of our beloved Empire!

Yea, for the land of our forefathers has always cherished the thought of Peace. It was the first to spread the word of God in those dark deserts of ignorance, where the British flag fluttered triumphant over the benign heads of Christ's missionaries.

Oh, eh, by the way Sir Weldon, I met the – ah – Bishop at Lady Winmore's bridge party last evening. He tells me that Vickers are doing very well indeed. Booming in fact. The Church is in dire need of funds, I am sad to say, and I – er – thought very seriously of investing two thousand pounds of the Church's capital in Vickers. That'll be four hundred shares, yes? Of course this is strictly between . . . ourselves, Sir Weldon. Strictly between ourselves. The fact is . . .

His Double. The flag of our fathers, the flag of Peace. The flag of our fathers, the flag of Peace . . . (*Repeat to end of speech.*)

As Pye's final speech fades down the lighting fades and then grows to a red spotlight. With this comes the voice of:

Radio Announcer. This is the Northern Programme. Here is the first General News Bulletin, copyright reserved. A report from Geneva states that the Peace Conference, for which Sir John Simon left London last night, broke down early today at the first morning's session. It had been decided to postpone the discussion on _____ to a later date. Consequently the first dispute item on the agenda was the discussion on the position between Japan and China. No decision was arrived at and the point was referred back. Princess Marina today opened the extensive new Convalescent Home for Disabled Ex-Servicemen. The Princess was wearing one of the new ostrich-feather muffs. The tension on the Italian–Abyssinian frontier was today heightened by the arrival of one hundred light Italian bombing planes. Market Report: Iron and Steel shares continued to command a big following and in every instance prices soared to still higher levels. Baldwins' rose to 110, Imperial Chemicals hardened at 114. British Oxygens continued to advance as did London Bricks and Tilbury Contracting. Oils were in heavy demand, Anglo-Iranians and Shells being favoured most. Wheat prices were the highest since 1914 and there was frenzied bidding for English Steels and Vickers. The closing prices were: Allied Iron 98, Baldwins 110, massed on . . . Famine sweeps the Balkan states Hitler says German nation will be Vickers 272 avenged France says pact was to be observed only in time of _____ Vickers 298 peace . . . Martial Law declared in Vickers 342 Brest Support your – Vickers by. . . . In time of . . . Vickers 385 . . . strife . . . you owe it to Vickers 395 your Empire Vickers 401–, 409 . . . 412 . . .'

The lights fade up drowning the Mutograph. With the lights 'The Steel Foundry' is faded up again; underneath it can be heard the sound of machine-gun fire. As the effects reach peak there comes a motor-horn telephone bell, then.

Fortune. Hi, Birthright! Vickers have blown up the market. Now we'll see the Germans march on Russia inside a week! Imperial Chemicals are touching 400! Yes sir 400 (*two motor horns on first 400*).

Winmore. (*Cross-fading with Fortune*) I say, Welly dear! I'm too utterly thrilled about your *sweet* company, too thwilled. My dear, how *naice* of them to send the shares up like that, just when I'm so frightfully broke. I say, old boy, do you know Dodie offered to buy my armament holdings at 500? But I'm not selling, old boy, no bally fear. I say, old thing, isn't it awful about those wretched Chinks absolutely impervious to all decent ideas of culture and all that sort of thing? The Pater thinks (*three motor horns*) that the only thing to do is to send half a dozen gunboats down the Kiang and mow the cads down.

Deafen'em. (*Cross-fading with Winmore*) Say, Sir B., yer know that ten thousand of Vickers asked you to get me? Well, can you make it twenty thousand to twenty five thousand? I've just heard that French planes have crossed the German frontier. That should send you up another hundred or so, eh, Birthright? Noni's rather anxious to invest some of the capital she holds, for the War Orphans' Fund. So do you think you could get her some more too?

[THE SIXTH MOVEMENT] As the lights come up on the 'Eh, Birthright' the four typists begin to move, in the rhythm of Mossolov's music. They move in line up the left sloping plane, across and down the right to Birthright's desk. They collect imaginary papers from him which he hands out with robot-like precision. At the beginning of Pye's speech the music fades down and the typists pause and stand, two on either side of Pye's pulpit. The inner two pose in attitudes of Salvation-Army sanctity, the outer two powder their noses. During the whole of Pye's speech the three Directors on the stools keep up a ceaseless and silent activity, miming telephoning, writing cheques etc.

Pye. (*Cross-fading with Deafen'em*) My dearly beloved brethren in Jesus Christ, I exhort you, in this our country's hour of need, to take up the cross of rightenousness and follow our Lord Jesus Christ to the tortured battleground of Golgotha.

Fortune. Hello Birthright! ten thousand more shares you hear? ten thousand more shares. Yes, ten thousand more, ten thousand more, ten thousand more etc. (*Guns on 'Yes, ten thousand more'.*)

Winmore. (*'On first ten thousand more'*) Hello Welly! Do get ten thousand more. What? No ten thousand more, Yes for me and papa what?

Deafen'em. (*On second 'what'*) Yes ten thousand more, ten thousand more etc. (*Increase guns on second 'what'*). Say, Sir B., gimme ten thousand more. Yeah! ten thousand more, ten thousand more etc.

Mossolov is faded up again at the end of Pye's speech. He comes down from his pulpit and embraces two of the typists. One typist sits on Birthright's knees swinging her legs to 'ten thousand more'. The other makes love to Fortune. As Deafen'em speaks, the sound of guns increases; 'ten thousand more' beats on like a hammer. It reaches peak, then drops, as three disabled ex-servicemen enter and cross the back plane from right to left. The 'ten thousand more' is now only hissed, the effects are very faint and the ex-servicemen can be heard whining 'matches, bootlaces, matches'. The lights fade down as they exit, Mossolov is faded up. During the blackout the three stools are taken off. The lights fade up to show two workmen, naked to the waist, throwing imaginary shells from one to the other on the upstage plane. They move to the rhythm of Mossolov and are silhouetted against a red light. Birthright is still seated at his desk down right.

After ten seconds the four typists with Pye behind them enter down right. They droop wearily, with their heads on each other's backs. They drag themselves up the left plane and down the right keeping time to the rhythm of 'the Steel Foundry'. Down left the three Directors enter and follow them. As the line crosses the stage from right to left Birthright rises automatically and leads them. The two workers continue to throw shells. The line drags on until a change of theme in the music, when they become stiff, machine-like automata moving their arms like a piston. At a second change in theme the line breaks up. Their bodies all sway in different directions. They become more and more savage, breaking into a frenzied dance of war like that of the witch-doctor in the first movement. At the height of the dance a savage voice shrieks out 'WAR'. The whole group fling out their hands and cry 'WAR WILL BE DECLARED!' Mossolov fades out on 'War'. At the end of their shout the group freeze and a Mutograph begins to pass slowly across the back wall.

Mutograph. French workers demonstrate for peace Martial law declared in Paris Uneasy situation of French Bourse . . . chorus girl says she was . . . British dockers refuse to load munitions . . . asked to dance Slight drop in Vickers . . . without any crisis intensifies Germany paralysed by political mass strikes. Clothes – Sporadic selling of Imperial Chemicals serious _____ . . . Vickers drop to 328.5 Italian strikers occupy munition factories Baldwins offer shares at 176 Baldwin warns the nation – Plan with the Planets Astrologer prophesies Vickers drop to 304 . . . riots . . . in Paris Pitiful case of Woolworth Heiress's Riots in Berlin . . . fifth husband . . . war . . . street chaos frantic . . . . Vickers 272 . . . Japanese soldiers fraternise with Chinese Red soldiers . . . War is the lifeblood of the nation says Mussolini, Italian soldiers say we will not fight Vickers 250 Steady decline in prices . . . Balkan states on verge of Revolution . . . Famous film star divorces Vickers 215 husband because Revolution in Spain . . . he bites his nails . . . British textile workers strike two hundred thousand say we will not work for war Alimony case Vickers 172 . . . . Vickers 164 Anti-war demonstrations and strikes paralyse Britain Riots in Vickers 123 all principal French towns Vickers 101 International anti-war movement's call for action answered by European strikes and demonstrations . . . Vickers 92 Anti-war organisations issue ultimatum Vickers 83 . . . All preparations for war sabotaged Vickers 60 strikes 54 Revolution in 31 30 29 28 the market is declared. . . . . comrades . . . . the electric newspaper has been taken over by the workers. A manifesto issued by the joint . . .

On the word 'declared' factory sirens are heard offstage. After 'comrades' the 'internationale' is heard faintly. It grows as the lights come up and the sound and light drown the Mutograph. The 'Internationale' flowers into several different languages. Workers march on to the stage from all sides. The two munition workers march forward to join them. The 'Internationale' floods the stage, the typists are lost among the workers. The four Directors and Pye collapse like deflated balloons in a heap down centre. The 'Internationale' reaches peak. The lights fade down to darkness and the voices are heard dying away as if marching on into distance.   *[The End]*

Newsboy

Workers' Theatre Movement

Co-ordinated and planned: Workers' Laboratory Theatre, New York, in montage from the poem by V. J. Jerome

English adaptation by G. Bluemenfeld

[SCENE 1] Amber spot thrown on Newsboy. As the play opens the News-boy, who represents the establishment bourgeois newspapers, stands in the amber spot and shouts in staccato symbolic fashion.

Newsboy. News Chronicle Empire (*repeat*). Plans for royal Jubilee. SIX KINGS AT ROYAL WEDDING. CUP FINAL LATEST.

As he talks the spot grows larger till it covers the entire stage. With the growth of the spot comes the growth of the Newsboy from a symbolic figure of all newsboys to an individual Newsboy, realistically selling his newspapers. This is the transformation to the Second Scene.

[SCENE 2] As the 1st Newsboy shouts his headlines, 2nd Newsboy walks across the stage. They glare at each other for a moment and the 1st Newsboy takes a kick at the 2nd, who runs off the stage.

Enter stage right a pretty girl. At the same time a well-dressed young man, left.

Throughout the entire scene, the Newsboy is shouting his words. The young man bumps into the young lady.

Young Man. (*Lifting his hat*) Awfully sorry. (*Young lady does not reply.*) But I say: I know you. Haven't I met you somewhere before?

Young Lady. No, I haven't been there. (*Sticks her nose in the air. Young man follows patiently behind. Enter blind woman, left.*)

Bl. Woman. (*Nasal whine*) Pity the blind, kind friends. Pity the poor blind. Pity the poor blind.

A charitable fat man comes across the stage from right to the blind woman. He drops a penny in her tin, buys a paper and exit.

[SCENE 3] Ballet scene. As the blind woman comes across the stage and turns to go back, all the figures who have thus far passed in the street scene come on stage and, working on three parallel planes with the same dance movement, go through movements which bring out their individual characteristic movements. All face the audience. They combine voices with characteristic gesture, i.e. the young lady keeps repeating 'Why don't you go away! I'll call a policeman! I'll call a policeman!' The blind woman repeats her singsong. The 2nd Newsboy shouts 'News Chronicle Empire. CUP FINAL DRAW. PLANS FOR ROYAL JUBILEE.'

In the meantime, the 1st Newsboy elevates himself above the others, upstairs centre. The characters keep moving back and forth across the stage, intermingling with their own words the words of the Newsboy: 'PLANS FOR ROYAL JUBI-LEE. SIX KINGS AT ROYAL WEDDING' etc. until the scene grows, their own words are completely displaced by the words of the Newsboy and all the characters are shouting his slogans. At the height of this chaos, the voices rise to a crescendo, terminating in the words 'HEY BOY!' which are the first words of the poem. As they say these words, all the figures veer towards the Newsboy upstage centre.)

Voice. How long are you going to stand there shouting yer guts out?

All the characters on the stage, still keeping their ballet formation, say the next words with a series of movements which bring out the ideas:

All. BECAUSE SOMEWHERE IN A WEST-END HOTEL A CHORUS GIRL SHOT out the brains of the old rip that kept her.

The figures freeze.

Voice. Don't you get tired, Newsboy, shouting all the time about

Char. Gent. Hold ups

Young Lady. And divorces

All. AND DUCHESSES IN GAMBLING DENS!

All through the play, the characters change from class-conscious workers to symbolic figures of an entirely different nature or realistic characters which vary greatly from scene to scene.

At this point in the play the characters become class workers, representing a picture of the Three Million Unemployed Men and Women. This is done through the characters facing the audience and saying the following words: 'THREE MILLION MEN AND WOMEN' as in rhythmic tread they form a miserable line outside the labour exchange, constantly repeating in low tones in mass: 'THREE MILLION MEN AND WOMEN.'

The spotlight changes from amber to green.

1st Voice. Fired from the mills.

2nd Voice. Fired from the docks.

3rd Voice. Fired from the coal mines.

4th Voice. Fired from the shipyards.

All. (*Louder and louder in desperation*) FIRED FIRED FIRED.

Voice (*Offstage*) No jobs today. You've had yer lousy money.

Grumbling rips in voices, then slowly retreating in distance as line breaks up and they all shuffle off the stage, except one.

[*SCENE 4*] *One figure, Unemployed, is left on the stage. Enter well-dressed man.*

Unemployed. (*Mumbling*) How about a tanner, Mister, for a bite and bed? I never done this before, Mister, but I gotta eat. Gotta sleep.

Man. Eat! Sleep! Huh!

Exit. A woman hurries by from the other direction, feeling the unemployed man's eyes upon her. Enter charitable gentleman.

Unemployed. (*A little more entreatingly*) How about a tanner, Mister, for a bite and a bed?

Char. Gent. (*Precisely, ethically offended*) I don't believe in it.

Unemployed. (*Not understanding*) What's that, Gov'nor?

Char. Gent. I don't believe in charity.

Unemployed. Oh! (*This strikes him as something new.*)

Char. Gent. (*Sententiously*) Why don't you do something? There must be lots of jobs for big strong fellows like you.

Unemployed. There just ain't, Mister.

Char. Gent. (*Cheerfully patting his shoulder*) Well, don't get downhearted. Keep on pegging away. Something's bound to turn up.

Unemployed. (*Raising his hands, clenching his fists as if he'd like to wring the man's neck*) GOD!

Exit charitable gentleman. Enter 3rd pedestrian.

Unemployed. (*Loud voice, angrily*) Hey, Mister! How about a tanner for a bite and a bed? This ain't charity. I'm hungry.

Pedestrian. Why don't you go to the Workhouse? What about your Parish Relief?

Unemployed (*Harshly*) I told you I ain't looking for Charity.

Pedestrian frightened, searches through his pockets for small change. He finds a sixpence and with hasty fingers offers it to man and starts to back away.

Pedestrian. Here . . . (*The coin drops.*)

Unemployed. (*Furious*) Too good to hand it to me, are yer?

Pedestrian. (*Terrified*) . . . I-It . . . it slipped!

Unemployed. (*Growling*) Get out of my sight.

Pedestrian scampers. Unemployed man looks after him angrily. Enter urchin. Urchin rushes for the money. Unemployed man kicks him away.

Urchin. That's mine. I'm seen it first.

Unemployed. It's mine. THAT'S MY SIXPENCE!

As he stands there, the money in his hand, a sibilant voice right whispers 'THAT'S MY SIXPENCE'. Following this, voice left ditto. Then voices everywhere. Voices of the three million unemployed. They come on the stage, the same people who were in the labour exchange scene, with their hands stretched out to the unemployed worker, pleading for the sixpence. All the time they keep repeating the phrase 'THAT'S MY SIXPENCE' so that it sounds like the murmuring of a hungry mob. Above this noise is heard the following line, repeated at intervals of about 45 seconds; 'THREE MILLION MEN AND WOMEN'. As this line is said, the desperation of the mob to get the sixpence rises, and the voices grow with it till by this time they have practically surrounded the unemployed worker.

Unemployed. (*Raising his fists, crying hysterically*) Tortured in hostels with hymns about Saviours.

All the other figures follow his hands, building a pyramid of grasping hands as they rise to the top. They do so saying the words 'THREE MILLION MEN AND WOMEN'. Then, deathly silence.
The silence is broken by the shouts of the Newsboy who is seen above the crowd, in the background, shouting his slogans.
Little by little the group with their hands outstretched draw their hands down and begin to laugh. It begins very quietly – a painful laugh that grows into hysteria as the scene goes on. The following lines are taken by different individuals. The characters again become ordinary workers, people conscious of the roles of the Newsboy.

1st Voice. And he stands up there shouting about Royal Jubilees.

2nd Voice. And Football Cup Draws.

3rd Voice. Six Kings at Royal Wedding.

4th Voice. Another flapper flies to Australia.

Hysterical laughter grows to a high pitch, and is broken by one of the characters who bursts through the mass and comes to the audience with the following lines. The role is still that of a worker who presents these lines with the sense of their class nature.

Worker. In America, 320 men left to burn in a jail so that one won't get away.

Negro Worker. Two hundred white men take a black man for a ride, string him up a tree, and shoot him full of holes because a white woman said he smiled at her.

Indian Worker. In India workers are bludgeoned – thrown in jail for daring to organize unions.

During these lines, those people who are not in the scene which follows move off the stage quietly. Four characters remain on the stage, the Indian worker and three others. The one nearest him grabs him and throws him upstage so that he falls.

[SCENE 5]

Indian Worker. Why are you keeping me here? (*Sitting in chair now.*)

Prosecutor. (*Sits in another chair facing him.*) What's it all about? (*Silence*) I've got some work to do. I've got a job to look after . . . Well, say something, can't you?

Everybody looks at him, except 2nd detective who is cleaning his finger-nails with his keys. After a long pause –

1st Detect. What's your name?

Indian Worker. Ali Singh.

1st Detect. What do you work at?

Indian Worker. On the railway.

1st Detect. You belong to the union? (*No answer*) Come on! Speak up! D'you belong to the union?

Indian Worker. Yes.

2nd Detect. Huh, a Red! I thought so.

Prosecutor. Now tell me, why did you fire those shots?

Indian Worker. Shots?

Prosecutor. Yes. You heard me. You're not deaf?

1st Detect. Come on, Ali Singh, spit it out. We'll see you get off light if you confess.

Prosecutor. Take my advice and don't play innocent. We know you fired those shots at the Governor. Lucky for you he wasn't hurt. So now, speak up. Why did you fire those shots?

Indian Worker. I tell you I don't know anything about any shots.

1st Detect. Where do you live?

Indian Worker. 179 Ragland Street.

1st Detect. Then what were you doing near the racecourse?

Indian Worker. I'm on a job round there, near the station.

2nd Detect. Don't tell lies. You're a Red. You were out to kill the Governor – now tell the truth. You fired those shots!

Indian Worker. No! No!

1st Detect. Then what was this revolver doing in your pocket? (*Taking out revolver.*)

Pause.

Indian Worker (*Jumping up*) That's not mine. I haven't got a revolver. You can't frame me! I was going to my work.

2nd Detect. God-darn you! Shut up. (*Pushes him back in chair.*)

[SCENE 6] *Played in the dark.*

Indian Worker. It's not mine.

Prosecutor. Be sensible, Ali Singh. You know we're going to make you talk.

1st Detect. Do you want us to knock it out of you?

2nd Detect. Come on, own up. Are you looking for a hiding?

Prosecutor. Now be sensible, Ali. Don't waste my time. Say you fired those shots, and get it over.

Indian Worker. No.

1st Detect. You still say this isn't your revolver?

Indian Worker. YES.

2nd Detect. But it was found in your pocket. It must be yours.

Indian Worker. No! I've never seen it before.

2nd Detect. Don't tell bloody lies.

Indian Worker. It's the truth. I swear it isn't mine.

Prosecutor. Then how did it come in your pocket?

Indian Worker. Someone must've put it there.

1st Detect. (*Angrily*) Stop lying. (*Threateningly*) – Now you little brown-skin-ned bastard, is this your revolver?

Indian Worker. No.

A loud crack. A yelp of pain.

1st Detect. Is it your revolver?

Indian Worker. (*Sullenly*). No.

Another slash. A yelp of pain.

1st Detect. Is it? Refresh your memory.

Indian Worker. No! No!

Two terrified screams, three loud cracks. Worker cries painfully. Silence!

Prosecutor. Now, Ali Singh, perhaps you will tell us. Is this your revolver?

A slight pause.

Indian Worker. (*Almost whispered*) Yes, it's my revolver.

Pause. In the silence, in the darkness, starting very slowly with pauses in between, in a stage whisper, the following lines are heard, each word spoken by a different person: 'Tortured' 'Framed' 'Imprisoned' 'Burned' 'Lynched' 'Murdered'. These words are repeated three times, growing louder each time until the words are heard: 'Have you heard of Sacco Vanetti?' Then the words travel round again until someone takes the line 'Have you heard of Thomas Mooney?' Once round again, then 'Have you heard of tortured Torgler?' and again 'Have you heard of Scottsboro? Scottsboro?' Each time a different voice takes up the line. This continues until the last time round, then the line is 'Have you heard of Thaelman? Thaelman?' And then the entire group, in mass 'HAVE YOU HEARD?' Lights go up on Scene 7.

[SCENE 7] As the lights come up on the words 'Have you heard?' all figures are facing the Newsboy, pointing up at him. Their hands slowly go down as Newsboy starts shouting headline: 'PLANS FOR ROYAL JUBILEE'. He

comes off chair, still shouting lines, and asks workers to buy papers. As he touches each on the shoulder the worker turns round with the 'Daily Worker' in front, until there is a full line of dailies. Newsboy walks to centre front as voice talks.

Voice. Get yourself a trumpet, sonny, a big red trumpet. Climb to the top of St. Paul's and blare out the news. TIME TO REVOLT! BLACK MEN, WHITE MEN, FIELD MEN, SHOP MEN – TIME TO REVOLT. Get yourself a trumpet, sonny, a big red trumpet and blare out the news –

All. TIME TO REVOLT! TIME TO REVOLT!

Newsboy discards his own placard, takes up trumpet and joins in chorus. Blackout.   *[The End]*

Extracts from a Living Newspaper

Last Edition

by Joan Littlewood *and* Ewan MacColl

THEATRE UNION
Presents

LAST EDITION

A LIVING NEWSPAPER
DEALING WITH EVENTS FROM 1934-1940
Edited by Theatre Union

AT THE ROUND HOUSE
EVERY ST., ANCOATS

on MARCH 14th, 15th & 28th, 29th at 7-30 p.m.
    MARCH 16th & 30th at 2-30 p.m.

ADMISSION BY MEMBERSHIP CARD ONLY
Collective Membership fee of 2ˡ6 per annum
for Trade Union Branches, Co-op. Guilds, Etc.

[THE UNEMPLOYMENT EPISODE]

Narrator. Last week, after vainly searching for work all day, William Castle at his last call, pleaded desperately with tears in his eyes. He was turned away. His wife met him with a brave smile. "Cheer up, Will' she said, "there's a letter for you, perhaps it's a job for the new year." It was an intimation that his employment benefit had ceased. He hid it from his wife, kissed her and left the room. His wife heard a strange noise downstairs. She found him on the floor. He had cut his throat. A verdict of suicide while temporarily insane was recorded.

Music; Vulcan theme

Voice   Down with the means test!
Down with the National Starvation Government!

Marchers enter on Platform 'A', singing

Marchers
March, march, men without work,
Scrapped by the cities.
March, march, men of the unemployed committees!

Narrator. Two hundred Scottish hunger-marchers set out from Glasgow.

Voice   Men from Govan and Cowcaddens,
Men from the Gorbals and the Broomielaw,
Men from Lanark and Kirkintilloch,
Men from Greenock, Partick and Parkhead.
The Clyde men.

Marchers.
For the right to work!
For the right to live!

Voice. Men from Newcastle, Gateshead, Durham, Morpeth, Willington, Sunderland, Shields; men from the shipyards, idle colliers.

Marchers. We refuse to starve in silence!

Voice: Men from Burnley, Barrow and Whitehaven,
Salford, Oldham, Manchester, Warrington.
Men from the loom and the derelict foundry.
Turners, puddlers, grinders, spinners,
The Northern men!

Marchers.
We've a right to live! We're human beings!
We've a right to work! We're men!

Light on platform 'C'. Hospital accident room. Doctor present. Nurse enters.

Nurse. There's a crowd of injured men outside, Doctor. Hunger-marchers. They've been fighting with the police.

Doctor. Better bring 'em in two at a time.

Exit nurse. She returns with two marchers, both injured.

Hello! You look as if you've been having a spot of bother.

1st Marcher. We've been having a spot of police brutality.

Doctor. That's rather strong, isn't it?

1st Marcher. They were strong men.

Doctor. Well, if you will go about the country disturbing the peace, you can only expect resentment.

2nd Marcher. Which peace? We've not heard about any peace. We only know about war. War with hunger and poverty, a war to keep ourselves and kids alive.

1st Marcher. A war to keep warm in the winter.

Doctor. I appreciate your difficulties, of course. But don't you think your methods of voicing your opinions are rather melodramatic?

2nd Marcher. Not so melodramatic as having your name in the paper with a verdict of 'suicide while of unsound mind' attached to it.

Doctor. That's a nasty blow you've given yourself.

2nd Marcher. I didn't give it myself. A cop gave it me as a sample of his resentment.

Doctor. Y'know, I think you're on the wrong track. These methods may be alright in Russia but the British people will never stand for them.

2nd Marcher. What do you think we are, Fiji Islanders? We *are* the British people; me and my mate here and the others outside.

Doctor. Now look here! You've got to admit that we have the finest democracy in the world here.

The patient slumps in the chair.

He's fainted. Some water nurse!

Nurse brings water.

I'm afraid you'll have to stay here for a few days.

1st Marcher. Don't you think we should leave half a dozen of our lads with him?

Doctor. Whatever for?

1st Marcher. Just in case the police try to get at him again in the interests of democracy.

Blackout.

[THE GRESFORD PIT DISASTER EPISODE] Newsboy
   dances up platform 'A'.

Newsboy.
   All the latest, last edition!
   Mr Eden's German mission.
   Paris riots, food shops looted,
   Van der Lubbe executed.
   Loch Ness monster seen again,
   Sentence passed on Ludwig Renn.
   News a'Chron, Last Edition!
   Last edition, Last edition!

   *A collier enters on platform 'A' carrying a lamp, whistles softly the Vulcan
   theme. Exit. Another comes and goes. Explosion. Woman runs along platform
   'A' to centre stage. Explosion. Blackout.*

Voice on Microphone. Hello! Is that the fourteenth district? You've got to
   get through. There's three hundred men there. Yes, in the Dennis Deep.
   One of 'em's got to answer. Three hundred men! There's been a second
   explosion and there's three hundred men there. You've got to get through!
   You've got to. Three hundred men!

   Explosion.

Hello, hello, hello, hello . . . There's been a second explosion in the Dennis
   Deep. There must be somebody there. There's got to be. There's three
   hundred men down there. Three hundred men! Hello! Hello! Hello!

   *Explosion. We hear a woman screaming. Woman runs on platform 'A'. She is
   in night attire and carries a miner's lamp. Stage lightens to a chill grey. She runs
   to various parts of platform 'A' knocking on imaginary doors.*

1st Woman. The Dennis is on fire! There's fire in the Dennis Deep. The
   Dennis Deep is on fire! The Dennis Deep is on fire! They're trapped down
   there! They're trapped!

   Women appear at various points along the platform.

Women. Trapped!

1st Woman. It's the pit. Wake up! Wake up! It's the pit!

Women. The pit!

   The women slowly, with dance-like movement form a compact group.

1st Woman. The pit's on fire, our men are trapped!

Women. My two sons. My husband and my two sons! All I have in the world!

1st Woman. They're in the Dennis Deep. We've got to get to them . . .

Women. My husband. My sons are down there! Hot as Hellfire! Gas! Falling
   rock! Burying them! Gassing them! Killing them! We've got to get to
   them!

As they begin to advance to centre stage there is another explosion and blackout.

Mic. Voice. Hello, hello, hello, answer me. Is that the 14th? Are you in the 14th? No, make for the bottom end, man. Make for the bottom end. Get out by the return airway. Get yourselves out. We'll get through to the Dennis. God help them, there's gas.

Lights up on women standing in two groups as at pit-head.

[THE GRESFORD PIT DISASTER TRIAL SCENE]
Fade up Vulcan theme simultaneously bringing up lights until it is possible to see the shadowy forms of men carrying empty stretchers.

Narrator. The Gresford Disaster. The explosion occurred about 2 a.m. on Saturday, the 22nd of September, 1934, in the Dennis section of the mine. The concussion was felt at the bottom of the pit and in the Slant district. Except for a few persons working near the pit bottom, and one deputy and five men who managed to escape from the 29's district, all the men who were working in the section at the time lost their lives the same day, which brought the total loss of life up to 265.

Towards end of foregoing speech, the light begins to fade again. Blackout. Sustain Vulcan theme then fade slowly behind following speech.

Narrator. The Board of Trade hereby direct that a formal investigation shall be held into the causes and circumstances of the explosion which occurred in the Gresford mine, Denbighshire, on the 22nd of September, 1934, and the board hereby appoint Sir Henry Walker, C.B.E., LL.D., His Majesty's Chief Inspector of Mines, as Commissioner to hold such investigation.

Half-way through foregoing passage lights slowly fade up to reveal group of women on platform 'A'. Group of miners enter downstage right. During the trial scene actors representing company interests use the extreme upstage area while those who appear for the prosecution use the downstage area. Cripps is situated between the two groups.

Cripps. And so, Mr Bonsall, you, the colliery manager at the Gresford pit, admit here that it was due to an oversight that the correct ventilation was not being obtained in this pit.

Bonsall. Yes, I admit it.

Cripps. You, as manager of course, were expected to run the mine as cheaply as possible. Is that so?

Bonsall. Yes, naturally.

Cripps. Mr Bonsall, was it a common practice for men to work overtime on Saturday and Sunday night? Apparently the men were working overtime on the night the explosion occurred, in fact many of them were doubling shifts, were they not? Working two shifts without a break.

Bonsall. They were not exactly doubling.

Cripps. They were working overtime?

Bonsall. Yes.

Cripps. Was it a common practice for the men to work overtime on a Saturday and Sunday night?

Bonsall. Yes, it was common practice.

Cripps. You knew, of course, that a breach of the Act was committed.

Bonsall. Many of them liked it.

Cripps. Did you know that it was a breach of the Act? (*Pause*) Did you know it was a breach of the Act? Did you know it was a breach of the Act?

Light fades. Spotlight on miners' wives who turn and face audience. Up Vulcan theme.

Women. Joseph Andrews, of Wrexham, dead.
Thomas Anders of Wrexham, dead.
George Anderson of Wrexham, dead.
Owen Andrews of Wrexham, dead.

The cause of death in each case was poisoning by carbon-monoxide. They sealed the pit two days after the accident but the force of a new explosion came and threw the seals off again. Sandbags and girders were thrown high in the air. My husband was down that pit.

Vulcan theme out. Women turn and face trial again.

Cripps. Mr Bonsall, there are forty-two days missing of fireman's reports, the forty-two days before the explosion. Those reports are vital to this enquiry. . . . We should like to have them.

Bonsall. They are down the pit.

Cripps. Is that the only excuse you have?

Bonsall. It is not an excuse.

Cripps. Was it not customary to keep those reports at the pithead?

Bonsall. In this case the reports were taken down the pit by a boy and lost in the explosion.

Cripps. Did you allow the pit to be run by boys?

Bonsall. How can I look after every boy?

Cripps. I am not asking you to look after every boy, I am asking you to look after the records.

Bonsall. I haven't the slightest doubt that they have gone down into the bottom.

Cripps. Whose responsibility was this?

Bonsall. The fireman's.

Cripps. I suggest that it was your responsibility. When did you last get the fireman's books to see if your orders were carried out?

Bonsall. I always left that to the clerk.

Cripps. In the same way you left it to the fireman. In the same way you tried to put the responsibility on to the fireman?

Miners' group turn and face audience.

Miners. Joseph Archibald of Wrexham, dead.
Thomas Archibald of Pandy, dead.

They found Thomas Archibald lying close to his tub. Somehow the tub had got turned over. His lamp they found at the face of the drift. All their lamps were at the coal-face. They left them at the coal-face because they were no use to them. Their lamps went out.

Women. They died in the dark.

Blackout.

[THE POLITICS OF DEMOCRACY EPISODE] Newsboy on platform 'B'

Newsboy. Disarmament conference decision! Anglo-German naval agreement reached. Last Edition.

Joe enters from centre stage and approaches Newsboy. Buys paper. Arthur enters from platform 'A'. Buys paper.

Joe. Funny kind of disarmament conference.

Arthur. Bloody funny. Ever since the last war Germany's been asking for equality. While it was a democracy nobody listened but as soon as Hitler comes they get a fleet.

Joe. (*Reading*) Lord Lothian says 'A stable Germany will ensure peace. Hitler has done much to bring order to Germany.'

Arthur. That's another way of saying he smashed the trade unions.

Joe. And now we're going to help him build a new German fleet.

Arthur. Yes, with our money. Listen to this: 'The Bank of England has granted a £750,000 credit to Germany in order to facilitate the mobilisation of German commercial credits.' That money comes from our pockets, every single penny of it.

Joe. They can't squeeze me any more. If there's another rise in the cost of living I'll be paying the boss a wage to let me work for him.

Arthur. They'll squeeze and squeeze until they've milked you dry and then they'll take the skin off your back to make purses with. Hitler's paved the way for this grand ceremony, that's why they're so friendly with him.

Joe. But why call the ceremony disarmament?

Arthur. For the same reason that they call hunger malnutrition or a blackleg a loyal employee. Because they want to give dung a fancy name and make it smell like a wallflower. Have you read what Sir Thomas Inskip said in an article to the press yesterday?

Joe. No.

Arthur. He said: 'In actual fact there is no great difference between the totalitarian and the democratic systems of government.'

Joe. He's talking through his hat.

Arthur. Think so? Listen to this: 'A widespread strike movement has broken out in Trinidad as a result of the rise in the cost of living and the refusal of the companies to increase wages. Serious rioting has occurred and many arrests have been made.' And we're still in the empire, see?

Newsboy. Part of our great democratic system.

Arthur. Right. Only six per cent of the population have a vote so that the only way they have of making themselves heard is to strike. They work in the oilfields. The islands contribute sixty per cent of the entire oil output in the British Empire. The other big industry is sugar. Look at this: 'Rioting still continues in Trinidad and in the police charges which took place last night many natives were killed and wounded.' Now we are going to act Trinidad. You and me will both play company detectives. He will be a Trinidad worker.

Newsboy. Me?

Arthur. Yes.

Newsboy. Can I make my face up?

Arthur. What for? You can be exploited without having a black face, can't you?

Newsboy goes up left. He is in a cul de sac.

We've got you in a side street by a deserted warehouse. There's no one who'll dare to interfere. You are on the strike committee, in touch with the leaders. Somebody's behind the strike, financing it.

Newsboy. That's not true. We made the strike ourselves.

Joe strikes him and he falls to the ground.

Arthur. Who gave the word for the strike? And don't say it was the committee.

Newsboy. We made the strike ourselves.

Joe. You're a liar! (*He hurls him downstage*) I'll make the black bastard talk.

Arthur. Just a minute, the Acting Colonial Secretary wants to talk first.

Spot on platform 'A'.

Act. Col. Secretary. In the past we have tried to ease our consciences with humbug and have had to satisfy Labour with platitudes but I would stress very strongly the view that an industry has no right to pay dividends at all until it pays a fair wage to labour and gives the labourer decent conditions.

Blackout on platform 'A'.

Newsboy. See, even the government is with us.

Joe. (*Kicking him*) Shut up!

Arthur. He's right, y'know. That was Red talk we just heard.

Spot on platform 'A'.

Charlton. I would like to draw the attention of the Secretary of State for the Colonies to the extreme view of the Acting Colonial Secretary for Trinidad.

Blackout on platform 'A'.

Joe. Who was that?

Arthur. It was Mr Alan Charlton, M.P. for Bury, Lancashire, speaking in the House of Commons, London, England.

Joe. How does he come into this?

Arthur. He's the director of the Trinidad Leasehold Limited which owns 85,912 acres of oilfields worth a capital of £1,639,452. His interest in this case is real interest, compound interest. Alright, get to work.

Joe. Who's behind the strike? Who financed it, eh? Who paid for the leaflets? Alright, if you don't want to say. If you want to keep quiet . . . But don't forget we gave you the chance. Don't forget that.

He shoots him. Blackout.

Narrator. Sir Thomas Inskip in a speech at Reading yesterday said that there was no great difference between the totalitarian and the democratic states.

Spot on three men on centre stage, facing audience directly.

Three Men. Which proves that a cabinet minister can sometimes tell the truth.

[THE SPANISH CIVIL WAR EPISODE]
Narrator.
>Wonderful days!
>So General Mola had to stop the advance on Madrid.
>For why? Because he had to wait for his white horse,
>So he could ride into Madrid in style.
>But while he was waiting, the internationals came in,
>And the anarchists from Barcelona,
>And the socialists from Asturias,
>And the communists from Guaderama,

And Mola's white horse turned out to be
A bloody white elephant.
Have a ride on it Chamberlain!

Spotlights on four men standing on platform 'A'. Each has a rucksack at his feet. They stand without moving.

Mic. Voice. Alec Armstrong of Manchester, building worker, communist. Can you see the people of Spain deserted by the government of your country, left to fight the combined armies of Spanish, Italian and German fascism? (*Pause*) Robert Goodman of Salford, printshop worker, communist. Can you see the women and children of Spain butchered without going to their aid? (*Pause*) George Brown of Manchester, building worker, communist. Can you see the workers of Spain fighting with obsolete weapons against the most modern instruments of war? (*Pause*) Bob Ward of Manchester, building worker, communist. Can you see men of all countries marching to the assistance of Spain and not march with them?

The four men lift up their rucksacks, turn to the audience, raise their hands in farewell.

Four Men. So long.

Slow fade out.

[THE MUNICH PACT EPISODE]

Actor. In accord with our policy of giving you as much variety as possible, what follows is in the style of an American gangster film. Sir Sigismund, or Siggy as he is known to the underworld, is expecting a visit from Sir Launcelot, now known as Lance the Umbrella Man. In the meantime he has summoned to a meeting the Italian killer, Muscle In. This scene is called: Who killed Johnny the Czech?

Central stage. Siggy discovered seated. He is playing patience. Enter Muscle In.

Siggy. Hi, Muscle!

Muscle. Hi, Siggy! I gotta your invitation. Say, what's the idea of all the chairs? A party?

Siggy. Yeah, a party.

Muscle. On my way here I see one of your boys. He says you gotta big job on. Plenty good pickings.

Siggy. Yeah, plenty good. Siddown, Muscle. Thi is the biggest job since we cracked the Spanish bank on 38th street.

Muscle. Yeah?

Siggy. Yeah. I need your help, see.

Muscle. Sure, sure, Boss. A fifty-fifty deal, ugh?

Siggy. What d'ya mean, fifty-fifty? What kinda talk's that? We fixed that you get the pickings from the Spanish job and I take the next. Well, this is it. See?

Muscle. Okay, okay. I get ya boss. I get ya. What's the layout?

Siggy. There's a store at the corner of 18th street and west 39th. It's kept by a guy called Johnny the Czech. You know him?

Muscle. Sure, he's gotta plenty big dough. Not so long ago he live in a cheap tenement joint on 14th street. Now he's on velvet. He gotta plenty cash, plenty boys to take care of him and plenty good business. Sure, sure I know him . . .

Siggy. The guy's poison. He's gotta go.

Muscle. Boss, this guy's plenty tough. Every one of his boys packsa the rod. My boys tell me every joint on his block gotta machine-gun and we wouldn't stand a chance in them streets. Oh no, I think this is not such a good idea. No?

Siggy. Yeah.

Muscle. Listen, Siggy. My boys don'ta feel so good. Look at that Spanish job. I told the boys it was easy but it took them three years, justa the same. Don'ta forget Spanish Joe. He was as full of holes as a sieve before he lay down. I lost plenty of my good boys and plenty cash. Siggy, you know me. Muscle In is your friend but no, I can'ta do this.

Siggy. Ease up, ease up. What do you take me for? A hick from the sticks? (*Pointing to his head*) what do you think this is for, a ball game? Now look. (*He arranges bottles and glasses on table.*)
This is Johnny the Czech's joint. And this is a speakeasy I control – the Viennese Cafe. This is the territory of Lance the Umbrella Man and just across the street is Eddy, his echo. Now Johnny the Czech thinks these two guys are his buddies. See? Well, are they?

Muscle. Boss, those-a guys is nobody's buddies.

Siggy. That's just what I think. Now listen. Who is it that nobody loves?

Muscle. I don'ta think that nobody loves me, Boss.

Siggy. Don't be so dumb. The guy nobody loves is Joe the Red. See?

Muscle. Oh, sure. That guy gives me a pain.

Siggy. He gives Lance and Eddy a worse pain. Them two guys is scared stiff of him. They'll play ball with any guy who's willing to take a poke at him.

Muscle. I geta you, boss. I geta you. You means that you're the guy.

Siggy. I mean I want them guys to think I'm going to take a poke at him . . . And in exchange, they double-cross Johnny the Czech. And then . . . well, I double cross them. A double double-cross.

Muscle. Gee, Siggy, that'sa beautiful. You tell 'em you fighta Joe the Red if they take a run-out powder on Johnny the Czech and thena you take a powder on them. You know what I think? I thinka that'sa beautiful. Boss, you're a genius.

Siggy. Sure, we got the Indian sign on 'em.

There's a knock on the door. They dive for their guns.

Siggy. Come in.

Enter Lance and Eddy.

Well, boys, you know what my terms are. Johnny the Czech's joint in return for a battle with Joe the Red. O.K.?

Lance. Well, we don't know. Eddy here aint so sure. I aint so sure we can trust you, Sig.

Siggy. I'm trusting you, aint I?

Lance. What d'ya mean?

Siggy. Siddown, punk! Right now my boys are breaking in on Johnny's territory. All you gotta do is send some of your boys over and tell Johnny to quit or else. Tell him you say so.

Eddy. I think Monsieur Siggy does not realise that this job is so difficult. Do not forget Johnny the Czech is under the impression that I am his friend. The double-cross is not so good for one's reputation.

Siggy. Aw, can the bull. Stop talking like a sky pilot. Let's have the answer, yes or no . . .

Eddy. Monsieur, you forget Joe the Red. He also is Johnny's friend.

Siggy. That's where you come in. You gotta make Johnny break with the Red.

Eddy. But how?

Siggy. You know how. Just give him some of that highfalutin talk. Put it over big. Tell him Joe's bad for his health. And if that don't work, threaten him. Tell him he'll be taken for a ride.

Lance. What about Joe? When do we start operations on him?

Siggy. As soon as I've cleaned out Johnny.

Lance. Can we count on that?

Siggy. Yes, I give you my word.

Muscle. Sure and I givea my word too. My boy's shirts may be blacka but they sure do hate that Red nogood.

Siggy. Is it a deal then?

Lance.
Eddy. (*together*) It's a deal.

Eddy. And now that's settled I think we'd better be getting back.

Siggy. Just a minute, the job aint finished yet. I gotta make sure you guys don't double-cross me and I gotta way of making sure . . . (*He shouts into the wings*). Okay, bring him in, boys.

Two henchmen drag in Johnny the Czech.

Lance.
Eddy. (*together*) Johnny the Czech!

Siggy. Yeah, Johnny the Czech. We're gonna bump him off, the four of us.

Johnny. Listen Eddy, you too Lance. You're my buddies. This guy's nuts. You can't let him croak me just like that.

Lance. No? You were tied up with Joe the Red, weren't you?

Johnny. Sure. But I was tied up with you too. Look I ain't done a thing. I kept out of your territory, didn't I? I kept to myself. All I did was run my own joint and try to keep the peace with you boys.

Siggy. Aw, can the sob stuff. You gotta go, Johnny.

Lance. Sure and after you, Joe the Red.

Eddy. I'm afraid so, Johnny, It is destiny.

Muscle. That's very good worda.

Johnny. Okay, okay. But don't forget, you birds, that Siggy'll double-cross you. He'll two-time ya. Then you'll be on the spot.

Siggy. Shut up! Okay, boys. Give him the works.

All four draw their pistols.

Lance. Hold on a minute.

He opens his umbrella and covers the four guns. They fire. Johnny falls, Lance takes a rubber ball out of his pocket.

He's all washed up. Okay, let's play ball.

He throws the ball to Eddy who throws it to Muscle. He is about the throw it to Siggy who turns his back on him.

Siggy. What's the prize?

Lance. Joe the Red's territory.

Siggy. No. I don't play.

Lance. Did you hear what I did? He won't play ball. You dirty little double-crossing rat! What about you, Muscle?

Muscle. If he don'ta play, I don'ta play.

Lance. Okay. This is war, war to the knife! This is war!   *[The End]*

An episodic play with singing

Johnny Noble

by Ewan MacColl

The curtain opens on a completely dark stage draped in black curtains. On either side of the stage stand two Narrators, a man and a woman dressed in black oilskins. They are pin-pointed by two spotlights. Very simply the man begins to sing.

[MUSIC CUE 1]

1st Narrator. (*Singing*)
  Here is a stage –

2nd Narrator. (*Speaking*) A platform twenty-five feet by fifteen.

1st Narrator. (*Singing*)
  A microcosm of the world.

2nd Narrator. (*Speaking*) Here the sun is an amber flood and the moon a thousand-watt spot.

1st Narrator. (*Singing*)
  Here shall be space,
  Here we shall act time.

2nd Narrator. (*Speaking*) From nothing everything will come.

1st Narrator. (*Singing*)
  On this dead stage we'll make society appear.

An acting-area flood fades up, discovering three youths playing pitch-and-toss upstage centre.

  The world is here –

2nd Narrator. (*Speaking*) Our world.

Up boogie-woogie music. A woman enters, dances across the stage and off. Fade out music.

1st Narrator. (*Singing*)
  A little gesture from an actor's hand creates a rolling landscape:
  (*Speaking*) or a desert.

2nd Narrator. (*Singing*)
  A word from us and cities will arise;
  The night be broken by screaming factories.

Up burst of machinery. A red spot is faded up discovering a half-naked figure of a man. He mimes raking out a furnace in time to machinery. The light and machine-noise fade out together. The man goes off.

1st Narrator. (*Speaking*) Yes, we speak of days that linger in the memory like a bad taste in the mouth. Come back with us a dozen years or so, back to the early thirties, to the derelict towns and the idle hands, the rusting lathes and the silent turbines.

An unemployed man enters, stands left centre, yawning.

Unemp. Man. Time to sign on. (*He exits*)

A child enters, a small lonely figure in a pool of white light. She begins a queer abstracted hopping dance.

2nd Narrator. (*Speaking*) Here a child grows up in a desolate land.

1st Narrator. (*Singing*)
>Here is a street
>In any seaport town.

Two distant blasts of a ship's siren.

>It could be anywhere
>Where a man's work is the sea.

The pitch-and-toss players begin to intone their calls.

1st youth. Heads.

2nd youth. Tails.

1st youth. It's mine.

2nd youth. What is it?

1st youth. Heads.

2nd youth. Tails it is.

1st youth. My shout.

2nd youth. Shout!

1st youth. Tails.

2nd youth. It's mine.

Fade and hold behind following sequence. Two small girls enter and are joined by the first little girl in a singing game.

[MUSIC CUE 2]

Three girls. (*Singing*)
>Have you seen owt o' my bonnie lad,
>And are you sure that he's weel, O?
>He's gone ower land wiv his stick in his hand,
>He's gone to moor the keel, O.

One girl. (*Singing*)
>Yes, I've seen your bonny lad,
>Upon the sea I spied him,
>His grave is green but not wiv grass
>And thou'll never lie beside him.

The song fades but is held faintly behind following sequence. The unemployed man enters, takes a newspaper out of his pocket and begins to read it. Johnny Noble enters and starts to watch the gambling game.

Unemp. man. Hello, Johnny.

Johnny. Hullo.

[MUSIC CUE 3]

1st Narrator. (*Singing*)
>Now come all you good people and listen to my song,
>It's of young Johnny Noble and I won't detain you long,
>Young Johnny lived on the north-east coast where trawler men
>>are made,
>And he was quite determined for to follow the sailor's trade.

Unemp. man. Courting again, Johnny?

Johnny. You can call it that.

Unemp. man. If you ask me, it's a mug's game.

Johnny. Nobody asked you.

2nd youth. It's still a mug's game.

Mary enters. The youths whistle appreciatively.

Johnny. Hullo, Mary.

Mary and Johnny dance. The gamblers play. The unemployed man reads his newspaper. The children play.

[MUSIC CUE 4]
2nd Narrator. (*Singing*).
>Now Johnny loved a neighbour's lass, young Mary was her
>>name.
>His love was deep and tender and burned him like a flame
>And Mary had loved her Johnny since she was but a lass,
>But you shall soon know their tale of woe and all that came to
>>pass.

2nd youth. You're a liar! It was tails.

1st youth. I tell you it was heads.

2nd youth. Don't try and fool me. I saw you turn it over!

1st youth. Are you calling me a cheat?

2nd youth. Yes, and a dirty rotten one at that!

The 1st youth strikes the 2nd.

2nd youth. You pig!

1st youth. Take your coat off and I'll show you!

They prepare to fight.

Little girls. A fight! A fight!

Mary. O stop them, Johnny!

1st youth. Him and who else?

The other characters form a ring round the fighters.

Unemp. man. Now take it easy. Do it proper. Make it a fair fight.

2nd youth. I'll kill him!

They dance a fight. A fisherman enters, watches the fight for a moment and is then noticed by Johnny.

Johnny. Whitey!

Seaman. Hi, Johnny!

The others crowd around the newcomer, the fight forgotten.

1st youth. I'll settle with you later.

2nd youth. Any time you like.

Johnny. When did you get in?

Seaman. About an hour ago. We've been lying off the point since early this morning.

Unemp. man. What kind of a catch did you have?

Seaman. More than four hundred cran.

2nd youth. Then there'll be work at the fish dock! Come on, let's go.

Seaman. You won't be needed.

2nd youth. Not with a load like that?

Seaman. They're back in the sea.

Johnny. You mean you dumped the whole catch?

Seaman. The whole catch. Five shiploads of dead herring caught off the Faroes.

Mary. But why?

Seaman. Owner's orders.

Enter Mary's mother.

Mother. Ted White! I didn't know you were back. Where's Dan?

Seaman. He's not with us.

Mother. Didn't he come back with you?

Seaman. No.

Mother. Well, where is he?

Seaman. Big John was to break the news. He'll be waiting back at your house now.

Mother. Ted, what is it? He's not . . .

Seaman. Tuesday night it was. The wind came up as we were drawing our nets just north of the Skerries. One minute it was dead quiet with nothing but the slip-slap of the water against the ship and the next it was all wind and thick sky bruised and angry. I never saw the sea in such a rage. It looked as if we'd have to cut the nets, but Dan was for facing it out. We worked there till the wind howled and the sky was in ribbons. By the time we got the nets aboard the sea was in the sky and roaring like a beast and then there came a great black blast and the sea gathered into one big fist of wave. It caught young Syms, the deckie, and crushed him against the cabin. He went limp and spun round like a stick in a cross-current. I saw Dan leap at the wave as a swimmer with a knife might leap to gut a barracuda. I tried to shout a warning but there was no room in the world for any voice but the sea's. The wave took them both.

While he has been speaking, the general lighting has faded leaving only Whitey and the mother spotlit. The other characters have retreated and formed a large semicircle half-hidden in shadow.

Mother. Dead!

Chorus. (*whispering*). Dead! Dead!

Mother. First my son and then his father. Lost, both of them lost, for a handful of fishes. For twenty years I have lived with a fear of this night and cursed the cunning of it. I've prayed that the sea would be swallowed up and silenced forever. Curse on the sea that a man should be less to it than a fish.

Mary. O, Mother!

Johnny. Mary . . .

Mother. Stay away from her! The sea's taken all it's going to take of my life. Stay away from her. No child of mine is ever going to suffer what I've suffered. I'll wash clothes, I'll scrub floors, I'll beg in the street, but no child of mine will ever give her life to the sea or to anything or anyone that belongs to the sea.

During the foregoing passage the lights have faded, leaving only mother and Mary and Johnny surrounded by shadows. Mother and Mary go off. Johnny stands centre stage. He looks round in perplexity. In the distance a barrel-organ plays. The stage becomes dark.

[MUSIC CUE 5]

2nd Narrator. (*Singing*)

Now two years pass and Johnny Noble's

Parted from his dearie;

And still she yearns for his return

And her heart is sad and weary.

> The lads all throng at Mary's side
> For she has grown full bonny,
> But the fairest flower amang them a'
> Is the sailor lad called Johnny.

Distant blast of ships' sirens. Enter Mary and Eddie, laughing.

Mary. I live just near here.

Eddie. That's a pity.

Mary. Why?

Eddie. Do you have to ask?

Mary. Well . . . goodnight.

Eddie. Don't go. It's early yet.

Mary. Do you call this early?

Eddie. Look, when am I going to see you again?

Mary. Oh, some time.

Eddie. How about tomorrow night?

Mary. No, I can't, I . . .

Eddie. Thursday, then. Listen, I'll tell you what. Let's have tea in town and then go on to the Plaza. They've got a marvellous band there; not like that bunch of amateurs at The Jig. Well, what do you say?

Mary. I'm sorry, but I can't.

Eddie. Why not? You like dancing, don't you?

Mary. I love it.

Eddie. Well, say you'll come. I'll see that you have a good time. Look Mary, I want to get to know you better.

Mary. You'd better ask someone else.

Eddie. I don't want anybody else, that's why I'm asking you. You know, you're too good to waste your time dancing with a bunch of louts at social club hops. I knew that the first time I saw you. You've got style and when you and me dance together I feel like we've been practising all our lives just for that one dance. You see, dancing with you isn't just routine, it's . . . O, I can't explain it but when I get that beat . . . one . . . two . . . da di di, da di . . .

Faint dance music.

. . . and feel you in my arms. (*He takes her in his arms.*) Well, it's more than just dancing.

The music grows louder. They dance. Johnny advances out of the shadows.

Johnny. Mary!

The music stops. The dancers fall apart.

Eddie. What's the idea?

Johnny. Mary, I've got to talk with you.

Eddie. Now look here, whatever your name is . . .

Mary. Alright, Johnny . . .

Eddie. I seem to be in the way. If you'd told me about him in the first place I wouldn't have bothered.

Johnny. Beat it!

Eddie. I seem to be losing my grip. (*He goes.*)

Mary. Well?

Johnny. Mary, I had to see you.

Mary. Did you have to spy on me?

Johnny. I wasn't spying. I've been waiting here for hours in the hope that I might see you.

Mary. You're shivering. You'll catch cold.

Johnny. I'm on fire Mary, I can't go on like this.

Mary. But what can I do? I told you everything was finished between us.

Johnny. I don't believe it. If you said it a thousand times I still wouldn't believe it. You and me couldn't live in the same world and not be close to each other. If you and me were finished then the sun would hide its face and the sea stop rolling, the wind would never blow again and every man and woman in this town would talk in whispers. Listen, you can hear the town breathing in its sleep. Do you think it would be so quiet if we were really through?

Mary. Is this what you wanted to say?

Johnny. I'm trying to wake you up out of this bad dream.

Mary. I'm sorry.

Johnny. Don't talk as if I am trying to sell you something. You remember me? I'm Johnny, the bloke who loves you. Remember?

Mary. I don't want to remember anything.

Johnny. Why not?

Mary. Because remembering hurts and I'm tired . . .

Johnny. Not too tired to dance.

Mary. Is this all you've got to say?

Johnny. I once knew a girl who looked just like you. Her hair was softer than a summer's night and her eyes were as deep as the ocean. Even to look at her made me feel good.

Mary. Don't, Johnny!

Johnny. Her voice was like yours too, only warmer.

Mary. Oh, why don't you let me forget?

Johnny. I keep remembering the things she used to say, the memory of her words won't let me sleep.

Mary. Forget her, Johnny, forget her.

Johnny. Sometimes we would walk together along the old moorland road and the feel of her arm in mine made the stars nearer and the sky wider. Everything was different when I was with her. This place wasn't half so dark nor the streets nearly so deserted . . .

Mary. Please, Johnny, please don't go on.

Johnny. Have you forgotten, Mary?

Mary. How could I forget?

Johnny. I love you, Mary.

Mary. No, don't say it . . . it's no good . . .

Johnny. I love you like the earth loves the sun, or the sea the sky, and what's more, you love me, don't you?

Mary. Yes, yes, but what's the good? Oh, Johnny, I'm so miserable I wish I could die. I'm tired of all the pain and hurt that's in loving. Do you think I don't feel all the things that you feel? I think of you all the time. Sleeping and waking, you are part of me, a part that never lets me rest.

Johnny. Then why do we act like strangers to each other?

Mary. Because it's the only way for us.

Johnny. Mary, you can't let your mother come between us like this. It's our lives . . . Oh, I know how she feels about the sea, but . . .

Mary. It's not how she feels. It's the way *I* feel. I hate the sea, too. Not just because it took my father but because of you. When I was little I used to lie awake at night and listen to my mother in the next room, lying awake and waiting. Sometimes I'd hear her moaning in her sleep and . . . Oh, don't you see I couldn't live like that? I couldn't. I love you too much.

Johnny. Alright, you won't have to.

Mary. What do you mean?

Johnny. Mary, if I could get a regular job, a land job, do you think you and me could get together again?

Mary. Do you mean it?

Johnny. Of course I mean it. Trawling's finished. They tied up another five boats last month, that means the end of the fleet. I've worked fifteen days in the last four months and three of those were a dead loss. I can't sit around waiting forever, and in any case if I have to choose between you and the sea . . . I don't care if I never see the sea again.

Mary. But where will you find work?

Johnny. There must be one job somewhere that I can do. Anyway, if there is, I'll find it.

Mary. You mean you're going away?

Johnny. Yes, Mary, I'm going to fish for work the way we fish for herring. I'll drag a net over the whole country if I have to, and one of these days I'll be writing to you and asking you to come to me. Will you?

Mary. To the end of the earth.

Johnny. And you'll wait?

Mary. Till the seas run dry.

They dance to the following song.

[MUSIC CUE 6]
1st Narrator. (*Singing*)
        Fare you well, my dear, I must be gone,
        And leave you for a while.
        If I roam away I will come back again
        Though I roam a thousand miles, my dear,
        Though I roam a thousand miles.

2nd Narrator. (*Singing*)
        The salt sea will run dry, my dear,
        And the rocks melt in the sun;
        But I never will prove false to the lad I love
        Till all these things be done, my dear,
        Till all these things be done.

The lights fade. Up music behind the following. The lights fade up and a chorus of unemployed men enter dancing.

Microphone voice. Crew of the Trawler 'Mary Ellis': Paid off!

Chorus. No change! No work!

Mic. voice. Trawler 'Sun-bird', in dry dock, all repairs at a standstill.

Chorus. No change! No work!

Mic. voice. Crew of the trawler *Merrily*: paid off!

Chorus. No change! No work!

Mic. voice. In future, trawlermen will apply for work at their labour exchange. Ships' husbandmen will no longer book their crews at this dock.

Chorus. No change! No work!

Johnny. What's wrong with the world? What's wrong with me? Don't people need clothes and shoes and houses any more? Don't they need fish out of the sea and coal out of the earth?

Mic. voice. The unemployment figures can now be said to be stabilised at two and a half million. No immediate deterioration is expected.

Roll of drums. The chorus fall into line.

Mic. voice. Two hundred Scottish hunger-marchers set out from Glasgow.

The chorus begin to march, marking time.

Mic. voice. November 1931. The unemployed of the north-east coast are marching.

1st man. Men from Newcastle!

2nd man. Gateshead!

3rd man. Durham!

4th man. Jarrow!

5th man. Morpeth!

6th man. Sunderland!

All chorus. Shields!

Mary. (*Offstage*) Wait, Johnny! Wait!

A newsboy carrying papers and a poster dances on.

Newsboy.
        All the latest! Last Edition!
        Mr Eden's German Mission.
        Paris riots, foodshops looted,
        Van de Lubbe executed.
        Loch Ness Monster seen again.
        Sentence passed on Ludwig Renn.
        All the latest!
        All the latest!
        All the latest!

He goes off. The chorus read their newspapers.

1st man. Plenty of words!

2nd man. Plenty of promises!

3rd man. Plenty of circuses!

All chorus. But no bread!

Mary. (*Offstage*) Wait, Johnny! Wait!

Johnny. Not me, I'm not waiting. I'm going out to find what's wrong with the world. And if there's a job anywhere, I'll find it!

Chorus retreat, waving slowly as light fades.

Chorus. So long, Johnny! So long, Johnny!
        So long!

Chorus goes off.

[MUSIC CUE 7]

1st Narrator. (*Singing*)
        Johnny Noble has left his home,
        He has walked over moss and moor;
        And he has gone to the banks of Clyde,
        To try his luck in the shipyards there.

Johnny dances across to the Narrator who suddenly takes the character of an unemployed man.

Johnny. How's things around here, Mac?

Clydesider. Deadly.

Johnny. Anything doing in the yards?

Clydesider. No, we've been idle for the last six years. Where are you from?

Johnny. Hull way.

Clydesider. Engineer?

Johnny. Fisherman.

Clydesider. No work?

Johnny. That's right. I thought I'd try the shipbuilding game.

Clydesider. It's a lost trade, chum.

Johnny. Are there no jobs at all?

Clydesider. None at all.

Johnny. They sound busy enough in there.

Clydesider. That's the wrecking gang. They're breaking up the equipment. Better go south. I'd be there myself if it wasnae for the wife.

The light and the Narrator fade. Johnny dances.

[MUSIC CUE 8]

2nd Narrator (*Singing*)
        In Durham County it is the same,
        The pithead gear is standing still,
        And men are filled with a sense of shame
        For idle hands and wasted skill.

A miner enters and stands in a pool of light, centre stage.

Durham miner. Why, but you've come to the wrong place, mon. There's no work here. Number Three was working until a year ago but that's finished now. The Ballarat seam's flooded out. They'll never get it working again. Why, there's not enough work to keep three men and a boy busy.

Johnny. How do you manage to keep going?

Durham Miner. Well, we've got our bit of dole and we scratch for coal on the screens to keep a bit fire in the house. Why . . . aye, but it's bad . . . it is that . . . bad all over, though they say things are better in the south . . .

Music. Man goes off. Unemployed men enter, dancing.

Johnny. Which is the road to Darlington, mate?

1st man. Follow the road . . . straight on.

Dance.

Johnny. Which is the road to Leeds, mate?

2nd man. Follow the road . . . straight on.

Dance.

Johnny. How do I get to Manchester?

3rd man. Follow the road.

All. Follow the road, chum. Follow the road. Follow the road, straight on.

Johnny. Where are YOU going?

All. We don't know, chum. We don't know. We just keep going.

Johnny. Well, good luck!

All. Good luck, chum!

Slow blackout.

[MUSIC CUE 9]

2nd Narrator. (*Singing*)
> Winter is past and the leaves are green,
> The time is past that we have seen.
> But still I hope the time will come,
> When you and I shall be as one.

The light fades up to half, showing a group of men sitting and lying on the stage.

Narrator. Men on the roads, men on the streets. The traversing of the endless circle. Hey, you there!

Chorus. Yes?

Narrator. What are you waiting for?

Chorus. For time to pass.

Narrator. Who are you?

Chorus. We are the disinherited.

Narrator. Where are you from?

Chorus. From everywhere.

Narrator. Where are you bound for?

Chorus. Anywhere. We walk between one meal and the next.

Narrator. And this is your life?

Chorus. We sign away our lives . . . every morning.

They lie down and sleep.

[*MUSIC CUE 10*]

2nd Narrator. (*Singing*)
> My Johnny's gone, I mourn and weep,
> But satisfied I ne'er can sleep.
> I'll write to you in a few short lines,
> I suffer death ten thousand times.

One of the men sits up and begins filling his pipe.

Johnny. My, but I could do with a breath of air.

Taffy. Well, there's no shortage of that outside, and no charge either.

Johnny. I like my air to be well seasoned.

Taffy. What do you mean by that?

Johnny. My lungs are in need of salt . . . Oh, for some sea air!

Taffy. Are you a matlo then?

Johnny. Fisherman.

Taffy. You are a long way from home, bach, there are no fish here.

Johnny. No . . .

Taffy. You are looking for work.

Johnny. Work? What's that?

Taffy. Yes, things are bad. Tell me, have you ever heard of Potato Jones?

Johnny. Potato Jones? Isn't he the skipper of the 'Seven Seas Spray'?

Taffy. The very man. Captain Jones, the blockade runner. I am sailing with him next trip.

Johnny. Oh, you're a seaman.

Taffy. Ship's cook for thirty-seven years. A galley-slave, my boy.

Johnny. Where are you bound for?

Taffy. Barcelona. We're carrying a cargo of canned milk.

Johnny. Dangerous work, isn't it?

Taffy. Well, I've known safer trips. Master Franco doesn't like people who feed children. Captain Jones makes him very angry.

Johnny. It's good work.

Taffy. You know, I think the captain is short of a deckhand. (*Pause*). I thought you might be interested. (*Pause*). Perhaps I shouldn't have mentioned it. Just forget everything I told you.

Johnny. Where are you sailing from?

Taffy. Liverpool.

Johnny. When?

Taffy. Thursday night.

Johnny. We'll have to be on the road early, then.

Taffy. I thought you were the right sort.

Johnny. Good night, Taffy.

Taffy. Good night, bach.

The light fades.

[MUSIC CUE 11]

1st Narrator. (*Singing*)
      So Johnny shipped aboard a craft well known in the coasting
                                    trade,
      She sailed for Barcelona through the fascist sea blockade.
      They beat the German submarines, and floating mines as well,
      And then they lay in the sheltered bay, a-heaving on the swell.

[MUSIC CUE 12]

2nd Narrator. (*Singing*)
      But back in the home town,
      Where time passes slow,
      There Mary sits waiting
      For Johnny, her jo.

      Her trust has not faded
      Though they are apart
      And the love has not withered
      That grows in her heart.

The stage is flooded with light. Two youths stand upstage right, arguing. Mary sits downstage left. Her mother sits nearby gossiping with a neighbour. The unemployed man stands upstage reading a newspaper.

1st youth. It was in the fourth round.

2nd youth. No, you're wrong –

1st youth. But I tell you, I saw the film four times!

2nd youth. I don't care if you saw it twenty times, it was at the beginning of the fifth round, a technical knockout.

1st youth. That wasn't the Baer fight – it was the Mexican champion.

2nd youth. It was the Baer-Louis fight!

1st youth. Now look, in the third round, Joe Louis began to work on Baer, didn't he? He got Baer into a corner, see, and began by giving him a few short jabs to the side, I tell you. I can remember every single punch in that fight. He stands there like this, see, crowding Baer . . .

2nd youth. So?

1st youth. So Maxie's getting tanned good and proper, so he tries to slip by on the ropes. Well, Louis waits till he's off-balance, see, and then he wades in with a smashing left drive. Maxie tries to side-step it, but Joe follows through with his right and closes Maxie's left eye for him.

2nd youth. Well, who's arguing about that?

1st youth. You are. Anyway, Maxie's minus a lamp now, see, and this time he doesn't know what day it is. He's been punched around so much. Well, the bell goes for the fourth round. 'Seconds out of the ring! Time!' Clang! Louis crossing the ring looking determined, like, but not tough. He looks like what he's going to do is for Maxie's own good. Now Maxie comes in sparring, but Joe won't play. He leads with his left to Maxie's side. Bang! Bang! Then with his right he breaks Maxie's guard. Bang! Wallop! And then that terrific left swing comes from nowhere and Maxie's out for good. One-two-three-four. . . I tell you, the referee could have counted up to a thousand. The fourth round it was, and still three-quarters of a minute to go.

2nd youth. It was the fifth round.

1st youth. You're punch-drunk.

The 1st youth takes a newspaper from his pocket and begins to study it. The 2nd smokes a cigarette.

Mother. My, but it's close, isn't it?

Neighbour. Terrible. It's just like an oven in the house.

Mother. Mary, why don't you go for a walk in the park?

Mary. I'm alright.

Mother. It would do you more good than sitting around here brooding.

A man enters reading a newspaper.

1st youth. What won the 3.30, Larry?

Man. Castle in Spain at 8–1.

1st youth. I had a bob on Blue Silk!

Man. Didn't stand a chance. Came in sixth.

Enter Eddie.

Eddie. Hello, Mary. Going to the dance?

Mary. No, I don't think I'll bother.

Eddie. Still waiting for Johnny?

Mary. What if I am?

Eddie. I think you're crazy. I bet you've almost forgotten how to dance.

Mary. I'm not complaining.

Eddie. Mary, how would you like to take a run into the country this weekend?

Mary. No, Eddie, I've told you, I . . .

Eddie. Alright, alright! I know the answer. It's a pity though, I've just bought a car.

Mary. A car? Well!

Eddie. Yes, I've been doing alright.

Mary. You certainly have.

Eddie. Seriously, though, Mary – you look as if you need some air.

Mary. Well, some other time.

Eddie. Some other time! I seem to have heard that before. How's Johnny going on? Got a job yet?

Mary. Not yet.

Eddie. What a mug you are. Hullo girls? Looking for me?

Enter two girls.

1st girl. Hullo, Eddie.

2nd girl. Coming to the dance, Mary?

Eddie. No, she's got a date with a ghost.

1st girl. How's Johnny?

Mary. He's alright, thanks.

Mother. Why don't you tell them he never writes?

Mary. Why should he? He said he wouldn't write till he found something.

2nd girl. I'd want a better excuse than that.

A youth enters playing a mouth organ. The two girls dance.

1st youth. Break it up, the experts are here.

They partner the girls.

Eddie. Come on, Mary, you're safe enough here.

They dance. Enter 1st Narrator with a letter.

[MUSIC CUE 13]

1st Narrator. (*Singing*)
        Which of you is Mary Marsden?
        I've a letter for you.

Girls. (*Singing*)
        Mary, hear what he is saying:
        Here's a letter for you.

1st Narrator. (*Singing*)
        The lad that gave it to me said
        His name was Johnny Noble.

Girls (*Singing*)
        Well she knew her love was true,
        Her handsome Johnny Noble.
        Oh, oh, oh, oh, Seaman Johnny Noble.

Mary. Oh, let me see it quickly!

She opens the letter.

Girls.   Oh, read it quickly, Mary, do
        And tell us what Johnny says to you.

Man.   Is his search for work now done?

Girls.   And does he write for you to come?

All.   Oh, read it quickly, Mary.

Girls.   Oh tell us, Mary, do!

[MUSIC CUE 14]

1st Narrator.
        Why do you grow so pale?
        What is so alarming?

1st girl. (*Singing*)
        Is it then bad news
        Makes you weep and mourn?

2nd girl. (*Singing*)
        Here begins the grief,
        Pain without relief –
        Has he then forsaken his love?

Girls. (*Singing*)
>She is left forsaken,
>Another she is taken,
>Johnny, Oh why do you so?

Mary. This letter – it's from Spain.

1st Narrator. Well?

Mary. He promised me that he was finished with the sea.

Men. (*Singing*)
>Oh, oh, oh, oh, faithless Johnny Noble.

[END OF SONG SEQUENCE]

Mother. I warned you, you should have left him when I told you.

1st Narrator. But why? What's he done except try and keep famine from the door of a brave people?

Mother. That's not his business.

1st Narrator. If a man in Spain dies because he opens his mouth to speak his mind, that's everybody's business.

Eddie. We've enough trouble of our own without going out to look for more.

1st Narrator. You don't have to go out to look for it. It's staring you in the face every time you open a newspaper. Look!

He takes a newspaper out of his pocket.

'Men and women are dying in China.'

A girl. That's a long way from here.

1st Narrator. They are dying in Spain and that's not so far away. Aye, and Germany and Austria aren't far away. Look at these four lines in a newspaper: 'It is reported from Hamburg that Rudolph Schwartz was executed this morning for attempting to organise a trade union.' Instead of Rudolph Schwartz it could be you – or Johnny. And we would be his executioners.

1st youth. Who, me?

1st Narrator. Yes, you. Look, we'll act it.

1st youth. But don't I need a black shirt?

1st Narrator. Don't worry – Fascism doesn't always wear a black shirt.

Mic. voice. It is early morning. The city is still asleep. You have lain awake all night waiting for this moment, the moment when time stops. This is the last time you will ever know the cold air of morning or the streets in the moment between sleeping and waking. This is your last walk.

During the foregoing passage, the lights fade until only the condemned man and the guards are clearly visible – the chorus stands on the periphery of the light. A man advances from the body of the chorus and begins to sing. The rest of the scene is danced.

[MUSIC CUE 15]

Singer. In the yard of a prison
                    That at last they might shoot him.
                    He stood, back to a wall,
                    Built by men such as he was.

Guard. Eins! Zwei! Drei!

Chorus. We mixed the lime and carried the hod
                    We laid the bricks for seventeen pfennig a day.

Singer. Even the rifles that were levelled against his breast
                    And the bullets had been made by men like himself –

Guard. Vier! Funf! Sechs!

Chorus. We watched the lathe and turned the steel
                    For twenty-two pfennig a day.

Singer. They were by this time long departed or were scattered,
                    Yet for him they lingered,
                    Still present in the work of their hands . . .

Guard. Achtung!

Singer. Even the men who would shoot him
                    They were not other than he
                    Nor forever cut off in their blindness.

Chorus. Kill him! Kill him! Kill him! Kill him!

A woman leaves the chorus and advances downstage.

Woman. Now memory comes, sharp and poignant
                    Filling his eyes with tears,
                    Trembling with distant music.
                    The suns of past summers
                    Stir in the blood
                    And the little roots of remembered springs tear at the soul.

Chorus. (*Gives a long shuddering sigh.*)

Woman. Oh, let there be night without stars
                    Body without movement,
                    Mind without thought.
                    Let me die unseen in the night
                    Feeling nothing but the body's anguish
                    Under the teeth of the wolves of darkness.

Chorus. (*Moans*).

[MUSIC CUE 16]

> Bravely he walked still encumbered with fetters,
> With fetters forged by his comrades,
> And hung on him by his comrades,
> And though it was morning then
> For at daybreak they marshalled them out,
> The buildings were empty and still.

Guard. Links! Recht! Links! Recht! Links! Recht!

Woman. Remember the days of hope,
> When the night had ears to hear the words
> That leap from house to house
> In little blades of fire,
> And men had the keen, sharp sight of birds
> To recognise the first, trembling spasm of revolt.
> Remember the song that thrilled the heart
> And made the air itself respond
> With brittle murmurings of dreams.

> Remember the shared desires and the shared hunger,
> The shared belief that all men are brothers,

> Remember the sudden crack of voice
> That made the streets rise up
> And bar the way to soldiers.
> These same streets, these same houses.

Guard. Links! Recht! Links! Recht! Halt!

[MUSIC CUE 17]

Singer. But to his eyes they sheltered now
> A numberless host of workers,
>   whose strivings and aims are his own –
> Now they led him forth against the wall,
> And all this he perceived,
> Yet understood it not.

The guard dances the shooting of the prisoner. The prisoner falls. Blackout. Up music and hold until the lights go up again. All the persons on the stage are discovered in their original positions, asleep.

Singer. You see?

Mary. They're asleep.

[MUSIC CUE 18]

1st Narrator. (*Singing*)
> Wake you up! Wake you up!
> You seven sleepers!
> And do take a warning from me,

> Be prepared to defend
> Your freedom to the end,
> Make a stand now for your liberty.

Sound of aeroplane.

2nd Narrator. (*Singing*)
> The night is disturbed,
> The calmness is broken,
> And death overshadows the world,
> You can hear the beat
> Of an army's marching feet
> And the war flags are being unfurled.

Sound of distant bombing.

Mary. What was that?

Unemployed man. It sounded like thunder.

Eddie. We could do with a storm. My, but it's close.

Mother. This kind of weather always puts me on edge. I think I'll go in.

She goes in.

1st youth. It's a good night for a swim. What do you say?

2nd youth. O.K.

They go.

Eddie. Sure you won't change your mind about the dance, Mary?

Mary. Not tonight.

Eddie. (*To first girl*) Come on, kid. You and me's going places. So long, Mary!

They go.

Mary. (*Reading Johnny's letter*) O, Johnny, I wish you were here.

Johnny has entered silently.

Johnny. Do you?

Mary. Johnny! (*They embrace.*) I can't believe you're here!

Johnny. Oh, I'm here, alright. (*He kisses her.*) Does that convince you?

Mary. Oh, Johnny, I've missed you so much. Don't ever go away again, will you?

Johnny. I had to go, Mary. I had to find out. You know, Mary, I used to feel lost, as if there was no place in the world for me. There seemed to be no sense in being born. But I've learned something. There's a lot of people like me in the world. We're everywhere, and we're important. Yes, we are, Mary! Oh, I know they let us starve and they don't care what happens to us, but when there's big trouble anywhere we are the ones they call upon for help. You know what, Mary? I've discovered that everything that's worth looking at in all the towns and cities of the world was built by people like us. I don't feel lonely any more because I know there's a man in Madrid just like me and at this moment he's fighting a German tank with a bottle of petrol. There's a million like me in China picking off stray Japs with obsolete rifles. I used to walk around like a mongrel dog begging for a bone but that's all over. I know who I am now, and I know why I'm here. I don't know why I'm saying all this to you, but . . .

Mary. I want to hear it.

Johnny. It's funny, but it's not what I intended to say.

Mary. No?

Johnny. No – I was going to ask you to marry me.

Mary. What, now?

Johnny. Well, not tonight, say in a week's time.

Mary. Ah . . . (*She weeps.*)

Johnny. What's wrong? Did I say something?

Mary. Oh, I'm so happy.

Johnny. Then you will?

Mary. Of course.

Johnny. I've done it! I've done it! I've done it!

First youth enters.

Johnny. Hey, cocky! I'm going to be married!

He whirls the youth in a dance.

1st youth. Hey, Johnny's gone crazy.

Enter 2nd youth.

2nd youth. What's wrong?

1st youth. He's getting married.

2nd youth. Larry, they've fixed up. They're getting hitched.

Unemployed man enters.

Man. Congratulations, Mary – and you too, Johnny.

Both. Thanks, Larry.

Enter Mary's mother.

Mother. What's happening?

Mary. Johnny's asked me to marry him.

Mother. Ah, well, I knew it would come to it some day.

Mother kisses Johnny. The others enter.

1st girl. Is it true, Mary?

Mary. Aye, it's true.

Johnny. And the whole street's invited to the wedding.

1st youth. Will there be a dance?

Johnny. Aye, you can dance yourself down to the knees.

He plays a jig on a mouth organ. The others dance until suddenly the jig is drowned out in a great sustained phrase of music. Slow fade-out.

Mic. voice. I am speaking to you from the Cabinet Room of Number 10 Downing Street. This morning the British Ambassador in Berlin handed to the German Government a final note stating that unless their troops were withdrawn from Poland by eleven o'clock this morning a state of war would exist between us. I have to tell you now that no such undertaking has been received and that, consequently, this country is at war with Germany.

Up level drone of planes behind the foregoing sequence. Cut in on last word with music, hold at peak and cross-fade with heavy ticking of clock. Hold behind the following.

Mic. voice. Passengers for Preston, Lancaster, Carlisle and Glasgow will leave on number 3 platform at 5.43. The train for Preston, Lancaster, Carlisle and Glasgow will leave number 3 platform at 5.43.

Another voice. Not much time left.

Two groups of figures, each composed of a man and a woman, are discovered embracing in two yellow pools of light.

1st woman. Don't forget your sandwiches, Jim. I've put them at the top of your case. And let me know your address as soon as you get there. I'll send you a parcel. Must keep talking, Jim, we must keep talking. It's queer, the minutes are bleeding away and all I can talk about are the things furthest from my mind. Do look after yourself, Jim, and don't forget to send anything you want washed. Four more minutes and it'll be the end. Oh, God!

Towards conclusion of foregoing fade up clock backed by voice.

Voice. (*Whispering*) Hurry, etc.

Mic. voice. The train for Crewe, Hereford, Birmingham, Pontypool and Bristol, will leave number 11 platform at 5.58.

Mary. Go on talking, Johnny, please go on talking. If we stop talking we'll start thinking. Take care of yourself, Johnny. And please write as often as you can. Oh, so much to be said and no words to say with. If you need anything just write and I'll send it to you. Only a few minutes left and then

. . . Perhaps it won't be for long. I'll be waiting for you. Oh, if only the clocks would stop forever!

Ticking of clock at peak. Sudden high-pitched blast of train whistle.

Mic. voice. Johnny Noble, able seaman!

Johnny looks round.

Johnny. It's time, Mary.

Mic. Voice. James Munroe, bricklayer!

1st man. It's time, lass.

Mic. voice. Young men, it's time to say goodbye.

The couples embrace. The men go off. The two women, lonely figures in the pools of yellow light, stand without moving. There is a sudden, loud, blast of escaping steam and the women begin waving handkerchiefs. The train gets under way and as the light fades there are two, short, melancholy blasts of the engine's whistle as it passes into a long tunnel.

Mic. voice. If only one could choose one's moments of eternity – but inexorable time divides and sub-divides and sub-divides again until nothing is left of a moment but an insubstantial memory.

Complete blackout.

Mic. voice. And everything is left unsaid except – Goodbye.

[MUSIC CUE 19]

2nd Narrator. (*Singing*)
        Westryn wind, when wilt thou blow?
        The small rain down doth rain,
        Oh, that my love were in my arms,
        And I in my bed again.

        Deep and wide the river runs
        That steals my lad away,
        And I must bide it here alone
        And cannot bid him stay.

[MUSIC CUE 20]

1st Narrator. (*Singing*)
        In nineteen hundred and forty two,
        In November, the thirteenth day;
        The 'Liberty Star' her anchor weighed
        And for Murmansk bore away, brave boys,
        And for Murmansk bore away.

        Our course was set for nor'-nor' east,
        Through the raging arctic sea, brave boys,
        Through the raging arctic sea.

Fade up throb of ship's engines. Light fades up discovering Johnny seated on a box playing 'On top of Old Smokey' on a mouth organ. A stoker enters. Johnny stops playing.

Stoker. Go on playing, Johnny. I just came up for a breather.

Johnny. My hands are too cold.

Stoker. What's her name, Johnny?

Johnny. Mary.

Stoker. The wife?

Johnny. Not yet.

Short blast of ship's siren.

Stoker. That'll be the 'Sverdrup'. She should be astern of us.

Two short blasts of ship's siren.

Johnny. My, but it's cold!

Stoker. Is this your first trip up here?

Johnny. Well, I was up as far as Iceland once.

Stoker. Iceland! That's the tropics. Wait till we reach the Behring Sea, then you'll know what cold is.

Johnny. How long have you been at this job, Frank?

Stoker. Thirty-seven years.

Johnny. That's a long time.

Three short blasts of ship's siren.

Stoker. Yes, I know these waters better than I know the back streets of Salford. I remember sailing up into the Kara Sea when the insurance risk was only three shillings to the ton. That's going back a bit. And I'd been up to the Chukotsk Sea twice by the time I was twenty. The first skipper I ever sailed with was one of the old timers of the Hull whaling fleet, never felt happy unless he was freezing off the coast of Greenland. A fine man. I was off Bear Island with the trawlers when this lot started. We were lucky to get home. I'll bet the halibut wondered what was happening.

The repeated alarm signal of a destroyer is heard. The clanging of bells. Red and green warning-lights flash.

Stoker. Back again!

Johnny. Well, come on then.

They race off. Blackout. Fade in droning of plane. Build to peak and hold with backing of music.

Voice. (*Above music*) Enemy, Green Nine-O!

Siren. Music out.

Voice. Action station!

Fade up lights. Gun crew discovered stage centre. In the following scene they dance a gun crew in action. Up sound of circling plane.

1st Seaman. What is it? Dornier 109?

Gunner. Well, it's not a seagull.

Voice. Bearing Green Nine-O!

Gunner. Bearing Green Nine-O!

1st loader. Bearing Green Nine-O!

Music. In dance mime the crew load and fire the gun.

1st loader. Load!

2nd loader. Load!

1st loader. On!

2nd loader. On!

Gunner. Fire!

Music.

1st loader. Load!

2nd loader. Load!

1st loader. On!

2nd loader. On!

Gunner. Fire!

Bomb explosion.

Voice. Bearing Red Five-O!

Loaders. Bearing Red Five-O!

Gunner. Red Five-O!

1st loader. Load!

2nd loader. Load!

1st loader. On!

2nd loader. On!

Gunner. Fire!

1st loader. Load!

2nd loader. Load!

1st loader. On!

2nd loader. On!

Gunner. Fire!

Sound of dive-bombing and machine-gun fire. Crew drops to ground. One loader is killed.

[*M U S I C   C U E   2 1*]

Narrator. (*Singing*)
> The Nazi planes from Christiansund
> Above our ships did fly,
> But our ack-ack guns got the measure of the Huns,
> And we blew them from the sky, brave boys
> And we blew them from the sky.

The members of the gun-crew re-form and resume the dance.

1st loader. Load!

2nd loader. Load!

1st loader. On!

2nd loader. On!

Gunner. Fire!

Seaman. He's falling! Look! Look!

2nd Seaman. There he goes!

Drone of plane falling followed by explosion. The crew cheer and the lights fade out.

[*M U S I C   C U E   2 2*]

2nd Narrator. (*Singing*)
> And back in the homeland,
> Where time passes slow,
> There Mary sits waiting
> For Johnny, her jo.
>
> Her trust has not faded,
> Though they are apart,
> And the love has not withered
> That grows in her heart.

Full lighting. Johnny and a woman neighbour enter from opposite directions, dancing.

[*M U S I C   C U E   2 3*]

Neighbour. (*Singing*)
> O Johnny, O Johnny, O Johnny,
> And is it yourself that I see?
> I thought you were on the Atlantic.

Johnny (*Singing*)
> I've been up through the cold northern sea.

Two girls enter, dancing.

Two girls. (*Singing*)
> It's Johnny, it's Johnny, Johnny Noble's come home,
> He left his love, Mary, the wide world to roam;
> But now he's come back from the ocean.
> You're a welcome sight, Johnny, to me.

Two youths enter, dancing.

1st youth. (*Singing*)
> Tonight let's all go out upon a binder.

Two girls. (*Singing*)
> There's a girl who's waiting patiently
> To hear that you are safe.

All. (*Singing*)
> Hurry up, man, hurry up, man,
> And find her.

Mary enters, dancing. She dances with Johnny.

[MUSIC CUE 24]

Two girls. (*Singing*)
> Winter is past and the leaves are green,
> The worst is past that we have seen;
> And now at last the time has come
> When these two hearts shall be as one.

Unemployed man. (*Singing*)
> O Johnny lad, and are you glad
> To be with us back home?

Johnny. (*Singing*)
> Why aye, but man, of course I am,
> No more I wish to roam.
> I've done my share of freezing
> As you may understand,
> And I've known some cold Nor'westers
> On the banks of Newfoundland.

All. (*Singing*)
> He's done his share of freezing
> As you may understand,
> And he's known some cold Nor'westers
> On the banks of Newfoundland.

Youth. (*Speaking*). Never mind, Johnny, that's all over and done with.
You're back home and that's all that matters.

The roaring boys, two grotesque figures wearing black tights and bowler hats, leap on to the stage.

Roaring boys. Yes, it's over and done with.

All. The war is over now.

1st R. boy. No more government attacks.

2nd R. boy. No more excess profits tax.

1st R. boy. No more joint production groups.

2nd R. boy. No more nonsense from the troops.

All. No?

R. boys. No!

1st R. boy. Time we got back to normal. Can't go on being a hero forever, Johnny. The heroes have had their day. Now it's our turn. Business as usual, that's our slogan.

All. Which business?

R. boys. Money business.

1st R. boy. Time we got back to normal.

2nd R. boy.
> Time we got back to the good old days,
> The happy-go-lucky production ways.

1st R. boy.
> Back to the dignified position
> Of unrestricted competition.

2nd R. boy.
> Back to surplus and higher rent,
> And a profit of eighty-four per cent.
> Back to normal.

1st R. boy. Back to normal.

Both R. boys. Back!

The chorus have retreated in the face of their dance. Now, the 1st Roaring boy produces a whistle and blows a sharp blast on it. The chorus turn stiffly and go through the motions of clocking-in. Each time one moves a bell rings. When they have all clocked in he blows another blast on the whistle. The chorus dance a machine which the two Roaring boys accompany with the rhythmic reiterations of:

R. boys. Time! Time! Time! Time!

The machine speeds up. At peak, Johnny interrupts.

Johnny. Stop!

The members of the chorus straighten up like men coming out of a dream.

Johnny. The war wasn't fought for this. They said it would be different. They said . . .

1st R. boy. Time to forget. Time to get back to the good old days. The days of plenty.

Johnny. Plenty of what?

Chorus. Hungry bellies and long queues,
    Plenty of time and nothing to do with it.

1st R. boy. That's life, Johnny. Survival of the fittest.

Johnny. We fought for something better.

Chorus. Yes!

2nd R. boy. Time you forgot the fighting, Johnny. You can't fight tradition. You can't fight history.

Johnny. But they said . . .

Bell clangs.

1st R. boy. Time to forget! Seconds out of the ring! Time! On my right, ladies and gentlemen, standing in the shadows of protective might is Battling Johnny Privilege the heavyweight champion of the world. On my left, the challenger Johnny Noble, representing the pipe-dreamers. The prize is the Universe. Seconds out! Time!

A bell clangs. Johnny comes out fighting and then drops his guard and looks round in daze.

Johnny. I can't see him.

1st R. boy. Never mind, kid. Forget it. We've got a boom on our hands. A trade boom. Now you go home and leave everything to me. I'll fix things so that you don't have to think about anything.

He begins to shepherd Johnny off the stage.

Man. (*In audience*) Hey Johnny!

Johnny. Who was that?

Man. It's me, Johnny.

Johnny. I seem to recognise the voice.

Man. Do you remember a trimmer called Johnson who was drowned in the Barents Sea. That was me, Johnny. I was a little-piecer from Bolton called Arkroyd. I died screaming in the Burmese jungle. There was a bricklayer called Brown with a wife and three kids in Birmingham. The Germans burned him with a flame-thrower. That was me, Johnny.

1st R. boy. It's time we forgot about the war.

Man. It's time you remembered why the war was fought. There's a job to be done, Johnny.

Johnny. But what can I do?

Man. You've two hands and a brain and there's plenty of you. Take the world in your hands. Johnny, and wipe it clean. It's up to you, Johnny.

Johnny. Do you hear that? It's our world. It's up to us. We can do it, can't we?

Chorus. Yes!

Johnny. Thanks, pal, for reminding me.

Man. That's all right.

Man turns and walks slowly up the centre aisle. Turning, he addresses the stage.

Man. So long, Johnny. Good luck!

Johnny. So long, pal.

Chorus. So long.

[MUSIC CUE 25]

Man. (*Singing*) This is the end.

2nd Narrator. (*Singing*) The end of the story of Mary Marsdon and Johnny Noble.

[The End]

MUSIC CUE 1

MUSIC CUE 2

Have you seen owt o' my bon-ny lad, And are you sure that he's weel, O? He's

gone ow-er land wiv his stick in his hand, He's gone__ to moor__ the keel, O.

MUSIC CUES 3, 4, 11

Now, come all __ you good peo-ple and lis-ten to my song, It's of young Johnny

No-ble and I won't de-tain__ you long, Young John-ny lived on the North East coast where

traw-ler men__are made, And he was quite de-ter-mined for to fol-low the sail-or's trade.

MUSIC CUE 5

Now, two years pass and John-ny No-ble's Part-ed from__ his dear-ie;

And still she yearns for his __ re-turn And her heart is __ sad and __ weary.

MUSIC CUE 6

Fare you well, my dear, I must be__ gone And__ leave you__for a-while. If I

roam a-way I will come back a-gain, Though I roam a thousand miles, my dear, Tho' I roam a thou-sand__

miles.

MUSIC CUES 7, 8

MUSIC CUE 9

MUSIC CUE 10

MUSIC CUES 12, 22

MUSIC CUE 13

Johnny Noble

MUSIC CUE 14

stately, recitative style (traditional)

Why do you grow so — pale? What is so a-larm-ing? Is it then bad news makes you weep and mourn? Here be-gins the grief, Pain with-out re-lief — Has he then for-sak-en his love? She is left for-sak-en, An-oth-er she is taken, John-ny, Oh why do you so? Oh, oh, oh, oh, faith-less Johnny No-ble.

MUSIC CUE 15

steadily, recitative style

In the yard of a pri-son That at last — they might shoot him. He stood back to a wall, Built by men such as he was. Ev-en the ri-fles that were lev-elled a-gainst his breast And the bul-lets had been made — by — men like him-self. They were — by — this time long — de-part-ed or — were — scattered, Yet for him they lin-gered, still pre-sent in the work of their hands...

SLOWER

Ev-en the men who would shoot — him They were not oth-er than he — Nor for-ev-er cut off in their blind-ness.

MUSIC CUE 16

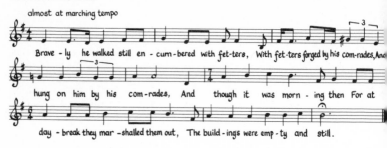

Brave - ly he walked still en - cum - bered with fet-ters, With fet-ters forged by his com-rades, And hung on him by his com-rades, And though it was morn - ing then For at day - break they mar - shalled them out, The build - ings were emp - ty and still.

MUSIC CUE 17

But to his eyes they shel-tered now A num-ber-less host of work-ers, whose striv - ings and aims are his own Now__ they led__ him forth a-gainst the wall, And all this he per - ceived,___ Yet __ un - der-stood it not.

MUSIC CUE 18

Wake you up! Wake you up! You sev - en sleep-ers! And do take a warning from me, Be pre -pared to de-fend Your free-dom to the end, Make a stand now for your li - ber - ty.

MUSIC CUE 19

Wes-tryn wind, when wilt__ thou __ blow? The small rain down doth rain, Oh, that my love were in my arms, And I in my bed a - gain___.

MUSIC CUES 20, 21

with determination   (traditional)

In nine-teen hun-dred and for-ty two, In No-vem-ber the thir-teenth day; The
'Li-ber-ty Star' her an-chor weighed And for Murmansk bore a-way, brave boys, And for
Mur-mansk bore a-way. Our course was set for Nor' Nor' East, Through the
rag-ing Arc-tic Sea, brave boys, Through the rag-ing Arc-tic Sea.

MUSIC CUE 23

cheerily   (by Ewan MacColl)

O, John-ny, O John-ny, O John-ny And is it your-self that I see? I
thought you were on the At-lan-tic. I've been up through the cold nor-thern sea. It's
John-ny, it's Johnny, Johnny No-ble's come home, He left his love, Ma-ry, the wide world to roam; But
now he's come back from the o-cean. You're a wel-come sight, Johnny, to me. To-
-night let's all go out up-on a bin-der. There's a girl who's waiting pa-tient-ly To
hear that you are safe, Hur-ry up, man, hur-ry up, man And find her.

Johnny Noble

MUSIC CUE 24

Win-ter is past and the leaves are green, The worst is past that we have seen; And now at last the __ time __ has __ come When these two hearts shall be as one. O John-ny lad, and are you glad To be with us back home? Why aye, but man, of course I am, __ No more __ I wish to roam. I've done my share of freez-ing As __ you may un - der - stand, And I've known some cold __ Nor' wes - ters On __ the banks __ of New - found - land. He's done his share of freez-ing As __ you may un - der - stand, And he's known some cold __ Nor' wes - ters On __ the banks __ of New - found - land.

MUSIC CUE 25

This is the end. The end of the sto-ry of Ma-ry Marsdon and John-ny No - - - - ble.

An episodic play in two parts

Uranium 235

by Ewan MacColl

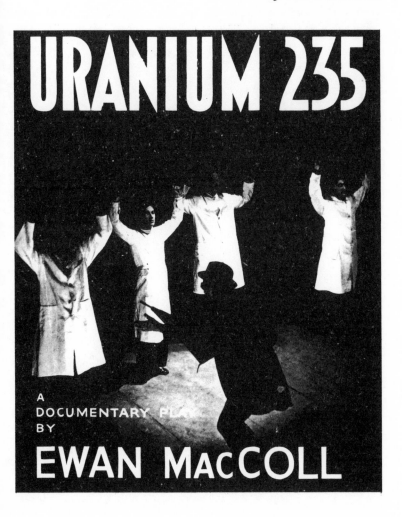

NOTE ON CASTING

A company of twelve actors, seven men and five women, made up the original cast of the Theatre Workshop production. Occasionally, this number would be enlarged by the addition of one or two more actors. On other occasions, the cast was reduced to ten.

AUTHOR'S NOTE

Uranium 235 was written for Theatre Workshop and produced by Joan Littlewood in 1946. During the four years it was in the company's repertoire, it underwent constant revision. The present script is the result of yet another revision, the most extensive to date.

[**PART ONE**] *The stage is dark. Spot comes up on the Firewatcher and then, on another level, Scientist is seen at a bench covered with apparatus. Air-raid sirens are heard. A girl hurries past.*

Firewatcher. Good night.

Exit girl.

> God, what an empty wilderness is time.
> A universe of endless desolation
> In which the hours are weary refugees
> Bent in a hopeless search for lost relations.
> Six till six my shift and three hours gone.
> This is no occupation for a man,
> This senseless peering into night
> As still and imperturbable as death itself.

A plane is heard.

> This is the hour
> When death is rationed out,
> When iron eggs, fruit of some monstrous coupling in Hell
> Are hatched in blood.
> This is the hour when cities rise up
> Shrieking in the night
> And lamentations sound from iron throats,
> This is destruction's hour.
> Oh God, protect this night
> From evil birds of prey,
> If not for man's sake
> Then for the sake of heaven's dignity.
> Dignity. What word is that?
> A hollow echo, a forgotten dream.
> A horse has dignity, a tree, a rock,
> An ant, a fly, a dog, a metal bar,
> Even a codfish, bleeding at the gills,
> Just gutted, outdoes man in dignity.
> Tonight they'll come again
> Chanting their bloody serenade
> And all the stars and wheeling suns of space
> Will vanish from men's minds
> As night stares down at us with bloodshot eyes.
> No more.
> This night will pass and so will other nights,
> Just as this war will pass.
> Men have survived catastrophes before
> And those who crouched despairing in a pit
> Have often lived to tell their friends of it.

Crash of bombs. Blackout on Firewatcher.

Man in Audience. Hey, there! You in the white coat! Is it always to be like this? Nothing but death and destruction?

Scientist. It depends.

Man in Audience. On what?

Scientist. On you.

Man in Audience. Us? Come off it! You're the ones who're supposed to know all the answers.

Scientist. Not *all* the answers but some of them . . . yes. We have, if I may say so, in the course of the last few years brought about considerable changes in what might be called the map of human knowledge. We have conquered power and explored the innermost secrets of the origin of matter. There are no closed doors to us now. We can choose our own road and send fate scurrying before us like an idiot beggar. We have opened a door on the future and on that door is written Uranium 235.

Blast of jazz music. Enter a couple jitterbugging. Music stops. They embrace. The scene should be played with frantic excitement.

Frank. Jessie, I love you. Honest to God, I love you. Gimme a kiss, Jessie. Do you love me, Jessie?

Jessie. Of course I do. I love you, Frank.

Frank. Do you, Jessie?

Jessie. You know I do, Frank.

Frank. Gimme a kiss, Jessie.

Jessie. I love you, Frank.

Frank. I love you, Jessie.

Scientist. Excuse me, but . . .

Frank. Look at the moon, Jessie.

Jessie. The moon in June . . .

Frank.   And time to spoon,
         My heart goes boom,
         Honest it does, Jessie!
         Boom diddy boom
         Diddy diddy diddy boom,
         Boom, boom, boom!

Music blares up. They execute hysterical dance.

Scientist. I wonder if you could spare a minute . . .

Frank. Are you an eyeful tonight! Honest, Jessie, you knocked 'em cold back there.

Jessie. Did I Frank?

Frank. Honest you did, Jessie, and you're my girl.

Jessie. Your girl . . .

Frank.   With your teeth like pearls
    My heart's in a whirl . . .

Scientist. I hate disturbing you, but . . .

Jessie.   Gimme a kiss. (*They kiss.*)
    You awaken such bliss.

Frank.   On a night like this.
    Just wait till the war's over, Jessie,
    And the lights go on again
    All over the world.
    I love you, Jessie,
    I love your eyes
    Blue as summer skies.
    And the touch of your hand
    Makes me understand
    And your bonnet of blue
    Reminds me of you . . .

Scientist.
    Now look here . . .

Frank.   I like your little turned-up nose
    Your little these and those,
    I like your lips, I like your hips,
    I like your feet, I think they're sweet,
    I like the way you take a chance,
    I like the smashing way you dance,
    I like your boundless energy.

Scientist.
    It's about energy I wanted to talk . . . (*Music and dance drown
    him. He continues to talk unheard.*) We can change the face of the
    earth in two generations.

Man in Audience. Speak up!

Scientist. (*Shouting*) I wanted to tell you that . . .

Two girls enter. They dance like sleepwalkers.

1st Girl. Tyrone Power's nice.

2nd Girl. Errol Flynn's nicer.

1st Girl. He's rough.

2nd Girl. He makes me feel all funny inside.

1st Girl. I dream of Tyrone Power.

Scientist. Now about power – I've discovered something very interesting . . .

1st Girl. He's got lovely eyes.

2nd Girl. Van Johnson's nice.

1st Girl. In his last film, Tyrone Power got killed in the last scene. I cried all night.

2nd Girl. Errol Flynn's nice.

1st Girl. I like Laurence Olivier – he's so handsome.

2nd Girl. I like Clark Gable – he's so strong.

1st Girl. James Mason's nice.

2nd Girl. Franchot Tone's nice.

1st Girl. Frank Sinatra's nice.

2nd Girl. Ray Milland's nice.

Both Girls. Nice. Nice. Nice. Nice . . .

Enter Every Girl's Uncle/Aunt reading newspaper. He walks around reading while crooner sings.

Crooner. (*Singing*)

> Love, love alone,
> Causes me to weep and moan.
> Love, love alone,
> Causes me to weep and moan.
> You can have my brain,
> You can have my bone,
> But leave me and my sweetie alone,
> Love, love alone,
> Causes me to weep and moan.

Every Girl's Uncle. The defendants first became intimate in the autumn of 1939 when they met at a reception given by Herr von Ribbentrop at the German Embassy. The plaintiff states that he visited the Conservatory between the soup and the fish at dinner and discovered his wife lying in a bed of arum maculatum. He attempted to remonstrate with her, but . . .

He turns a page.

Scientist.

> I should hate to be thought importunate . .

Every Girl's Uncle. Chats with the stars. Lovely ladies learn basic English. Film fans fan flames for Flynn. Knock his eye out with a teenage bra . . . let Priscilla take care of your pimples . . . let me take two stone off your middle . . . let me add six inches to your bust . . . Advice to the lovelorn.

Don't worry, little miss Eighteen, the one man is more important than half-a-dozen others . . . Do you envy her streamlined figure? The new Orion belt will take ten years off your stomach.

Scientist. Now for the last time . . .

Every Girl's Uncle.
        Tales of vice,
        Tales of spice,
        Juicy details, very nice.
        Facts about an opium den,
        Special remedy for men.
        All the latest rapes and killings.
        Seaman said: 'The girl was willing.'
        Strip-tease dancer's bravery.
        Exposure of white-slavery.
        Girl says she acted under dope.
        Higher birth-rate Britain's hope.
        Cottage slayer gets the rope.
        Murder weapon found in soap.

Enter sportsman.

Scientist. Is no one interested in what goes on in the world? I tell you, the entire race is in danger!

Sportsman. What race?

Scientist. The human race.

Sportsman. God! For a moment I thought you meant the two-thirty. Got five bob on Whirlwind. Dead cert, eight to one. Inside information, but don't let it get round or the price'll drop.

Scientist. I too have inside information.

Sportsman. Reliable source?

Scientist. Very! Direct from the solar system.

Sportsman. Don't talk to me about systems. I've tried 'em all. It's just a matter of luck. If it's your turn, yet get it. If it isn't, you've had it. Take the Pools – who wins the big money? The experts? Not on your life! It's the mugs who've never even seen a game of football. Last week an old biddy in Liverpool won ninety thousand quid! Think of it!

Scientist. It's not important.

Sportsman. Not important? Listen to him! Ninety thousand quid not important!

Scientist. Listen . . .

Sportsman. Take me, now – been studying form for years and what have I won? Not a bloody sausage! Last week I should have won a packet by all the rules. I'd got Arsenal to win. Dead cert! Five minutes to go and the score even. Matthews gives Stevenson the ball and he's got a clear field. Thompson tries to intercept him – not a chance! Stevie has him cork-legged. Right down the field he goes with the ball at his feet. The crowd's going crazy.

All. Come on, Stevie! Come on!

Sportsman. Parker's coming up behind him like a bleedin' tank. Stevie makes like he's going to shoot. Parker swerves and Stevie gives the ball to the Bomber. He gives it back to Stevie. There's nobody between him and the goal.

All. Shoot! Shoot!

Sportsman. Terrific kick! The ball goes sailing through the air, straight as a bloody arrow to the top left-hand corner of the net. Impossible to miss! Beautiful goal!

All. Goal! Goal!

Sportsman. No . . . no! Just at the last minute there's a sudden gust of wind and the ball curves and misses the net.

Groans from everybody.

Luck! Just luck. That goal would have won me a fortune. Could happen to anybody.

Scientist. Listen, everybody. What happens during the next few months depends upon your decision. There is very little time left.

Crooner enters with microphone on a long lead. He dances as he sings.

Crooner. (*Singing*)

> Enjoy yourself, it's later than you think,
> Enjoy yourself, while you're still in the pink.

The people on stage reassume their mantles of frantic gaiety, reciting their characteristic lines at greater and greater speed. Build up to a peak. Explosion and simultaneous blackout. After a short pause, a spotlight beam begins to wander aimlessly across the stage area. It finally comes to rest on a female, headless lay-figure. The head, wearing a blond wig, lies at the mannikin's feet. Close by is an old-fashioned portable gramophone on which turns a cracked record so all that we hear is the repeated phrase, 'Enjoy yourself, it's later than you think.' It finally runs out of power. During the narration which follows, members of the cast drift on to the stage.

Microphone Voice. 1945–Atomic bombs on Hiroshima and Nagasaki. 1946–the Cold War begins. 1947–Chiang Kai Shek launches full-scale offensive against the reds. War in Burma. 1948–Extension of the Cold War. British troops fighting in Malaya. France defends Indo-China . . . from the Indo-Chinese. Dutch troops defend Indonesia against the

Indonesians. 1949–Britain saves Greece . . . from the Greeks. 1950–War in Korea. 1951 . . . 52 . . . 53?

1st Actress. Must it happen?

2nd Actress. I can't bear to think of it.

1st Actor. You have to think of it or you won't have anything to think with. That's the way it's always been. People couldn't bear to think about it. So they turned their faces away and refused to see what lay under their noses. It was none of their business, they said, and by the time events had proved them wrong, it was too late. They were either dead or dying, killing or being killed. Their homes were rubble and their towns were graveyards. Men, women and children dying in countless millions because we couldn't be bothered to think.

2nd Actress. And now there's fission.

Mic. Voice. Calculations for the case of masses properly located at the initial instant indicate that between one and five per cent of the fission energy of the Uranium should be released at a fission explosion. This means from two to ten times 108 kilo calories per kilogram of Uranium 235. The available explosive energy per kilogram of Uranium is thus equivalent to about two thousand tons of T.N.T.

1st Actor. That's Greek to me.

Scientist. Actors, of course, are not meant to be physicists.

3rd Actress. They're not supposed to be anything but actors, but it isn't enough.

2nd Actress. It should be.

1st Actor. I don't agree.

3rd Actress. We are part of society whether we like it or not. If we don't eat we go hungry, and according to you (*indicating the Scientist*), if we don't think, we die.

2nd Actor. And now there's fission.

2nd Actress. Yes, and who gave us that great gift?

Scientist. Atomic fission doesn't necessarily mean atomic bombs.

1st Actress. What else does it mean?

Scientist. Why are you so aggressive?

1st Actor. Maybe she's prejudiced against people who make things that kill other people, if you see what I mean.

Scientist. But you can't just shift the responsibility for progress and . . .

3rd Actress. Progress! Is that what you call it?

Scientist. There are problems, I grant you that, but . . .

2nd Actor. Perhaps we ought to examine those problems in our own way.

2nd Actress. Which way's that?

2nd Actor. As actors.

1st Actress. Where do we begin?

2nd Actor. At the beginning, where else?

1st Actor. That's about three thousand years ago, isn't it?

Scientist. It begins with Democritus of Abdera. (*He is handed a chiton by one of the actors. He puts it on.*) In the course of putting on this chiton I have ceased to be a twentieth-century physicist, gone through a transition phase of being myself playing an actor, and finally taken on the external habiliments of an old Greek gentleman.

2nd Actor. Athens, 470 BC., a city built on a rock. Houses of white stone, stucco and marble, occasionally alabaster. Wide streets flanked with statues. The pillar of the ancient world.

A pillar which has been lying on its side upstage centre is raised upright by two actors. On a raised platform which runs against the back wall of the stage a priest enters, followed by a group of worshippers. They sing and dance across the stage.

Priest. City of wise Athene.

Chorus. Io, Io, Io, Io.

Priest. Child of Zeus and Ceres,

Chorus. Io, Io, Io, Io.

Priest. Mother of birds and the wise owl,

Chorus. Io, Io,

Priest. Master of the golden ocean,

Chorus. Io, Io.

Priest. Out of the void and the chaos of nothing,

Chorus. Io, Io, Io, ayee.

Priest. Out of the darkness and the night,

Chorus. Io, Io, Io, ho.

Priest. Zeus, the father and begetter of Gods,

Chorus. Io, ayee, ayee,

Priest. Fashioned the earth from a pebble of clay.

Chorus. Ayee, ayee,

Priest. Fashioned the earth with the sun to warm it;

Chorus. Ayee, ayee,

Priest. Fashioned the moon as a lamp of night.

Chorus. Io, Io, Io, ayee.

They kneel.

Democritus.
All this is false.

Priest. Who speaks against the Gods?

Democritus.
I, Democritus of Abdera.

Priest. Who is greater than Zeus?

1st Chorister.
Did man fashion the earth out of nothing?

Democritus.
Nothing can come from nothing.
Nothing can be reduced to nothing.
The universe does not change.

Throughout that period of time long past elements have existed out of which our world of things is composed and remade. These atoms are endowed with an immortal nature, none of them can turn to nothing.

An eternal substance holds them fast,
A substance interwoven part with part
by bonds more or less close;
But since the mutual fastenings of the atoms are dissimilar,
and their substance is everlasting,
things endure with bodies uninjured
till some force arrives which proves
strong enough to dissolve the texture of each.
Therefore no single thing ever returns to nothing
but at their disruption, all pass back
into the particles of matter.
None of these things that seem to perish
utterly perishes, since nature forms
one thing to another and permits nothing to be forgotten
unless first she has been recruited by another's death.

The 1st actor suddenly steps out of his role and interrupts the proceedings.

1st Actor. God! What a load of codswallop!

1st Actress. Why? What's wrong?

1st Actor. The whole bloody scene's wrong.

3rd Actress. I thought it was quite effective.

1st Actor. Oh, come on! It's an absolute travesty of the truth. What are we trying to show?

2nd Actor. We're helping to perpetuate a myth.

1st Actor. That isn't our job. Can you imagine the rulers of the ancient world wafting around like a bunch of flat-footed Isadoras, spouting bad poetry?

2nd Actress. You got a better idea?

1st Actor. We could try using some common sense. Athens wasn't the paradise the Victorians cracked it up to be. It was a powerful military state founded on slave labour.

The 2nd actor assumes the gestures and vocal delivery of a market-spieler. He grabs hold of the arm of the 3rd actress.

2nd Actor. Ladies and gentlemen, what am I offered for this choice piece of merchandise? This is no sullen captive from the stews of Syracuse but a willing servant, the result of scientific breeding on our state farm at Pylos. As you know, ladies and gentlemen, we deal only in pedigree stock. Strength plus comeliness, that is what we offer you. Look at her, friends – not a blemish anywhere. Feel that firm flesh. Prime condition! Look at the hair; see how it glows. And the teeth! Look at the teeth! There's thirty years' hard work in her, maybe more. And she's fully trained. Guaranteed to give satisfaction both in the kitchen and the bed. She can cook, carry, wash, launder, is proficient at needlework and is an excellent proposition for breeding purposes. Now, what am I offered?

During the foregoing passage, the rest of the company have entered into the spirit of the scene and created the atmosphere of a busy and colourful market. A woman calls her wares: 'Ripe melons, whole or by the piece!' Another carries a basket and advertises ripe figs.

Silk Merchant. Genuine Persian silk! The last piece! You'll never see workmanship like this again. They've stopped producing it. Twenty drachma! That's all I'm asking for, twenty drachma! A bargain at double the price!

Woman. I'll give you ten.

Silk Merchant. Ah, a lady who's fond of a joke, eh? Well, I like a joke myself, but we live in a hard world, lady. Ten drachma wouldn't pay the tax. I'm giving it away at twenty!

Woman. I'll give you ten.

Silk Merchant. I'll tell you what I'll do . . .

They move upstage, still bargaining. Two businessmen stroll downstage, deep in conversation.

1st Businessman. I think it would be a mistake to sell now.

2nd Businessman. The market's good!

1st Businessman. It'll be better still if you wait.

2nd Businessman. You're really banking on the rumours of war, aren't you?

1st Businessman. War is necessary to the economy, it's inevitable.

2nd Businessman. But the cost!

1st Businessman. The cost will be shared by a great number of citizens; the profits, on the other hand, will belong to a small group of far-seeing investors like ourselves.

They move off upstage, talking. Democritus and a youth walk downstage, talking.

Youth. And these atoms – what exactly are they?

Democritus. They are the elements out of which everything is made.

Youth. Everything?

Democritus. Everything. The soil and the seed in it. The sun which warms it and the rain which moistens it. The rocks and mountains, the seas, the birds in the air and the blind worm. All are made of the same elements.

Youth. And man?

Democritus. Yes, man too. All men, the senator, the merchant, the soldier, the slave.

1st Businessman. What's that you say?

Democritus. We were discussing philosophy.

1st Businessman. Philosophy? It sounded like treason.

Silk Merchant. Did somebody say 'treason'?

Democritus. I assure you, sir, you are mistaken. I am Democritus, a philosopher and no politician.

1st Businessman. I distinctly heard him say that the slave is equal to the senator.

Democritus. I merely said that, in my opinion, all men – indeed all things – shared a common origin.

Woman. Does that include women?

Democritus. Everything that is.

2nd Businessman. Is this slave my equal then?

Democritus. In the eyes of nature, yes.

Silk Merchant. Treason!

1st Businessman. And more than treason, for what this man says strikes at the very heart of religion, our social order, our thinking, our way of life. For if everything that is has a common origin then there is no difference between Gods and men, between men and women, between rulers and ruled, between master and slave. Can you imagine what will happen if such ideas are allowed to pass unchallenged? Every slave in Athens would soon be asserting his right to equality; women would question their husbands' authority; the poor would demand a seat in the Senate and the soldier would challenge the general's right to give orders!

All. Treason! To the Senate with him! Stone him!

Democritus. My friends . . .

Silk Merchant. No slave-lover calls me a friend!

Democritus. If you choose to interpret an abstract philosophical idea in social terms, then the fault is not mine. I am not responsible for the way nature organises her resources and neither threats nor arguments can alter the fact that life is constituted in a particular way. I am an old man and I have pondered deeply on these matters and my observations . . .

Priest. Why do you listen to this old fool! Will you match your strength against the high ones on Olympus? Athens asks more of her sons than idle speculations on things that are not. Let us have men like the heroes of antiquity, men like those who fought at Troy awhile back. Not broken seers but warriors like Achilles and he that darkened the Cyclops' eye and trampled the great oceans under his feet. Give us men of the sharp sword and the swift galley . . . men who tame rivers and the high mountains. Would you be great? Would you be noble and remembered in the songs of the bards? Then rise up against the barbarians of Lacedaemon, strike down all the false traitors throughout the Peloponnese. Listen to the drums and the sound of many feet. That is the Thebans on the march. The men of Chios and Lesbos are ready. The Acharnians are waiting for the word. Ionia and Thracia wait only for the men of Athens to begin the war that will carry our power to the uttermost ends of the earth!

Towards the end of the above speech, the crowd encircle Democritus and the murmurs of approval of the priest's remarks turn into shouts of anger directed at the philosopher. They finally close in on him and trample him underfoot as the light fades.

After a moment of complete darkness, the roving spotlight fades up and its beam wanders about the stage, finally revealing a skeleton holding a tattered flag and occupying the place on which the priest stood to deliver his tirade. Blackout.

Mic. Voice. War! Athens against Sparta. Broken Thebans dying of cold on the tracks of mountains. Corcyrian sailors – food for fishes at Syracuse. Siege, hunger, plague! Athenian bodies rotting on the roads of Sparta. Ionian dead feeding the Cretan vines. War and more war! Rome against Greece, against Gaul, against the Iberian peninsula, against the Scythians. Rome against the world. And everywhere the sword triumphant, everywhere the tramp of legions, from the equatorial forests to the congealed sea of Thule. War everywhere! The last flicker of learning and then . . . darkness.

Halfway through the speech the light has faded up again and the Singer has entered half-dressed in mediaeval costume. He carries a doublet over his arm.

Singer. I must apologise for not being properly dressed, but who would have thought the glory that was Greece would have passed by so quickly. But that is the way things happen – events won't wait for the last button to be buttoned and momentous happenings often catch one with an unzipped fly. Hence the ruins of empires. The next scene should, by rights, deal with the Romans, you know the kind of thing, the legions on the march.

(Singing)

> Twenty leagues a day, that's the Roman way,
> Our swords are sharp, our enemies are weak,
> Make the vanquished pay, that's the Roman way,
> The world is there to win and travel's cheap.

But you probably know all about Rome and the Romans, how they brought civilisation to the inferior peoples of Europe and Africa. I would guess you've all read about the wonderful roads they built and how their barracks were bigger and better than anybody else's and how their plumbing was the wonder of the age. Therefore we'll pass on without comment. In any case we couldn't afford to put Roman soldiers on the stage. For that kind of thing you need subsidies, which we don't have. We're not a rich company, at least not rich enough to be able to afford armour and weapons. And so we pass the Roman era and feel our way through the darkness of seven hundred years, years which passed like a bad dream. And now that I'm suitably dressed, the play can continue. The time is . . . let's say 1300 A.D. The place? Anywhere in Europe. The characters . . .

(Singing)

> The people whose names are not remembered,
> Names that don't get in the history books;
> The smith whose shoulder bears the baron's brand,
> The serf who nourishes his master's land,
> Villeins, sundry servants, greasy cooks.
> The woman bending double in the field,
> The handless beggar tapping with his hooks,
> The legless soldier limping on the road,
> The porter dragging at his load,
> The brutal, toiling, uncomplaining band
> Who, by and large . . .

(Speaking) . . . make up the population of this land.

During the above, various characters enter and move about the stage.

Singer. *(Singing)*

> The cripple crawls upon his knees.

Cripple. Alms! Alms!

Singer. (*Singing*)
> The leper parades his foul disease.

Leper. Unclean! Unclean!

Singer. (*Singing*)
> The spotted plague walks through the land,
> And hunger's rife on every hand.

Blind Man.
> A crust, for the love of Christ!

Singer. (*Singing*)
> Death is each man's neighbour,
> Death it is who plays the pipe
> And beats the tabor.

Music: The Fool's Jig. Ragged figure enters playing pipe and tabor followed by beggars, serfs, etc., dancing. All except the Singer join in.

Blind Man. For the love of Christ!

Mad woman enters carrying bundle as though it were a child.

Mad Woman. Sweet Jesus, restore my babe!

The music fades out but all continue to dance to the slower rhythm of the Singer's tune.

Singer. (*Singing*)
> New-risen from the rags she calls a bed
> The babe she bore and bears is newly dead.

Mad Woman. No! No! No! No!

Singer. (*Singing*)
> And now she needs a scapegoat for her blame,
> Someone to bear the burden of her pain.

An old woman enters.

Old Woman. Tibby! Tibby! Come on, Tibby!

Singer. (*Speaking*) Most convenient.

(*Singing*)
> And now this feeble-minded, poor old bitch
> Must stand accused and die,

(*Speaking*) for she's both old and helpless – must be a witch.

Mad Woman. (*Pointing at the old woman*) Witch!

All. Witch!

The old woman laughs, bewildered.

Man. In the book it says: 'Thou shalt not suffer a witch to live.'

Old Woman. Tibby! Tibby!

Woman. Her familiar – she calls on her familiar.

Mad Woman. Murderer!

Man. Let her burn!

All. To the fire!

They drag the old woman off. The light dims until only the Singer can be seen.

Singer. (*Abandoning his role*) What we might call 'The Years of Darkness'. A convenient label though a less than accurate one since the years in question are illuminated by the ruddy glare of fires used to burn old ladies, heretics, scholars, philosophers, towns, villages, cities, libraries – and eccentrics who refused to believe the world was a flat platter on the sideboard of the Lord. As for science, it was taking some odd turns, though things began to improve by 1450 when the first translations of the Arabic manuscripts began to appear in Europe and the art of Alchemy was reborn.

The lights go up and discover Bernard Trevisan who stands upstage centre and forms the pivot of a group of six alchemists who throughout the scene which follows perform a slow, ritual dance, the movements of which are largely made up of cabbalistic signs.

Alchemists. Who art thou?

Trevisan. Bernard Trevisan.

Alchemists. From whence art thou come?

Trevisan. From the city of Padua.

Alchemists. For what art thou searching?

Trevisan. For the philosopher's stone. For the father of rocks and the mother of metals in the same organism.

Trevisan attempts to dance but his way is constantly blocked by the cloaked alchemists.

I shall find the seed which will grow into great harvests of gold. For doth not a metal grow like a plant? Lead would be gold if it had time to grow. For it is absurd to think that nature in the earth bred gold perfect in the instant. Something went before. There must be matter more remote. Nature doth first beget the imperfect then proceeds she to the perfect. Hast thou the secret of the stone?

1st Alchemist. Hast thou rectified spirits of wine?

Trevisan. Thrice ten times till I could not find glasses strong enough to hold it.

2nd Alchemist. Then thou should search at Avignon in the books of Pope John the Twelfth.

Tevisan. Hast thou the secret of the stone?

3rd Alchemist. Go thou to the shores of the Baltic Sea. Take thou the salt of the sea, rectify it day and night until it is as clear as crystal. That is the dark secret of the stone.

Trevisan. I seek the philosopher's stone. Hast thou the secret of the nature of it?

4th Alchemist. Dissolve silver and mercury in aqua fortis. Concentrate the solution over hot ashes and reduce them to half. Pour the mixture into a clay crucible and leave in the sun's rays. For gold is merely the rays of the sun condensed to a yellow solid.

Trevisan. Hast thou the secret of the stone?

5th Alchemist. Whatever is below is like that which is above. And that which is above is like that which is below, to accomplish the miracle of one thing.

Trevisan. The stone . . . the philosopher's stone . . . I must find the secret.

6th Alchemist. The father thereof is the sun and the mother thereof is the moon. The wind carries in it his belly and the nurse thereof is the earth. This thing has more fortitude than fortitude itself for it will overcome every subtle thing and penetrate every solid thing. By it this world was formed.

Trevisan. The stone . . . the stone . . . what is the secret?

The alchemists make cabbalistic signs.

Alchemists. God made one and ten, one hundred and one thousand and then multiplied the whole by ten.

Trevisan. But I do not understand this mummery.

Alchemists. We can tell you no more.

They exit. Trevisan sinks to the ground.

Trevisan. I have burned out my life at a laboratory furnace and I still have not the secret, but a time will come when nature will unloose the bonds of things and man will stand triumphant on the peak of a great mountain.

Snatch of a Gregorian chant. The lights fade.

Bruno. Oh, black wall of ignorance, night of fear! Who will tear the shroud off the world?

Lights go up and discover Giordano Bruno standing centre in a monk's habit. Near him lies a figure half-emerged from a tomb. Death holds him in an embrace.

Is there in all Christendom a place where man can speak his mind? Is there a village anywhere where ignorance does not parade the streets in silks and golden mantle of authority? Is there? In the places of learning I have spoken and my voice was lost in a wilderness of skulls. The universities of

Paris, Prague and Pisa have become night stools where darkness can relieve himself. Truth is banished to the stews where apes can use her for their pleasure and reason is scourged through the streets in a fool's cap.

Recumbent figure moves and then laughs.

Why do you laugh?

Paracelsus. I see myself in you.

Bruno. A sponge made like a man. Another drunken fool whose breath poisons wisdom.

Paracelsus. I am drunk with dust and worms have made me wise.

Bruno. What do they call thee, wineskin?

Paracelsus. Paracelsus, a dust mote caught in the sun's web, a voice riding the wind.

Bruno. Paracelsus – he that is called the sword of reason, the Luther of Chemistry?

Paracelsus. The same.

Bruno. Thou hast been dead a hundred years

Paraclesus. I speak across a grave with a voice full of earth and stars.

Bruno. From what deep hell hast thou returned?.

Paracelsus. I have lain in a worm's belly with the dreamers of dreams, with Copernicus who rode a galactic ride and bloodied the sun's flanks with jewelled spurs, with da Vinci whose brain was a crystal span across the universe.

Bruno laughs.

Why do you laugh?

Bruno. I speak of the seed of life and my only audience is a dead man.

Paracelsus. Thy voice is still unblunted and can cut holes in the night.

Bruno. But the living?

Paracelsus. Fools for the most part, pathetic fools who walk a road of terror between one breath and the next.

Bruno. Is there no hope then?

Paracelsus. There are always some who listen, whose eyes can penetrate the shades. You know that, Bruno.

Bruno. I am a hunted man, an exile. I walk the road by night to avoid the church's spies. I speak to men in Genoa, Florence, Milan, but wherever I go the Inquisition's ears are cocked wide to snare my words. I, who love men, am ringed about with loneliness. Those whom I would teach look at me with fear.

Paracelsus. What would you teach them?

Bruno. A single truth so that all truth should prosper. I would teach them the law of Copernicus which says that the sun is immovable in the centre of the universe and the earth has a diurnal movement of rotation.

Paracelsus. And it is for this . . . truth you would sacrifice your liberty?

Bruno. There can be no liberty without knowledge. Only by understanding the world can we learn to understand ourselves.

Towards the end of this speech, a hooded figure, an officer of the Inquisition, is revealed.

Inquisitor. The truth you teach is heresy! It is an evil lie!

Bruno. The violation of reason is the real heresy and what you call evil is the degradation of man. By denying men the truth, you make them vulnerable.

Inquisitor. It is not the church which seeks to dethrone man as the image of God. It is not the church that would banish the earth to a lower place in the universe and make the sun the centre of the world.

Bruno. It is the church which burdens the mind of man with chains.

Inquisitor. Silence, heretic!

Bruno. I will not be silenced!

Inquisitor. Perhaps when you feel the fire . . .

Bruno. You cannot burn the truth. Rome has excommunicated me, Geneva has stoned me – but while I have breath in my body I will speak the truth for men to hear. I will sing a song of truth as will charm the shackles off their leaden souls.

Inquisitor. You poor, stupid fool! They will not listen.

Bruno. I will make them listen!

Music: The Fool's Jig played on pipe and tabor. Fool enters dancing, leading a procession of dancing men and women. Bringing up the rear is the figure of Death.

Listen, and I'll slake your thirst with wisdom's vintage. I'll spin you an endless universe – on the loom Copernicus built.

Paracelsus. Dance, my pert flesher! Jig it, my she-cadaver! Give us the dunghill galliard!

Bruno. Good people, I have a wondrous tale of sun and stars that will amaze you.

Paracelsus. In upon them, Bruno! Breach the walls of their stupidity with the culverins of reason!

Bruno. Here is a charge of cavalry to put ignorance to flight: the sun is immovable in the centre of the universe and the earth has a diurnal movement of rotation.

The Inquisitor throws off his cloak and reveals himself dressed in the military costume of the period.

Inquisitor. Here is a fine jigging madcap folic for a man of mettle. Here is a lusty hot-breathed gallop for a spirited wench. Come, you lusty boys! Come, you dams of future Alexanders and lend your hearts for drums. Would you be kings and emperors? There are kingdoms waiting for each of you in the Americas. Will you be noble and great and have your name the title of a ballad? Let him that will win renown and a king's booty follow me! I have wars for you in France, in Spain, in the Low Countries, on the seas and oceans of the world.

During this speech a drum has begun to beat. It gets louder and louder. The dancers, led by Death, go off.

Bruno. Fools! How they love the darkness and hold in contempt all that is not contemptible. But it is inconceivable that . . . they will not dance forever. A time will come!

Paracelsus. You will have to die for them first, Bruno. They understand no language but the language of violence.

Fade to darkness.

Mic. Voice. 1550 – War!

Music.

England against France. Poland against Hungary. 1560 – War! Spain against Tripoli. The first religious war in France. 1570 – War! Spain against Turkey. England against Scotland. Venice against the Porte. 1580 – War! Spain against Portugal. Poland against Russia. The seventh religious war in France. 1590 – War! Turkey against Persia. Spain against Aragon. Italy against Provence. 1600 – War! France against Savoy. Spain against Africa. Sweden against Poland. 1600 – Giordano Bruno burnt at the stake.

The recorded voice of Paracelsus is heard whispering.

Paracelsus' Voice. You will have to die for them first, Bruno.

Lights fade up. The actor who plays the Scientist strolls on stage with the 3rd actress. An actor enters from the opposite side of the stage, only half-dressed.

3rd Actress. We seem to have mislaid the atom and . . . what was it you called it . . . fission.

Scientist. Ah yes, the atom. To see the next stage of the development of atomic theory, we have to go forward in time about 250 years.

1st Businessman. November 16th, 1807, to be precise. Where the hell's George? (*Calling into the wings*) George!

2nd Businessman. (*Offstage*) Won't be a minute.

1st Businessman. Hurry up!

2nd Businessman. I'm being as quick as I can.

Scientist. He'll have to move a lot quicker if he's going to keep up with the times. The Industrial Revolution's getting into its stride. Hargreaves' spinning jenny is forty years old and James Watt's steam engine is busy transforming the face of Britain. So unless George really gets moving . . . well, he's going to miss making a fortune.

The 2nd businessman enters.

2nd Businessman. Give me a hand with this cravat, will you.

1st Businessman. Relax, relax.

Scientist. We'll leave them to it.

All leave except the two businessmen.

2nd Businessman. Damn! Look at my hands. They're filthy!

1st Businessman. Well, I don't suppose many early nineteenth-century factory owners had clean hands. Where there's muck, lad, there's brass. And it's brass that counts.

2nd Businessman. How do I look?

1st Businessman. You'll pass. Where's Dalton?

2nd Businessman. He's got a difficult costume change. This jumping about from one character to another is bloody confusing. One of these performances I'm going to come on in the Greek scene dressed as a Manchester businessman. That'd shake 'em! A quick-change artist, that's me.

1st Businessman. Right, cut the chat and let's get the scene moving.

2nd Businessman. Right. November, 1807. Manchester, a meeting of the Literary and Philosophical Society at 35 George Street.

1st Businessman. That's here.

2nd Businessman. Right.

1st Businessman. We're waiting for tonight's lecturer to arrive.

2nd Businessman. Mr John Dalton, schoolmaster.

1st Businessman. We'd better get the table.

They go to the edge of the stage and mime picking up and carrying a table.

1st Businessman. You're not trying! This is a heavy table, solid mahogany. Everything connected with the Literary and Philosophical Society is solid, including the members: self-made, solid as the Stock Exchange, honest-to-God businessmen. Let's try again.

They repeat the mime.

2nd Businessman. Sceneshifters!

1st Businessman. The shifting Manchester scene.

He produces a square of velvet from his pocket and it becomes their table. They mime sitting at it. From now on, they speak in Lancashire dialect.

Both Businessman. Manchester, city of cotton.

Voice. (*Offstage*) City of Peterloo, city of poverty, four-fifths of the population living in cellars!

1st Businessman. Better close the window. We don't want any interruptions.

He rises, mimes closing window and returns to his seat.

Must try and preserve the right atmosphere for scientific speculation.

2nd Businessman. Aye.

1st Businessman. Pays to keep an eye on scientific progress.

2nd Businessman. Aye.

1st Businessman. What Manchester thinks today!

2nd Businessman. Aye. Anything in this Dalton chap's ideas?

1st Businessman. 'Appen there is.

2nd Businessman. Chemist, did you say?

1st Businessman. Schoolteacher.

2nd Businessman. Not too pedantic, I hope. I like a speaker who can make you sit up. No frills or fancies, mind.

1st Businessman. Might be summat in his atomic theory.

2nd Businessman. Where's Dicky Howarth? Ain't he coming?

1st Businessman. Havin' troubles with his weavers. Tried to burn down his mill on Tuesday.

2nd Businessman. Aye, I heard summat about it.

1st Businessman. Five arrested.

2nd Businessman. Well, they'll have plenty of time to repent. Dicky's their magistrate, i'n't he?

1st Businessman. Likely.

Dalton enters.

Ah, here's Dalton now! Good evening, Mr Dalton.

Dalton. Good evening.

1st Businessman. I don't think you've met Mr Butterworth, our membership secretary.

2nd Businessman. How d'ye do. I'm looking forward to hearing all about your . . . what d'ye call 'em?

1st Businessman. Atoms.

2nd Businessman. Atoms, of course! Stupid of me. I've a dreadful memory.

1st Businessman. If you're ready, Mr Dalton . . .?

Dalton. Yes. Perfectly ready.

1st Businessman. Fellow members, ladies and gentlemen. It gives me great pleasure to introduce tonight's speaker, Mr John Dalton, who will speak on 'The Atomic Theory of Matter'. Mr Dalton.

Dalton. Friends, I am a poor lecturer and not very gifted with amusing anecdotes – consequently, I must approach my subject in the only way I know how, that is, directly and without circumlocution. For more years than I care to remember I have been a keen student and observer of the atmosphere, and this has led me to speculate on a problem which no one has yet made clear. We all know that the atmosphere is composed of four gases – oxygen, nitrogen, carbon dioxide and water vapour. Priestley, Cavendish and Lavoisier have proved that point. But how are these gases held together? Are they chemically united or are they just mixed together as one mixes sand and clay? My own observations had led me to believe that air was a mechanical mixture of gases . . . and yet the chemical composition of the atmosphere is constant. My records prove that without question. I have analysed the atmosphere taken from hundreds of different places in England, over mountains, lakes, in valleys, in sparsely settled regions and in crowded towns and always the composition has been the same. Now why does not the heavier carbon dioxide sink to the bottom of the sea of air to be covered in turn by the lighter oxygen, nitrogen and water vapour? You must all have observed how oil floats on the surface of a heavier liquid such as water . . . and yet this does not happen with the gases which compose the air. Why?

Interrupter. (*From the audience*) Because of atoms?

Dalton. Exactly! Because of atoms! Everything in nature is composed of minute particles called atoms and the atoms of the different gases diffuse through each other and thoroughly mix, thus keeping the composition of the atmosphere uniform.

Interrupter. Show us these atoms.

Dalton. That is impossible, my dear sir. Even the most delicate instrument cannot render them visible to the naked eye.

Interrupter. And yet you would have us believe in these intangible toys.

Dalton. They are far from intangible. These atoms are indivisible – even in the most violent chemical change the atoms remain intact. Furthermore, the atoms of the same element are all alike, but the atoms of different elements differ in both size and shape.

Interrupter. How do you deduce that? By their smell?

Dalton. No, by their weight. I have drawn up a table of the atomic weights of the elements – that is their relative weights.

Interrupter. This is absurd: Mr Dalton admits that his atoms are smaller than anything ever seen even under the most delicate microscope, and yet suggests that he can weigh them. Mr Dalton, I'm afraid, is suffering from hallucinations, or something worse. What is Mr Dalton's theory but ridiculous pictorial juggling? Can any serious-minded chemist accept such a theory, which is, in fact, as baseless as the four elements of Aristotle? I am astonished that any man of science can be taken up with such a tissue of absurdities.

1st Businessman. I think the last speaker is being somewhat harsh in his criticism of our guest. At the same time, Mr Dalton, I feel there's summat in what he says. Don't misunderstand me, Mr Dalton, we're all interested in progress. Indeed, I would go so far as to say that without chaps like us there wouldn't be any progress.

2nd Businessman. Hear, hear.

1st Businessman. For while it's true that you are the chaps who do the dreaming, we are the ones who do the doing.

Interrupter. Hear, hear!

Woman in Audience. Don't take any notice of them, Dalton! You were right. Time has proved you right.

The Scientist enters. The two businessmen exeunt.

They were the ones who dealt in absurdities.

Scientist. Please, please, I'm afraid you're interrupting our play. In any case they can't hear you. Oh, the actors can but Dalton and the others . . . as far as they're concerned you don't exist except as a kind of generalised possibility.

Dissatisfied Playgoer. Get on with the play!

Scientist. We're trying to do just that.

Diss. Playgoer. All this awful speechifying! If I wanted to listen to that kind of thing I would go to the appropriate place for it, a lecture hall. The theatre is hardly the place for it.

Scientist. Ah, you wish to be entertained!

Diss. Playgoer. Isn't that what one normally goes to the theatre for?

Scientist. Have patience. We have a love story for you, the love of the proton for the neutron. The most enduring love story in history. And, if you like a good murder, we'll show you the greatest killing the world has ever seen, with the most efficient murder weapon. Just bear with us a little longer. Now, where were we?

Woman in Audience. Dalton and his atomic theory.

Scientist. Ah, yes. Were you able to follow him?

Woman in Audience. Yes, I think so. But where do we go from here?

Enter five scientists, wearing white coats and grotesque masks. They walk deep in thought and move like jerky puppets.

1st Scientist. Well?

Group of Scientists (Chorus). Exactly. Where do we go from here?

Enter Mendeleyev.

Mendeleyev. To the ends of the earth. Search in the bowels of the earth, in the dust of factories, in the waters of the oceans, search.

Chorus. For what?

Mendeleyev. There is an element as yet undiscovered. I have named it eka-aluminium. It will be easily fusible, it will form alums and its chloride will be volatile.

Derisive laughter from chorus.

1st Scientist. The age of miracles. Science has acquired a prophet, gentlemen; he can foretell the properties of elements even before they are discovered.

Chorus. That is ridiculous . . . that is absurd!

Mendeleyev. Seek it, I say, and it will be found.

2nd Scientist. Who is he?

3rd Scientist. Dmitri Ivanovich Mendeleyev. He's a Kalmuk or one of those outlandish creatures.

Mic. Voice. 1875 – Professor Duboisbaudron discovers the eka-aluminium in a zinc ore found in the Pyrenees. He has called the new element gallium.

Chorus dances, expressing consternation.

1st Scientist. Coincidence . . . mere coincidence! One of those lucky guesses which prove the law of averages.

Mendeleyev. There is another undiscovered element which I have called eka-silicon. It is dirty grey in colour with an atomic weight of 72, a density of 5.5 and is slightly acted upon by acids.

Chorus laughs derisively.

1st Scientist. Moses speaks from the laboratory. He gives us the tables of the law before the law is written. He brings metaphysics to bear on the science of chemistry.

Chorus. That is ridiculous . . . that is absurd!

Mic. Voice. 1876 – Winkler has isolated a new element from the silver ore, argyrodite. It has an atomic weight of 72.3 and a density of 5.5. Winkler has called the new element germanium.

1st Scientist. A lucky guess.

Chorus dances and exhibits first signs of panic.

Mendeleyev. The third undiscovered element I have called eka-boron. Its atomic weight is 45, its valency 3.

Chorus laughs weakly.

1st Scientist. I am afraid that our colleague Professor Mendeleyev has allowed himself to become intoxicated by the success of his first two guesses. He would reduce chemistry to the level of the crystal-gazer's art.

Chorus. That is ridiculous . . . that is absurd!

They slowly collapse like wax figures during the following speech.

Mic. Voice. 1878 – Professor Nilsen has isolated a new element from the ore euxanite. It has an atomic weight of 45.1 and a valency of 3. Nilsen has called it scandium.

Mendeleyev. Gentlemen.

Chorus begin to come to life again.

There is no secret, gentlemen. I have discovered that the properties of the elements are a periodic function of their atomic weights; that is, the properties repeat themselves periodically after every seventh element.

Chorus. This is amazing!

2nd Scientist. So beautifully simple!

Chorus. So obvious! This is our goal . . . the end of our search!

Mendeleyev. It is only a stage on the journey, a resting place while material is gathered for the next advance.

Lights fade. Music.

Mic. Voice. A stage in the journey.

Actor. (*Taking off mask and addressing the audience*) At this stage, we could, on this stage, show you the many detailed stages through which the science of physics passed before it reached the present interesting stage. But time and space, or to be more precise, space time, does not permit. And so we follow your example, take the events of the next few years for granted and draw a curtain over half a century. The curtain will be closed for ten minutes during which the lights in the auditorium will go up so that you may move about and restore your circulation. For the mind is always more receptive to ideas when the blood circulates freely. And although ten minutes is not long, it gives an audience time to pick the author's bones quite clean . . . don't you agree? In ten minutes then, we meet again at history's crossroads

where we shall endeavour to show you the point at which dreams and
reality meet. Blackout please.

Lights fade.   *[End of Part One]*

[**PART   TWO**] *The Puppet Master, his Secretary and Death are
discovered.*

Puppet Master. This looks like the place . . . what time is it?

Secretary. 1901, sir.

Puppet Master. Then there is no time to be lost . . . the show must open in
1914 . . . that's the deadline.

Scientist enters.

Secretary. Have you an appointment?

Scientist. Appointment? Isn't there some mistake?

Secretary. Everyone has to have an appointment.

Scientist. But look here, this is our stage, we're doing a show . . . you can't
just come in here and commandeer the stage . . . the audience is waiting
. . . they've paid to be entertained.

Puppet Master. Don't worry about the audience . . . I'm planning a big show
for them.

Scientist. What kind of show?

Puppet Master. A tragi-comedy with massed bands and fireworks. A passion
play of steel in which the audience are actors and the actors are children
lost in a wilderness of fire and screams. My play will draw your heart out of
your body and turn your eyes to scalding pools of salt. I'll touch your mind
with horror so that every tortured second will extend into eternity. Oh,
and there will be laughter too, shrill as a gull's cry; laughter that will cut
like a scythe and beat like a hammer against the roof of despair. Dancing
I'll show you, such as you've never seen! Jigs of legless men and eightsome
reels performed by faceless ghosts and over open graves of broken earth
one-armed heroes will tread in slow pavanes to the stinking songs of last
year's flowers.

Scientist. But this is our stage.

Puppet Master. Come sir, all the world's a stage.

Scientist. Yes, but we haven't booked the world for our production.

Puppet Master. No, but I have. (*He laughs.*)

Scientist. Who are you?

Puppet Master. My name is Legion. I am sometimes known as James Pierrepoint Rockerfeller Thyssen Zaharoff Vanderbilt Power. My friends call me Order, my enemies, Chaos. I'm the managing director of the biggest show on earth, I.P.I.

Scientist. I.P.I.?

Puppet Master. International Puppets Incorporated.

Scientist. (*Pointing to Death*) And who is that?

Puppet Master. He is the leading man in my next production.

Scientist. Why is his faced masked?

Puppet Master. He lives in the shadows. His skin dislikes the light. And now, if you are satisfied with our credentials, we'll proceed with our auditions.

Scientist. But what about *our* show?

Puppet Master. I'm sorry.

Scientist. Can't your auditions wait?

Puppet Master. Time will not wait . . . these auditions were fixed a hundred years ago.

Scientist. But look here, we have certain rights . . .!

Puppet Master. You have no rights.

Scientist. We have a contract with the management.

Puppet Master. I am the management.

Scientist. Suppose I refuse to leave?

Puppet Master. I think my secretary will convince you that that would be unwise.

Scientist. Are you threatening me?

Puppet Master. That won't be necessary.

Secretary interposes herself between the two men and produces a cigarette case.

Secretary. Cigarette?

Scientist. I don't smoke. Look here, this is a preposterous situation.

Secretary. Do you have a light?

The Puppet Master produces a lighter and thumbs a flame. He then withdraws to the shadows upstage. The Secretary blows smoke in the Scientist's face.

Secretary. Please don't be angry. There's nothing to be angry about.

Scientist. Nothing to . . . do you consider it normal behaviour to . . .

Secretary. Please! We want to help you.

Scientist. Help me? What do you mean?

Secretary. Just think of all the help you've given to others!

Scientist. I don't know what you're talking about!

Secretary. You work miracles with your science. The small flame that lit my cigarette, the lift which carries me to my apartment, the shaded light which stands beside my bed, the music carried on the air.

Music.

Scientist. You're confusing technology with science.

She begins to drift around in a kind of half-dance.

Secretary. How pleasant it is to let one's body be carried along on the music, to move silently hearing only the whisper of the blood.

Scientist. What are you trying to do?

Secretary. I am trying to make you forget the discomfort of knowing. I would like to stroke your mind with dreams.

Scientist. I have my own dreams, thank you!

Secretary. Why are you afraid?

Scientist. You're being ridiculous!

Secretary. Do your dreams frighten you?

Scientist. Not in the least. In any case, my dreams are my own. They are the logical outcome of my work.

Secretary. There are other things. Turn away from the things that disturb you. Is it for you to die of other men's complaints, to weep knives of tears and slow your blood with ice? Somewhere for you is a turquoise sky where the sun sings with the lark's voice. There are rivers and jewelled streams where the slender reeds whisper secrets. Nights when the moon caresses the thighs of hills with silver hands.

In the course of speaking the above lines she has moved close to the Scientist. Now they are both dancing together.

We dance well together.

Scientist. I feel rather hazy about . . . about . . .

Secretary. Don't worry about anything. I'll take care of you.

She dances off with him and after a moment returns alone.

Puppet Master. Well, is he quiet?

Secretary. Sleeping like a child.

Puppet Master. Good. We can begin the auditions. If the talent's good the show'll be good and if the show's good the money'll be good. Did you notify the applicants?

Secretary. Yes, sir.

Puppet Master. Are there many of them?

Secretary. The entire population of Europe.

We'll need more for the second act but that can wait. Let's have the double-act first. What do they call themselves?

Secretary. The Curies. Marie Curie of Warsaw and Pierre Curie of Paris.

Waltz music. Pierre and Marie Curie enter. They wear formal ballroom costume of the period and speak their lines as they dance.

Pierre. To serve humanity, that is the aim.

Marie. We speak in civilisation's name.

Pierre. A secret lies in uranium ore.

Marie. A secret imprisoned within the core

Pierre. Holding the secret of matter in store.

Marie. Together we'll find it!

Pierre. Pitchblende brought to the cleansing flame,

Marie. Dissolved in acids, boiled again.

Pierre. Banish impurities, crystallise,

Marie. Dissolved again, the crystal dies.

Pierre. Crystallise with barium salts,

Marie. Dissolve and remove the impure faults.

Pierre. At this first stage
The pitchblende takes
The form
Of crystalline concentrates.

Marie. Day after day
Week after week
We repeat the process,
We who seek:

Pierre. The shed is red with the furnace glow

Marie. But the seed in the crucible starts to grow.

Pierre. In return for the sweat and toil we've spent
A newly discovered element –

Marie. I will name it after my native land – Poland.

Pierre. But the restless, unfettered mind pursues
Still more reactive residues.

Marie. Seeking for matters' final grain
Repeating the process again and again.

Pierre. Purify further, no cessation.

Marie. Concentrate through crystallisation,

Pierre. Solution,

Marie. Fractional separation.

Pierre. Reduce still further, refine, distil,

Marie. Repeat the process again until

Pierre. There in the heart of the crucible
A steady phosphorescent gleam

Marie. The track where minuscular comets stream –

Pierre. Here is reward,

Marie. The final sum
Of all our labours,
Radium.

Puppet Master. Take the man away, he's spoiling the act.

Death dances off with Pierre, to the waltz tune.

Marie. Pierre, Pierre, where are you? Come back into the light, Pierre . . . oh, my love.

Puppet Master. Carry on, miss. Time's precious.

Marie. But my Pierre?

Puppet Master. Sorry, but the show must go on.

Mic. Voice. To serve humanity, that is the aim.

Marie (*Dancing*)
The long road is my road.
Mine the long journey.
Through the spinning void
I walk,
Through the great silences
Of matter's universe.
Behind are the low lands
The known lands of measured days
And landscapes of nights
Without feature.
Here there is no teacher
Lending experience,
No constant compass,
No dexterous hand
Sharing the net's drag.
Mine is the unshared dream,
And dreams are made of formulae
And hollow glass
Where little suns and blazing stars
Revolve and scatter
Microscopic nebulae.
Oh, there is music in my ears
And brittle songs of dying particles.
Hear how a metal sings
Under the acid's kiss,
Hear how the elements
Repeat their whispered
Scales of secrets.
Now through a darkness of numbers
I walk

Where X is the moon which harries the clouds
With planet packs.
Oh, scythe of wind,
Keen blade of wind,
Reason of wind,
You stir the leaves
With radioactive ecstasy.
And the mind leaps
With the speed of light,
And overtakes
The dream,
And the night
Recedes before
The impact of new suns,
And the mountains
Are broken
By the roads.

Shall I follow the sodium trail or the trail of mercury! Which is my road? How shall I go?

Puppet Master. That's enough, miss, we're short of time. Your act, I'm afraid, lacks popular appeal. Needs a little comic relief . . . and yet . . . and yet . . . we might build you up in a few years' time as a gallant little lady, a silver-haired old lady, the world's sweetheart. I'll think about it. Goodnight . . . the gentleman will show you out.

Death waltzes out with Marie.

Who's next?

Secretary. Joseph John Thomson of Manchester.

Enter Thomson, as ring-master. Circus music.

Puppet Master. Thomson?

Thomson. That is my name.

Puppet Master. What do you do?

Thomson. I am a small-game hunter in the borderlands where force and matter meet. I am an atom tamer.

Trumpets sound.

Puppet Master. What experience?

Thomson. The experience of Faraday in electrolysis. The experience of Helmholtz of Potsdam. Also many years as ring-master in the Cavendish Laboratory.

Puppet Master. I don't think we can use a circus act.

Thomson. My circus is in a cathode tube.

Puppet Master. Circuses are out of date. Horses have no sex appeal and clowns are corny.

Thomson. Sir, you are referring to my public.

Puppet Master. Why do you wear a bandage over your eyes?

Thomson. I move in an unseen world where only the mind's eye sees.

Puppet Master. All right. Let's have your act.

Fanfare. Thomson goes into his 'act', making like a circus-spieler.

Thomson. Ladies and gentlemen, walk up, walk up! See the greatest show on earth. For the first time in any public place of entertainment we present the smallest, fastest, most amazing particle the world has ever not seen. It's terrific, it's gigantic, it's infinitesimal! Ladies and gentlemen . . . the Electron!

Tremendous fanfare. Thomson ushers in the invisible Electron. He bows and kisses her hand and applauds. . . . Puppet Master begins to protest.

Ah, and you are wondering where I found her! Years ago, when I was prospecting in the heart of Darkest Electricity I discovered that an electrical charge possesses inertia, the distinguishing characteristic of all matter. Ever since that day I have hunted in the deserts of space, in the jungles of calculation, in the wastes of gases for this ever-elusive Electron and now, at the cost of great personal danger and sacrifice, I have torn such a corpuscle from the heart of that great continent, the Atom. Look, my friends, look and marvel! See how effortlessly she will speed round the ring at a breathtaking speed of 160,000 miles a second. Ladies and gentlemen, may I present the only Electron in captivity, about to perform in John Thomson's Cathode Circus!

Long roll of drums. Thomson rotates on his heels, apparently following the progress of the Electron. Finally he bows.

Puppet Master. Just a moment, my friend, I didn't see your Electron.

Thomson. Why do you wear a bandage over your mind's eye?

Puppet Master. Not what I would call amusing.

Thomson. I didn't claim that it was amusing, merely miraculous.

Puppet Master. A miracle without crowd-appeal is unacceptable.

Thomson. Peasant!

Secretary. I'm afraid your time is up, sir.

Puppet Master. (*To Death*) Show him out.

Thomson. I can find my own way.

Puppet Master. My friend will help you. Like you, he has solved many problems in his time.

Death dances off with Thomson.

Circus acts! Electron tamers! Are there no tightrope-walkers on the list?

Secretary. None tonight, sir. There'll be plenty next week when we hold the political auditions.

Puppet Master. Pity they're so second rate. Still, what would a circus be without clowns? I'm going out for some refreshment. Carry on with the auditions. You know what I'm looking for.

Death makes to follow him.

No, you stay here. I'm arranging a big banquet for you and I wouldn't want to spoil your appetite.

He goes off. The following scene should be played as knockabout comedy. Enter Einstein.

Einstein. Ah, guten abend, fraulein. Wo is der Herr Direktor?

Secretary. I beg your pardon?

Einstein. The Direktor, he is here, yes?

Secretary. No, he's engaged at the moment. I am his assistant. Who are you?

Einstein. Ich bin Einstein. Albert Einstein.

Secretary. You are a comedian?

Einstein. Bitte, was ist ein comedian?

Secretary. You are a funny man?

Einstein. Oh ja, please, sehr lustige man. Morgan früh hab' ich eine kleine joke gemacht. You like jokes?

Secretary. If they're funny.

Einstein. So. Hier ist eine kleine dichte, a poem I have made . . . listen:

> Der was ein young fraulein called Bright
> Who could travel much faster than light,
> She started one day
> In a relative way
> Und came back ze previous night.

(*He laughs*) Es is gut, no?

Secretary. It doesn't make sense.

Einstein. More than sense it makes. It makes scientific history. For you I will prove it mit die mathematik. There is a curvature in space . . .

Secretary. We have very little time . . .

Einstein. Please, there is no such thing as your 'time' – everything is a point-event in a space-time continuum.

Secretary. Is that supposed to be funny?

Einstein. The truth is never funny.

Enter the Puppet Master.

Puppet Master. On the contrary, the truth is always funny.

Secretary. This is Mr Einstein, sir. He is a comedian.

Einstein. But please, it is a mistake you make. Only in my spare time am I funny.

Puppet Master. Oh, an amateur.

Einstein. By profession I am an impresario for ze ballet. For you the greatest ballet of the age we have gebracht.

Enter Max Planck and Nils Bohr, arguing.

Planck. Nils, you are mein guter Freund; for you ze greatest admiration I have, but in this thing I must insist . . . ze electrons pirouette.

Bohr. For seventy times have I told you that this is not pirouette, but gargouillade, the spin around the fixed orbit.

Planck. Spin, pirouette, gargouillade, what you like call it, but the sequence follows so . . . first the spin, then the grand jetée en l'air tournant . . . then the spin again in the new orbit. Agreed, ja?

Einstein. Herr Direktor, meet my colleagues: Professor Max Planck and Nils Bohr, choreographers-in-chief of the great atomic ballet.

Puppet Master. How do you do?

Planck. How do we do what?

Einstein. This 'how do you do', it is idiomatic, no?

Puppet Master. Yes. Do you think you could explain to your friends that I am a very busy man?

Einstein. But of course. Der Herr Direktor sagt dass er sehr beschäftig ist und Mann muss zur Sache kommen – der Dummkopf! Aber, naturlich mussen wir die Ungestaltung der Masse in Energie-abgabe verstandlich machen, in Ubereinstimmung meiner Energie-gielchung . . .

Planck. But of course, we are all busy men.

Puppet Master. Well, go ahead then, show us your act.

Planck. Ein moment. First we must explain ze Quantum Theory.

Puppet Master. Is that necessary?

Einstein. It is very important.

Planck. (*With demoniacal intensity*) You think that energy can be divided up indefinitely, do you not? But you are wrong . . . this energy, it is discontinuous. It is atomic in structure.

Puppet Master. Really?

Planck. Ja wohl. It is emitted not in a continuous wave, but only in small, finite units which I have called quanta. So the amount of energy in a system is the number of quanta in it.

Bohr. Stop! Maxie, my friend, for me everything is clear. Your Quantum Theory explains why the electrons give off light and heat. It is so – the electron revolves in an elliptical orbit around the nucleus – yes?

Planck.
Einstein. (*together*) Ja wohl.

Bohr. Until it is disturbed by some outside force like the cathode rays or even heat. Und when it is disturbed so, the electron leaps from one orbit to another orbit farther from the nucleus.

Planck. So.

Bohr. So it is this leaping of the electrons to new orbits which causes the emission of light and heat. Es ist gut, nicht wahr?

Planck.
Einstein. (*together with enormous enthusiasm*) Wunderbar!

Puppet Master. Gentlemen, if you really have a ballet, I should like to see it.

Planck. But of course.

Bohr. Come, together we will go and prepare them for the audition.

They exit.

Puppet Master. What's the theme of your ballet?

Einstein. MC squared equals E.

Puppet Master. What?

Einstein. Here is the story. Attend! I will elaborate.

He calls to offstage.

Anastasia!

A pretty girl wearing a spangled leotard enters.

This is my assistant, Fraulein Mass. Now, together we will prove that a very small mass is equivalent to a great amount of energy, no? Now, please, very carefully you will attend!

He makes passes with his hands like a magician.

MC squared equals E!

A gong is struck and the light is blacked out. When, after a moment, it goes on again, Miss Mass has disappeared and in her place stands Energy, a muscular male figure.

You see! It is sehr simple, no? Und now the corps de ballet I will call. Ah, already they are here. So much activity, yes?

The corps de ballet have entered while he has been speaking. They immediately begin to limber up.

Puppet Master. Ballet, I'm afraid, is a little too precious for what we're looking for. Ours is a mass audience. And for that, a certain robustness is called for.

1st Neutron. But you haven't even seen us. How can you possibly judge us without seeing what we can do?

Puppet Master. And who might you be?

1st Neutron. Well, I might be Eleonora Duse or Catherine the Great, but I'm not. I am a neutron, one of Professor Chadwick's discoveries. I'm the neutral counterpart of the positive proton.

1st Proton. That's me, positively.

Alpha Particle. The pushy type.

Energy. Now you two, don't start again!

Puppet Master. And what do you do?

Energy. I'm Energy. I keep this lot under control.

Puppet Master. And the electron, where is he?

2nd Proton. Oh, you can't see him. He's whizzing round outside in a ten-mile radius.

2nd Neutron. If you're wondering who I am, I'm the extra neutron. I get shot into the heart of the nucleus.

Puppet Master. And I take it that all of you form an atom of uranium.

3rd Proton. Not really. A uranium atom has ninety-two protons and a hundred and forty-three neutrons. Who could afford a cast of that size?

1st Neutron. So you'll have to use your imagination.

Energy. O.K. Let's get on with it. (*Calling*) Music!

Music. Two neutrons, dressed in white, and two protons, dressed in red, whirl round the stage and finally form a compact group. They are joined by other protons and neutrons. An alpha particle attempts to penetrate the group but is deflected by an invisible force. Finally, Chadwick's neutron dances into the centre of the group and all leap away from her and land on their knees. End of music.

Puppet Master. Is that it?

Energy. What more do you want, the end of the world?

Puppet Master. Too abstract, too . . . it lacks . . . zing!

The rest of the scene is played like a 'thirties gangster film.

Energy. Quit shootin' off your mouth. Stick around, bub, and we'll go through the whole routine in another way. O.K., kids, let's show this mug what happens.

2nd Proton. Sure, we'll run a floorshow and mebbe get to Hollywood.

3rd Neutron. You don't object to a little naturalism with just a soupçon of symbolism . . .

Energy. Button up, Gabby, I do the talking in this outfit.

1st Proton. O.K., boss, O.K.

Energy. Get some furniture for this dump.

Protons go off and return with a table. Neutrons bring in chairs. Energy draws a semicircle in white chalk. Protons are now wearing gangster hats and the neutrons very modish headgear.

Now, if any of you mugs cross that line, I'll bust you wide open . . . see?

2nd Proton. Gee, boss, I'm getting tired of sitting around here doing nothing . . . I wanna go out and see the world.

Energy. Yeah? Now listen, sucker, I'm giving the orders around here, see? And nobody complains. There's plenty of guys would give their right arm to be in this outfit . . . how would you like to be a hydrogen proton and live in solitary confinement, eh?

2nd Proton. I wouldn't like that, boss.

Energy. Well, quit bellyaching.

He begins to play patience.

1st Neutron. It ain't so bad, honey . . . you still got me.

2nd Proton. Oh, sure, sure . . . still a change of scenery wouldn't do no harm.

1st Neutron. I think you're tired of me. (*She weeps.*)

2nd Proton. Aw, quit bawling!

1st Neutron weeps all the more.

1st Proton. That ain't the way a gentleman talks to a lady!

2nd Proton. No? D'ye wanna make something of it?

1st Proton. Sure I do.

2nd Proton. Why, you dumb flat-top . . .

Energy. Take it easy, take it easy, or I'll croak the both of you.

The two Protons retire.

2nd Proton. Gee, babe, I ain't tired of you. Honest, kid, I love you, don't I? Do you remember the promise I made when we first teamed up? Wherever you go, I go, and wherever I go, you go. Well, that's still O.K. by me.

1st Neutron. Oh, honey . . .

They embrace.

Mic. Voice. Calling Energy 235! This is the electron guard calling Energy. Reporting unsuccessful attempt by rival electrons to crash the outer ring. Signing off! Signing off!

Energy. Gate-crashers, eh? That's that guy Thomson again . . . imagine it! Trying to send a couple of dumb electrons into my territory . . . some people have no respect for private property.

Pause.

2nd Neutron. Do you know what day it is, sugar?

1st Proton. Sure, it's Thursday.

2nd Neutron. Yeah, but it's kind of special . . .

1st Proton. How come?

2nd Neutron. It's our anniversary.

1st Proton. Yeah? Imagine that.

2nd Neutron. You don't sound very interested.

1st Proton. Oh, sure, sure.

2nd Neutron. I bought a new hat . . . do you like it?

1st Proton. It stinks.

2nd Neutron. Why, you dumb cluck . . .

Energy. Pipe down!

2nd Neutron. But the dirty . . .

1st Proton. You heard: pipe down!

Enter Alfie Particle.

2nd Neutron. (*Flashing the old 'come hither' look*) Well, if it ain't Alfie Particle!

Alfie. Hiya, babe! You still stringing along with that heel?

2nd Neutron. He don't bother me.

Alfie. Why don't you give him the air, kid? I could show you the big time.

2nd Neutron. Mebbe.

Alfie. Aw, come on, babe, I got big ideas . . . this guy's just a stick-in-the-mud.

Energy. Beat it, punk!

1st Proton. Yeah, beat it!

Alfie. Why, I've a good mind to come in there and . . .

First Proton. Listen, needlenose, this is a high-class outfit and we don't take bums, so beat it before things get tough.

Alfie. If it wasn't out of respect for the ladies, I'd come in there and drill you!

Energy. Give him the bum's rush.

1st Proton kicks Alfie off.

Mic. Voice. Calling Energy 235! This is the electron guard calling Energy! A flash neutron dame known as 'Chadwick's neutron', alias Lola the Smasher, has penetrated the outer ring and is heading for the nucleus. Signing off! Signing off!

Enter Lola. Wolf whistles from the protons.

Lola. Hallo, boys . . . swell set-up you got here.

1st Proton. Boy, oh boy, is she a dish or is she a dish?

2nd Proton. Why don't you come on in?

Energy. On your way, sister. This is my outfit.

Lola. Yeah?

Energy. Yeah!

Protons. But, boss . . .

Energy. Nobody's going to muscle in on my territory.

Lola. Scared of competition, eh?

Energy. I'm warning you . . . I don't know my own strength.

Lola. You're kinda cute . . . my, what big muscles you got!

1st Proton. I got muscles, too, sweetie-pie!

2nd Proton. Quiet, fishface!

Lola crosses the chalk line and is in the centre.

1st Neutron. Look, she's crossed the line!

2nd Neutron. Oh, gee, something terrible's going to happen!

Lola. These your floozies?

2nd Proton. Kind of.

Lola. Kind of negative, ain't they?

Energy. All right, I warned you . . . don't say I didn't warn you!

Lola. Say, what's eating you? Do you two guys have to listen to this big lummox beefing like this all the time? What are you, men or mice?

1st Proton. What do you mean?

Lola. Why don't you run gangs of your own? You're tough . . . you've got experience . . . why, a coupla big jerks like you ought to clean up!

1st Proton. Say, that ain't a bad idea.

2nd Proton. It ain't at that.

1st Proton. We could see the world.

2nd Proton. (*To 1st Neutron*) Baby, this is where we blow.

Energy. For the last time . . .

Both Protons. So long, boss . . . it's been a long time.

1st Proton. There ain't room for all of us.

2nd Proton. California, here I come!

1st Proton. From now on, call me boss of the Krypton Gang!

2nd Proton. And I'm the big shot of the Barium Gang!

They go off.

Energy. O.K., sister, O.K. I ain't got no ties no more, no responsibilities. Hold me down to earth, I feel my powers a-working. Stand back and give me room according to my strength. I'm a rip-tailed snorting child of the elements . . . I'm half fire, half light, with a punch that can knock holes in the moon. I ride to town with a team of comets harnessed with cosmic rays. My whip is the North Wind and twin stars the rowels of my spurs. When I'm hungry I eat time and wash it down with the Milky Way. Yippee! Yippee! Bow down and wait! When I smoke I use a volcano for a pipe and thunderbolts for matches. I'm the father of the oceans, the guy who put the curvature in space. Bow down and tremble! I scratch my head with lightning and purr myself to sleep with thunder. Yippee! Owooo! I'm the toughest, roughest, goldarned particle in the Universe!

He leaps into the air. Loud and sustained explosion. Blackout. When the lights go on again, the Puppet Master, his Secretary and Death are discovered on stage.

Puppet Master. The release of Energy! What a closing act it'll make!

Secretary. Wonderful!

Puppet Master. With a show like that we'll clear the board of competition. We'll be running the entire show before we're through.

Death makes to leave.

Not yet, sonny! I'll give your cue when the time comes. (*Addressing Secretary*) You're quite clear about the schedule?

Secretary. Perfectly clear. Act One, 1914. Rehearsal for Act Two, 1936. Act Two, 1939. Act Three . . .

Puppet Master. Leave Act Three for the moment. The exact time will depend on the audience. Get your coat, my dear. It's time we were on our way.

The light fades down a little as they exit upstage right. At the same moment an actor and actress enter downstage left.

Actor. Put out the light – and then, put out the light!

Actress. Well, we've looked at the atom – now perhaps we ought to take a look at ourselves.

Actor. You mean us, personally, as actors?

Actress. No, just people . . . you know, people as in people.

Actor. Oh – that kind of people!

In the following scene, all the searchers wear rather nondescript outdoor clothes. Raincoats would serve perfectly. The first searcher, a man, enters and addresses the actor.

1st Man. I appear to have lost my way.

A girl enters.

Actor. Maybe the young lady can direct you.

1st Man. Excuse me, miss. I wonder if you can help me. I'm looking for the road that leads to a good life.

1st Woman. Sorry, I'm a stranger here myself.

2nd Woman. Can you tell me where I am, please? I seem to have been misdirected. I'm looking for the road to happiness.

1st Man. Did you come by the crossroads?

2nd Woman. No, I took the short cut. I thought it looked easier.

1st Woman. I came that way too, but it doesn't seem to lead anywhere.

Enter two women.

3rd Woman. It's awfully dark.

4th Woman. I'm afraid we're lost. We must have taken the wrong turning.

Enter man and woman.

2nd Man. We're looking for Freedom's road. Could you tell us the way?

1st Man. Sorry, but we're lost, too. This is a cul-de-sac.

2nd Woman. Well, what do we do now?

1st Woman. I suppose we'd better go back and start all over again.

3rd Woman. But it's so dark!

Actor. Oh, come on, you know the way.

4th Woman. We're supposed to be acting.

Actor. Maybe we need a different script. One that deals with a different set of facts.

1st Man. What kind of facts?

Actor. Well, we could show how the actors responded to the rehearsal of Act Two.

2nd Woman. Rehearsal?

Actor. I'm referring to Spain. Remember?

Mic. Voice. This is Madrid calling! This is Madrid calling! Belchite calling! Guernica calling! Hello! Hello! Are you receiving me?

Light changes. A single overhead spot makes a pool of light centre stage. The searchers and the two actors stand in a semicircle at the upstage edge of the light. Each of them takes a newspaper from his pocket and reads it throughout following episode. At the same time, two of them hurl themselves into the centre of the pool of light. One of them lies wounded, the other crouches over him. The scene is interrupted by the intermittant crash of bombs.

Soldier. It's not much further now, Jimmy! Can't be more than a hundred yards at the outside. Don't worry, we'll make it!

Distant artillery barrage.

They got all the bleedin' artillery in the world out there! German, Italian, Spanish . . . Christ! If only . . . never mind, we'll show 'em. The way we did at Teruel. (*Singing*) Forward, you must remember! (*Speaking again*) Who could forget the smell of Badajos . . . or the stillness of Guernica when they'd finished with it? Butchers!

Member of Chorus. A hundred and forty-three for four wickets! Hutton's coming in to bat.

Drone of planes and crash of bombs.

Soldier. Madrid's getting it bad tonight . . . they'll never take Madrid, not with all the tanks and planes in the world. (*Singing*) Forward, you must remember, herein our strength does lie. Forward, you must remember, in hunger or in plenty . . . (*Speaking again*) Remember how we drove 'em back at Guadarrama? Rifles against tanks! And Belchite! The Thaelmann brigade on our left flank and the French on our right. They won't forget those days, Jimmy. Nobody will.

Bombs.

Member of Chorus. There's Larwood coming now!

Member of Chorus. Shouldn't allow bodyline bowling. Not cricket!

Soldier. It'll be quiet back home now. People'll be asleep in bed and the streets'll be quiet with the roofs of the houses shining like silver under the northern moon. There'll be no fear of bombing, that's for sure. Not yet, anyroad. (*Shouting*) Hey, you in bed back home! Wake up! Wake up! (*To his companion*) Sorry, kid. Forgot.

Member of Chorus. A hundred and eighty-six for four wickets!

Member of Chorus. A hundred and ninety! Verity coming in to bowl.

Member of Chorus. Two hundred and five for four wickets!

Member of Chorus. Boundary! Bravo!

Member of Chorus. He'll make his century, easy.

Member of Chorus. Two-twenty-four not out!

Member of Chorus. Two-seventy-six for six!

Gunfire very close.

Soldier. Shut up! Shut up, you rotten bastards! My mate's trying to sleep. Can't even get a kip without some noisy bleeder banging away with all he's got! Go on, shoot, shoot! You can't bloody well kill all of us . . . you fascist bastards!

Burst of machine-gun fire. He falls over the body of his mate.

Jimmy! Jimmy!

Mic. Voice. All right, soldier, you can get up now. This is only a play, an attempt to discover the location of the audience's conscience.

Soldier. (*Rising to his feet*) There were more than a million men and women in Spain who didn't get up.

Mic. Voice. The rehearsal. The stage was Spain, Austria, the Saar, Czechoslovakia. But the stage management was provided by Germany. Germany calling! Germany calling! The Germany of Guns-Before-Butter, the Germany which was defending Europe from the menace of Communism. The Germany of the blond hero and the concentration camp. The Germany of Adolf Hitler and the Anglo-German Naval Agreement.

Two men, members of the chorus, man-handle a third man in the centre of the light.

1st Gestapo. All right, Eisler, talk!

2nd Gestapo. You heard what he said.

1st Gestapo. You might as well talk, Eisler, We've been on to you for a long time.

Chorus. (*Whispering*) Long time. Long time. Long time.

2nd Gestapo. We want to know where you got the leaflet.

1st Gestapo. And no lies, Eisler. We know you're part of the cell at Siemen's. We want to know who number one is. Who issues the instructions? You've got sixty seconds to talk!

Chorus. Quiet! Quiet! Quiet! Quiet!

2nd Gestapo. (*Striking him*) Talk, you red bastard!

1st Gestapo. Maybe you'd like me to jog your memory.

He produces a rubber blackjack from his pocket.

You had a sister once, Eisler. Remember?

Chorus. Elsa. Elsa. Elsa. Elsa.

1st Gestapo. You never knew what happened to her, did you? But we know, Eisler. We were there. Isn't that right, Kurt?

2nd Gestapo. We were there, all right. And did we let her know it!

1st Gestapo. Took her a long time to die.

2nd Gestapo. Sit down and think it over.

He kicks him in the stomach.

1st Gestapo. Thirty seconds left.

Chorus. Thirty seconds! Thirty seconds! Thirty seconds!

1st Gestapo. That's all you got. Speak up! Who printed the leaflets? Who are the other members of the cell? Who issues the instructions? Talk, you ghet!

They begin to beat him up.

Chorus. This is it! This is it! This is it!

2nd Gestapo. Do we take him in?

1st Gestapo. Haven't the time. I promised to take the wife to the pictures.

2nd Gestapo. Better finish him, then.

He produces a pistol.

1st Gestapo. Not that way. Too noisy! The town's full of foreign visitors. Hold him up.

They break his neck and he falls to the ground.

Mic. Voice. This scene is called 'Strength Through Joy'.

The two Gestapo officers become actors again and help Eisler to his feet. All three rejoin the semicircle.

1st Gestapo. The scene ends and the actor rises to his feet. But there were hundreds of thousands of real actors who never rose again.

Mic. Voice. And there were the refugees: the writers, doctors, students, scientists.

A woman leaves the semi-circle and stands downstage, waiting.

Chorus. He's late! Late! Late! Late!

A man leaves the chorus and joins her.

Lisa Meidtner. Thank God!

Frisch. Have you been here long?

Meidtner. No, I just arrived.

Frisch. Sure you weren't followed?

Meidtner. I came a long way round. Is something wrong?

Frisch. I had visitors today.

Meidtner. The Gestapo?

Frisch. I . . . think so.

Meidtner. Listen, something very important has happened. I have a contact in Strassman's laboratory. His neutron bombardment of uranium has produced an isotope of barium.

Frisch. You are certain?

Meidtner. Positive! The nucleus split into equal parts releasing enormous amounts of energy.

Frisch. I take it you understand the implications of this news.

Meidtner. Of course. The laboratory is already on a war footing.

Frisch. We've got to get out of Germany immediately.

Meidtner. I've made all the arrangements. Can you get a travel permit?

Frisch. I . . . yes, I think I can.

Meidtner. I have an aunt who lives in Schleswig. If you could get that far, it should be easy to slip over the border into Denmark.

Frisch. Denmark, Copenhagen and Professor Nils Bohr!

Meidtner. If anything should happen . . .

Chorus. Watch out! Watch out!

Frisch suddenly embraces her. A man enters, pauses, lights a cigarette, then walks off.

Frisch. Sorry, Miss Meidtner. To have to play such games!

Meidtner. We'd better go. It's dangerous being out so late.

Frisch. See you in Copenhagen.

They shake hands.

Both. Good luck!

They resume their positions in the semicircle.

Meidtner. We did not have to make the perilous journey through a hostile land.

Frisch. But thousands of others did.

Member of Chorus. It isn't pleasant to remember such things. It is so easy to forget other people's sufferings. And yet our century has taught us that disaster may result from a defective memory.

Mic. Voice. Is there a mental specialist in the house? The world's gone mad again! September the third, 1939. WAR!

Sound of marching feet. Five scientists wearing white lab coats enter. They form two small groups and stand deep in conversation. The Puppet Master enters briskly.

Puppet Master. Fall in!

The scientists form a straight line. The entire scene is performed as bayonet-drill, with Puppet Master as sergeant.

Puppet Master. Squad 'shun! Left turn! Tem-po!

1st Scientist. MC squared equals E.

2nd Scientist. B equals bracket ZMp unbracket minus M.

3rd Scientist. K infinity equals 0.87.

4th Scientist. K infinity equals 0.98.

5th Scientist. Epsilon pf eta equals K infinity.

1st Scientist. K infinity equals 1.007.

Mic. Voice. The piping must have a high neutron absorption cross section. The highest are lead . . .

All. Water corrosion.

Mic. Voice. Bismuth.

All. Water corrosion.

Mic. Voice. Beryllium.

2nd Scientist. There is no beryllium tubing in the country.

Mic. Voice. Aluminium.

All. Doubtful.

Mic. Voice. Magnesium.

All. Water corrosion.

Mic. Voice. Zinc.

All. Water corrosion.

Mic. Voice. Tin.

All. Water corrosion.

Mic. Voice. Try aluminium.

All. It works!

3rd Scientist. For a separation producing 90 per cent uranium 235 from natural uranium, r must equal 1,260 but alpha equals root 352 over 349 which is only 1.0043.

4th Scientist. 92 uranium 238 by neutron gamma reaction to 92 uranium 239.

5th Scientist. 92 uranium 239.

Mic. Voice. Half-life twenty-three minutes.

5th Scientist. By beta emission to 93 neptunium 239.

Mic. Voice. Half-life 2.3 days.

5th Scientist. By beta-gamma emission to 94 plutonium 239.

4th Scientist. 94 plutonium 239 by alpha emission to 92 uranium 235.

There is a blinding flash and a loud, sustained explosion followed by a blackout. The light comes up again and discovers the Puppet Master, his Secretary and Death, leading Energy on a leash.

Puppet Master. Let us pause here.

Secretary. But the audience . . .!

Puppet Master. The audience?

Secretary. Is it wise to let them see so much of you?

Puppet Master. They will have forgotten me by the morning.

Secretary. Are you sure?

Puppet Master. I know my audience. In a few minutes they will leave this building imagining that a man can walk out of his own life. They don't realise that they are the main protagonists in the play. They will go out into the night sharing the same dream until the dream is shattered by a stream of petty circumstances. In fifteen minutes, only half the dream will remain. In thirty minutes only half of half the dream and in an hour nothing will be left but a blurred image on the retina of the mind's eye. For the last bus home tonight is more important than the hearse which bears one to a worm's banquet in twelve months' time. Let us be thankful, my dear, that people have such short memories.

Secretary. Last night I dreamed of my dead lovers. They looked at me out of the empty sockets of their eyes and spoke of their unborn children.

Puppet Master. I will find you new lovers.

Secretary. But they will die like all the others.

Puppet Master. Because you break them. You always break the toys I bring you.

Secretary. Now you are scolding me.

Puppet Master. I? Now, why would I scold you? There are plenty more toys. Soon there will be another generation of young men and you shall have them all.

Secretary. Soon?

Puppet Master. As soon as the chorus is ready for the next scene.

Secretary. The young men who talk with voices of caressing hands . . . the young men of the red hands and the smoke of battle in their hair . . . the young men whose bodies live like a flame which burns the night and dies with burning . . .

Energy and Death rise up.

Puppet Master. Not yet! The actors haven't recovered from the Second Act. Give them a sporting chance, I say, and the hunt will be the keener.

Secretary. Why can't the play go on and never stop?

Puppet Master. Let them repair the broken cities first. Let them breed again. Let them erect a superstructure on their lives and we four will destroy it.

Enter a woman.

Woman. I had a son,
　　　　　A song in my veins,
　　　　　A green shoot in my heart,
　　　　　A flight of grace notes,
　　　　　That was my son.

Secretary. Where is he now?

Puppet Master. Yes, where?

Woman. Where?
　　　　　My heart is a barren field
　　　　　Where withered nettles whisper dry laments,
　　　　　Where the sun gives no warmth,
　　　　　Where the broken stars are fallen on a rubbish heap.

Puppet Master. You should apply for a pension.

Woman. Yes, I will apply for a pension.
　　　　　I will buy me an axe
　　　　　And lop off the dead branches of the world.

Puppet Master. You can't do that without a permit.

Woman. I will search for a man
　　　　　In whom there is no singing,
　　　　　No warmth, no light, no music.
　　　　　A man of shades and empty silence.

Secretary. I warned you. The audience!

Woman. I will find a man
        Who tears the young plants out of the earth
        And feeds his swine with roses;
        The man with the woodman's axe
        Who fells the striplings in spring
        Before their leaves are born;
        The smiler with the knife.
        A man like you who talks of pensions
        When the blade of anguish
        Turns within the womb.

Puppet Master. Dear lady, you are distraught. I am not the man you seek, for like you, I too know parental love. Sleep is what you need, good lady.

Woman. Sleep!

Puppet Master. My friend here is a famous sleep practitioner. He will give you something which will help you to forget.

Death approaches her but stops as a soldier enters.

Soldier. Can he give me something that will take the smell of burning flesh out of my nostrils, something to make my ears forget a screaming soldier?

Puppet Master. He can do all that.

Soldier. Can he show me the man who makes of my death a mockery, the commander who never leaves the field of battle for fear that life should grow there? Can he show me him?

Woman. Young man, you have looked at the stars and stumbled in a grave.

Soldier. I was a young man
        With eyes that looked to see things grow,
        Corn from the seed,
        Cities from the rock,
        Wheels from the iron-ore.

Secretary. What are you now?

Soldier. I was a man
        With hands that drew
        The goodness out of metals,
        The whirling shaft,
        The lunging piston,
        The hissing bar.

Woman. What do you do now?

Soldier. I plant corpses in a desert,
        Because a man with a barren mind
        Has forgotten what life is.
        A man like you.

Puppet Master. Come, come, young man! My grey hairs deserve respect.

Enter two men wearing garb of concentration camp inmates.

1st Inmate. Do my grey hairs deserve respect?

2nd Inmate. Do mine?

Both. We were men once.

1st Inmate.
> Hope, desire, pity, love,
> We knew them once.

2nd Inmate.
> Ambition, anger, laughter, tears,
> Familiar things.

1st Inmate.
> Familiar no more.
> All gone, destroyed.

Both. Reduced to ashes in the ovens of Auschwitz.

Secretary. Send them away – they frighten me!

1st Inmate. We frighten ourselves.

Puppet Master. People want to forget.

2nd Inmate. Who will help *us* forget?

Puppet Master. (*Indicating Death*) I have a friend here who is a specialist.

1st Inmate. I know his face. I've seen him in the camp.

Soldier. I know him, too!

Several Voices. He is the Puppet Master's friend.

Puppet Master. All this is foolishness.

Enter the Scientist.

Puppet Master. There is the man you seek. He it is whose brain conceives the tools of death. If the graves are now prepared for other wars, then he's the man who is responsible.

All. The enemy!

Scientist. Wait! Let me speak.

Puppet Master. Your voice is cracked.

1st Inmate. Let him speak. We have known too much of death to welcome it.

2nd Inmate. Let him have the benefit of the trial we never had.

1st Inmate. You are accused of conspiring against the world, of betraying mankind to war and wretchedness, of using the brain to do the work of Death.

Woman. You are accused of conspiring against tomorrow's generations.

Soldier. You are accused of planning to destroy the very fabric of the world, of having released the forces of death in everything that lives.

All. You are accused of conspiring against the human race.

Scientist. The road that we have built across the wastes of ignorance is not a road which leads to Death except for fools who would throw themselves over the precipice. It is a good road which can lead to peace itself if only men will stop wearing blinkers on their eyes. It can lead to peace such as you have never known.

Puppet Master. An empty dream!

Scientist.

> He is the man of the shades
> The woodman with the axe,
> The puppet-master who shapes the play
> Of death. He is the enemy.

All. The enemy!

Puppet Master. Good people, please. I am an old man interested only in my son here. (*He indicates Energy*). The very apple of his father's eye.

Scientist. He is no child of yours. I accuse this man of having kidnapped Energy, the child of my own brain.

Puppet Master. He's mad.

Scientist. I accuse him of conspiring against the peace of the world, of debauching science's discoveries, perverting progress, and of gross distortion of the truth.

Puppet Master. He is my child.

Scientist. You lie!

Puppet Master. Come, I will do the sporting thing. (*He produces dice.*) Let us decide with the dice.

Soldier. Let me see them first. (*He takes the dice.*) The dice are loaded.

All. He is condemned.

1st Man. Let Energy speak. Who are your parents?

Energy. Albertus Magnus, Einstein, Democritus, da Vinci, Planck, Dalton, Rutherford, Paracelsus, Thomson, Mendeleyev, Curie, Bohr, Chadwick, Dirac, Heisenberg. The men and women of the whole earth and of all ages. I am their child.

1st Man. But you cannot go with them all.

Woman. Which way will you go?

Energy. I will go where you go. If you work for war I will work with you. If you work for peace I will work too. There are two roads.

Puppet Master. My road is the familiar one. You can walk it blindfold. Come with me.

Scientist. Mine is the new road, where a man walks with his eyes on the future. The road out of the night.

Energy. There are two roads. It is for you to choose and for me to follow.

The crowd hesitates.

Which is it to be?

All. Which way are you going?   *[The End]*

NOTE

Following Theatre Workshop's practice of keeping the play up to date, the author has written a new ending, one more in accord with his present political position. After the Puppet Master's speech 'An empty dream' (p. 125), the play continues as follows:

The actress who has been playing the role of the mother suddenly abandons the role and becomes an actress again, talking to her workmates. The rest of the characters onstage follow her example.

Woman. You know, I think I agree with you.

Those onstage are put to a nonplus for a moment.

Puppet Master. That isn't in the script.

Woman. No, it isn't. At least, it isn't in the original script.

Soldier. Which original script? I understand there's half a dozen 'original' versions of the script.

1st Man. That's right – the original script was written in 1946 and played for just over an hour. Then a longer version was made in 1947 and then they kept altering it by subtracting scenes and adding others until about 1952.

2nd Man. And the final script is the one we've been performing tonight?

1st Man. Not exactly. A lot of it's from the original and the rest from some of the later versions.

Puppet Master. Confusing, to say the least?

Woman. (*To the audience*) Are you confused? Perhaps I should explain. What you have seen so far, is what the author wrote way back in the late forties and early fifties. At that time he believed, as many people did, in what Eisenhower called 'Atoms for Peace'. Indeed, he ended the play on a note of hope. 'We have the choice,' he said, 'between two roads: the road to war and the road to peace.'

Scientist. So?

Woman. Events have forced him to change his mind.

Scientist. Which events?

1st Man. The blow-out at Windscale in 1957 which released twenty thousand curies of radioactive iodine-131 into the atmosphere.

Soldier. The explosion of stored radioactive waste at Kyshtym in the Soviet Union in 1958, which resulted in more than a thousand square miles being contaminated by radioactive strontium-90 and caesium-137.

Secretary. The partial melt-down in the fast-breeder reactor at Detroit, Michigan, in 1966.

3rd Man. And similar accidents in West Germany, France, Switzerland, Japan – and of course, there was Three Mile Island.

Soldier. The U.S. Safety Information Center at Oak Ridge recently disclosed that of the two thousand incidents investigated in 1979, no fewer than thirty-two could have ended in a catastrophic melt-down of the core.

Scientist. That wasn't here in Britain, was it!

Soldier. No, that wasn't here in Britain. We don't know how many near catastrophies have occurred here as the British nuclear industry refuses to make its safety findings available to the public.

Secretary. What do you think they're trying to hide?

Scientist. Look, you talk as if there's some kind of conspiracy.

Woman. There is a conspiracy! A conspiracy to keep us in the dark, to keep us from knowing what they've got in store for us.

Scientist. This isn't some B-film about mad scientists intent on destroying civilisation.

Puppet Master. No? I think it *is*. And a bloody awful B-film at that! A cast of third-rate actors playing at politics.

Scientist. It's scientists we're talking about, not politicians.

Secretary. Are they any different?

Scientist. Of course they are! At least, their motivations are different.

1st Man. Grow up! Don't tell me you still believe all that nonsense about the scientist's pure motives, about his only interest being the furtherance of human knowledge.

Scientist. I don't think it is nonsense. There are scientists who . . .

Puppet Master. A minority. A small minority. Most of them are pretty much the same as everybody else.

Scientist. Exactly! So why suggest that they're all alike?

Soldier. You're the one who suggested that.

Scientist. I did nothing of the kind.

2nd Man. You implied it.

Puppet Master. Their motivations are different, you said. Well, perhaps that's true for a small handful of them but I'll bet that for every scientist who is a selfless seeker after knowledge there are a hundred or more who are as much on the make as any politician. Their motivations, as you call them, are ambition, the need to feel successful, to feel 'in the know', to have the symbols of success constantly in one's sight: the Mercedes, the modest estate, the fine house, the right school for one's children, a title possibly. And it's satisfying to be able to pontificate at high table or on TV or at conferences of experts. When you have achieved these things, you tend to put any doubts you may have about what you are doing into a locked drawer and forget about them.

Scientist. You're being cynical.

Puppet Master. Maybe. But not nearly as cynical as some of the people we're discussing who, in the course of their professional careers, have managed to put their conscience into a deep coma. They're clever people, yes! But the search for truth, knowledge, and all the other noble concepts . . . bilge! It's a bloody great fraud! They're con-artists! You'd better recognise the fact that a man or woman can be a brilliant nuclear physicist and yet be a third-rate human being.

Scientist. In which case, they're no different from the rest of us.

Woman. They *are* different. They're worse than the worst of us.

Scientist. How do you make that out?

Woman. They *know* what they're doing. They're not like someone who goes out and murders a child – some old man, sick in the head. Oh, no! We're talking about rational people: brilliant minds! People who're supposed to be more far-seeing than the rest of us. And what do these rational, brilliant, far-seeing people do with all that know-how? All that knowledge, that effort to understand the physical laws of the universe! What do they do with it? They turn to us, the stupid, gullible, easily impressed public and say: 'Here is a present for you, the wherewithal to destroy yourself and the world you live in. Our greatest achievement!'

Soldier. Isn't that something! Use a little of it to make a bomb, a small bomb just big enough to wipe out a town with maybe two hundred thousand inhabitants. With a slightly bigger bomb you could wipe out Liverpool or Edinburgh.

2nd Man. And with four or five such bombs you could eradicate London from the face of the earth. No more traffic problems, no housing problems . . .

Secretary. And no people problems. Period!

From now on, all the dialogue is directed straight to the audience.

Puppet Master. And if you want something really big, then there's the nuclear reactors dotted all over Britain, those old-fashioned Magnox reactors at Windscale and Hunterston, Chapel Cross and Dungeness. They are the time-bombs in the atomic nursery. And then there's the A.G.R.s at Hartlepool, Heysham and Hinkley Point, and the rapid breeder they propose to build at Dounreay. They'd really be effective at dealing with our problems, since there'd be nobody left to experience problems.

Woman. Each of those reactors is a weapon pointed at the heart of this nation.

Scientist. They produce power.

Woman. They only produce electricity and we've got more of that kind of power than we need. They produce radioactive substances which poison everything they touch – the land, the rivers, the seas, the air . . . they breed cancers in the bones and flesh of people like us. Man's greatest achievement! A device, a series of devices with which we can kill ourselves, our children, our families, our friends.

Scientist. You don't seem to understand . . .

Woman. And *you* don't seem to understand what is at stake. These people that you admire so much, these dedicated scientists are as venal, as corrupt as . . . you expect venality from business tycoons, you expect generals and professional hit-men to be ruthless but . . . you read about some old lady being beaten up by teenage thugs and we're all horrified! But these people plan the murder of cities, continents, millions of men, women and children! Even while we're talking, the reactors go on breeding more and more plutonium and more and more radioactive waste . . . plutonium has a half-life of twenty-four thousand years and it takes about ten half-lives for radioactive material to become harmless. That means plutonium has to be kept out of the environment for a quarter of a million to half a million years.

If at any time during that period it is released into the environment, land and water are poisoned forever. Forever! Forever! Who are the real vandals? The football gangs who tear up railway carriages or the glib engineering geniuses and men of science who are prepared to tear up the planet we live on? Why do they do it? Why? Why?

Scientist. (*Taking off his white coat*) It isn't so much a question of why they do it, it's why do we let them do it?

2nd Woman. Yes, why? Are we too lazy, too preoccupied with other things? Don't we care? What about those we love and those who love us? Are we prepared to stand back and do nothing to stop them from being murdered? What about our children? Do we really love them? Enough to save them from this horror?

Soldier. Yes, that is the question. And it isn't only human life that is threatened – it's all life. And it's forever.

All. (*Quietly*) Forever!

Woman. Have you decided where you're going on your holidays next year? Have you made your plans yet? Perhaps you shouldn't bother. There may not be any next year or next month for that matter, or next week . . . or tomorrow . . . forever is an awful long time.

3rd Woman. It really depends on us. On you, me, him, her, all of us. We're all responsible for what happens. This is one situation we can't opt out of. In any case, there's nowhere to opt out to.

Puppet Master. We can stop them, you know! It'll take courage, determination, nerve and the capacity to put up with a hell of a lot of double-talk.

1st Man. Of course, you may prefer to gamble, staking humankind's future against the slow burn or the big bang. It really depends on whether you think the world's worth saving.

Puppet Master. Do you think you might give it some thought? It's worth thinking about. And remember what's at stake: our future and our past, all two or three million years of it. Anyway, think it over.

Woman. Yes, think it over. But don't take too long. Please don't take too long.

A brief pause and the light begins to fade.

All. (*Quietly*) Remember – forever is an awful long time.

The stage is left in darkness and the theatre is filled with whispers . . . 'Forever . . . forever . . . forever . . .' [The End]

The beaten track is beaten frae the start
– Hugh MacDiarmid

The
Other Animals

by Ewan MacColl

CENTRAL LIBRARY THEATRE

ST. PETER'S SQUARE · MANCHESTER
GENERAL MANAGER & LICENSEE
CHARLES NOWELL, M.A., F.L.A., CITY LIBRARIAN

JULY 5th to 24th   Evenings at 7   Matinee: Saturday at 2-15   Box Office: CENtral 5972 (10-30 a.m.—7 p.m.)
House Manager, Peter Carpenter.

THEATRE
WORKSHOP

presents

THE OTHER
ANIMALS

Ewan MacColl's new play

Produced by

JOAN LITTLEWOOD

The Other Animals was presented by Theatre Workshop at The Library Theatre, Manchester, on 5 July 1948, with the following cast:

HANAU	Ewan MacColl
ROBERT	David Scase
DOCTOR GRAUBARD	Peter Varley
1st GUARD	John Blanshard
2nd GUARD	Denis Ford
MARIA	Julia Jones
ROLF	Howard Goorney
ANDERSON	Edmond Bennett
THE MOON	Jean Newlove
THE GIRL IN WHITE	Doreen Warburton
THE GIRL IN GREEN	Leila Greenwood
THE GIRL IN CRIMSON	Kristin Lind
A NURSE	Leila Greenwood
AN ARCHITECT	Edmond Bennett
A YOUNG LABOURER	Denis Ford
AN OLD MAN	Howard Goorney
A YOUNG WOMAN	Doreen Warburton
AN OLD WOMAN	Jean Newlove
FRANCISCO PIERA	Howard Goorney
CLEMENCE GAUDRY	Julia Jones
JAMES GUTHRIE	Edmond Bennett
A COMMERCIAL TRAVELLER	John Blanshard
BRAVE LITTLE WOMAN	Leila Greenwood
DEATH AS AN OLD WOMAN	Kristin Lind
MORNING AS A YOUNG GIRL	Jean Newlove

Directed by Joan Littlewood. Sets designed by Joan Littlewood. Costumes designed by Bernard O'Connell. Lighting by John Bury. Choreography by Jean Newlove.

[**PART ONE**] *The curtain rises on a stage draped in black. In the centre stands a circular steel cage, broad at the base, narrowing as it reaches up into the darkness. Left and right of the cage and as far back as possible are two platforms raised above stage level. At first there is little light on the stage, just one dim spotlight beam falling into the cage, which becomes brighter during the announcer's introduction.*

Announcer. (*Intimately*) The word 'cage' is a noun. 'Old French from Latin Cavea – cavity, from CAVUS – hollow. A box or enclosure wholly or partly of openwork for confining birds or other animals.'

1st Voice.

        Thus, in our dictionary,
        Simply and precisely,
        Is defined
        The penultimate abode
        Of those marked down for death
        By history's enemies.

Somewhere in the night a man screams.

        Here in this purgatory
        Set between two hells,
        The hell of blindness
        And the hell of seeing,
        The species wages war
        Upon the genus.

Phrase of music.

2nd Voice.

        Both are the other animals,
        Alike in external features as two peas,
        Two spirochetes or two baboons,
        And yet dissimilar as a thing
        And its reflection in a mirror;
        A difference measured
        In the terms of dreams.

Phrase of music.

3rd Voice.

        Both are the other animals.
        One is the hawk, keen-sighted, solitary;
        The other a jackdaw, noisy, gregarious.
        One is the white, poised gull,
        A visual song of infinite variation,
        Counterpoised on wind and sky;
        The other, the snot-green shag,
        A stomach with wings, haunting its ichthyic past
        In worlds of fishes' bones and coastal silt.
        One is the eagle, rejecting the valley's scars

For the utmost pinnacle of vertiginous dream;
The other, the small, nocturnal owl
Avoiding abacination from the candle's gleam.
These are the other animals.

*A metallic tapping becomes audible. A voice keeps pace with the tapping: 'They
– are – bringing – him – back.' The echoes die away.*

1st Voice.

They envied his keen sight,
His quick perception;
The perfection which lies
In co-ordination of mind and eye.
And he would not join their chorus.
And fearing his silence
And hating what they feared,
The jackdaws fell upon the lark,
Mobbed him,
Crowded his flight with clumsy jackdaw wings,
Tore at his silence with blunt jackdaw cries,
Robbed him of that fine co-ordination,
The essence of his being.
And his seeing eyes glazed over,
Leaving a lesser world
For jackdaws
And the other animals.

Music.

2nd Voice.

Shags opened the breast of the wheeling gull
As he rode the shifting currents of the air.
His perfect flight
Was a reminder,
Constantly before their eyes,
Of the gulf
Which lies between
Their world, half-fish, half-bird,
And his,
All bird,
Perfect.

Music.

3rd Voice.

Behind the walls of darkness,
Where he wields dominion over frogs and mice,
The captive owl conspires against the eagle:
Plans a regime where night
Will be perpetual and universal
And sight limited to those things
That avoid the light and love the darkness.

The tapping and the voice are heard again. 'They – are – coming. Pass – it – on.'

1st Voice.

>   Where there were eyes
>   Of suns and stars,
>   Gouging batrachian thumbs
>   Left only cavities,
>   Hollows of darkness
>   Where life festers
>   And cries out with iron voice,
>   In words of rust,
>   Inflicting ferrous wounds
>   Upon the silence.
>   That they can still be heard
>   Above the twittering, bat-voices of the dead,
>   Is a tribute
>   To the light behind the eyes,
>   The dream behind the fact,
>   Which characterise
>   That Individual.
>   (genus Homo, family Hominidae, class Mammalia)
>   Of the highest type of animal
>   Existing
>   Or known to have existed,
>   Differing from other high types of animals
>   Especially
>   In his extraordinary mental development.

All.

>   Man – the other animal.
>   Men – the other animals.

In the distance a steel door clangs. The tapping begins again accompanied by the voice. 'They – are – bringing – Number – Three – back.' The tapping and the voice increase in volume until it seems that every nook and cranny of this dark, sub-world is alive with hoarse, tearing echoes. The sounds reach a peak and then stop with sharp and terrific finality. Two guards enter, half carrying, half dragging the prisoner, Hanau, known to the other prisoners as Number Three. Though still in his early forties, weeks of captivity and torture have given him the appearance of an old man. His hair is streaked with grey and the stubble of his beard bloody from countless beatings. At the moment he is unconscious of his surroundings, the wide, staring eyes see only the phantoms which people his private world of delirium and pain.

1st Guard. Home again, brother! There's no place like home.

2nd Guard. Christ, how this place stinks!

1st Guard. You get used to it. A matter of time, that's all.

2nd Guard. Hope you're right.

1st Guard. With time you can get used to anything. Take me, now – I've seen the day my stomach was as queasy as a bitch's belly full of its first load. The slightest whiff of anything that disagreed with me and I'd be off my food for days. Now I could eat my dinner off the floor of a privy and not even notice. Habit, that's all!

2nd Guard. At the training centre we used to turn the hoses on the prisoners.

1st Guard. This is a prison not a bath-house.

2nd Guard. I still don't like the way the bastards smell.

1st Guard. Maybe you'd like some eau-de-cologne. If you want to make good in this world then you've got to be master of your own stomach. A rebellious belly is like a spoiled woman: both have to be tamed or they'll tame you.

Hanau. One . . . two . . . three . . . four. There's one too many.

2nd Guard. Shut up!

1st Guard. Here, hold him up while I unlock the door.

Hanau. All except the fourth. Anderson . . . Rolf . . . Maria . . . Maria . . .

1st Guard. Sure, Maria . . . we'll send her to you later.

Hanau. Was it safe to bring him here?

2nd Guard. You heard me, be quiet!

1st Guard. He can't hear you. As far as he's concerned you don't exist.

Hanau. There is a certain familiarity . . .

2nd Guard. If I had my way I'd talk to him with my boot.

Hanau.   He looks as if he slept too much;
It leaves a mark, makes a man look
Like a blurred reproduction of himself.
Just stand aside a little! You see,
He has the sleeper's voluntary deafness.
And do the sleeping bedrooms hear
The statement of the streets,
The factual report of feet on pavements?
Sleep is a perpetual multiplication
Of dead tissue, a parasitic growth
Which feeds upon awareness,
Dulling the pitch and volume
Of infinite, stratose gradations
Of acquired perception.

1st Guard. All right, professor, the party's over. (*He stands by the open door of the cage.*) Right! Release the prisoner.

The 2nd Guard throws Hanau into the cage. He falls flat on his back and lies quite still.

He's tired. Wants to lie down.

2nd Guard. It beats me how the sod manages to go on living.

1st Guard. Habit, just habit!

2nd Guard. If the commandant would give me three minutes of the prisoner's time, I'd break him of all his habits.

1st Guard. And then Graubard would break you.

2nd Guard. What's Graubard got to do with it?

1st Guard. Why don't you ask him?

2nd Guard. I thought he was only the doctor here.

1st Guard. That's right, only the doctor. Listen, I'm going to give you some advice. Whether you take it or not is none of my business, but if you don't I'll guarantee you'll be in the front line within a week, and a front line which is always falling back is a very unhealthy place to be in.

2nd Guard. Well, what's your advice?

1st Guard. Just this: remember that it's Doctor Graubard who writes the prescriptions. The commandant is only the dispenser.

2nd Guard. But I don't see . . .

1st Guard. Think it over, just think it over. Let's go!

They make to leave, but stand back to allow Dr Graubard to enter. He is a man of about forty-five years of age, alert and vigorous, but possessing an air of detachment. In spite of holding the rank of a major, he consistently wears civilian clothes, conscious of the fact that this makes him conspicuous in a world where everyone wears a uniform.

Graubard. And how is my patient?

1st Guard. Still out, sir.

Graubard. Out? He appears to be very much 'in'.

1st Guard. Yes, sir. I meant he's still unconscious.

Graubard. Has he said anything since he had his treatment?

1st Guard. Only in delirium, sir. He spoke of sleep.

Graubard. Hallucinate, no doubt.

1st Guard. Sir?

Graubard. Did he appear to be seeing things?

1st Guard. Yes, sir. Definitely, sir!

Graubard. And he spoke of sleep?

1st Guard. Yes, sir.

Graubard crosses to the cage and stands looking down at Hanau.

Graubard. Beware of dreams, Hanau! Beware of dreams!

The 2nd Guard laughs obediently. Graubard comes back and stands facing him.

Do you have dreams?

2nd Guard. No, sir.

Graubard. Then why did you laugh?

2nd Guard. It was what you said, sir. It struck me as funny.

Graubard. It did? I see. So you think I'm a humorist.

The Guard is silent.

You're new here.

2nd Guard. Yes, sir.

Graubard. Where were you before?

2nd Guard. Training course, sir. Number Five Interrogation Centre.

Graubard. Did you volunteer?

2nd Guard. Yes, sir.

Graubard. Why?

2nd Guard. (*Flustered*) Why, sir?

Graubard. Yes, why did you volunteer? Do you like the work?

2nd Guard. Oh, yes sir!

Graubard. Why?

2nd Guard. (*Very confused*) I . . . I don't know, sir.

Graubard. Doesn't that strike you as strange?

2nd Guard. No, sir . . . I mean, yes sir.

Graubard. Make up your mind. Tell me, was the killing of prisoners part of your training?

2nd Guard. Yes, sir.

Graubard. And how did you react?

2nd Guard. I don't quite know what you mean, sir.

Graubard. Did you enjoy it?

2nd Guard. I . . . it was an order, sir.

Graubard. I know it was an order, and I'm asking you whether you enjoyed carrying out the order. What were your personal feelings towards the prisoners?

2nd Guard. I hated them!

Graubard walks slowly round the Guard, like an officer inspecting a private on parade.

Graubard. You're a neurotic. Did you know that?

2nd Guard. No, sir.

Graubard. Well, you know it now. (*To the 1st Guard*) See that he keeps away from Hanau. Understand?

1st Guard. Yes, sir.

Graubard. (*Speaking softly, but with great emphasis to the 2nd Guard*) Hanau is my masterpiece and I want no psychopathic scribblings on the canvas. This place is not an abattoir, remember that: it is a laboratory where I carry on my research. Is that clear?

2nd Guard. Yes, sir.

Graubard. Remember also, that the prisoners in this wing are necessary to my work. They are not brought here for the gratification of your neurotic impulses. Your experience in dealing with peddlers of badly written leaflets is, no doubt, extensive, but . . .

Hearing Hanau's voice, he stops abruptly.

Hanau. The decision was clear . . .
　　　　Cell nuclei composed
　　　　Of three and only three.
　　　　Three shadows in all the streets
　　　　Of all the cities, combining
　　　　To form the nervous system
　　　　Of October.

He falls silent again. Graubard crosses to the cage.

1st Guard. Do you need us, sir?

Graubard. No, you can go.

The Guards exit.

Hanau! Hanau!

Hanau. A trinity of shadows,
　　　　Answering to names
　　　　Assumed and thrown aside
　　　　At the dictation of events.
　　　　The struggle of the living nucleus
　　　　Against dead tissue.
　　　　That was it.

Graubard. Was, Hanau, was! The past tense.

Hanau. We plotted the course of unseen stars
　　　　 Across a stinking wilderness.
　　　　 Night was the enemy we fought
　　　　 In groups of three.
　　　　 Three who cheated death
　　　　 By simulating death;
　　　　 Three pairs of eyes
　　　　 Concealing vision
　　　　 Under the habits of the blind.
　　　　 Three minds that still know how to think
　　　　 Even when thought was outlawed.

He becomes silent again.

Graubard. Hanau, can you hear me?

Hanau. Rolf, will you vouch for him?
　　　　 Will you, Maria?
　　　　 Why was he brought here, then?

He sinks back and his speech becomes increasingly incoherent.

　　　　 One . . . two . . . three . . .
　　　　 The stable atom.
　　　　 Rolf . . . Anderson . . . Maria . . .
　　　　 One . . . two . . . three . . . four . . .

　　　　 Four is the extra proton.
　　　　 Seen his face but not
　　　　 The recognition which
　　　　 Is swift and yet
　　　　 And yet seen somewhere . . .

His words are lost in a low muttering.

Graubard. Destroy the enemy's lines of communication. That is a classic
axiom of war and the fact that this is a war of ideas fought on the battlefield
of your mind makes it none the less relevant. Yes, Hanau, your defence
was strong, perfectly co-ordinated, I'll grant you that, but it is broken
now, and your fortress is a ruin haunted by shadows. Later, you will
introduce me to these phantoms and we will interview them together.
Later . . . when you have returned from that strange and fascinating
region to which you have retreated. I shall be waiting for you at the border,
on your side of the border, so that we can discuss your experiences while
their impression is still vivid in your mind. The battle is almost finished,
my friend; it only remains for us to take the citadel and the best time for
storming the barricades is at the moment when night and morning are still
joined. If it were possible, I would stay and follow all the stages of your
journey, but my time is not my own. Today is the twenty-second of
December, the Day of National Deliverance; a pompous title I agree, but
then fools love pompousness and most people are such fools. Your refusal
to realise that was the cause of your downfall. It was your greatest

weakness, Hanau. Ah well, you won't have to listen to the Command-mant's speech, you have been spared that. You can rest assured, though, that our separation will not be prolonged. I'll be back before the applause has died away. Au revoir, and a safe return.

He goes out. The metallic tapping and the voice are heard again, quiet at first, but gathering volume and intensity.

**Voice of the
Prison.** Number Three! Number Three! Are you all right? Are you all right? Answer, Number Three! Are you all right?

There is a pause. Hanau groans and attempts to drag himself up into a sitting position.

Why don't you answer? Number Three . . . hold out! Hold out! Hold out, Number Three! We are with you! Hold out! Hold out!

The voice has been joined by other voices filling the night with whispers. Hanau is seized with a sudden spasm of fury. He grasps the bars of his cage and tries to shake them.

Hanau.   They have murdered light
           And nothing is left
           But a bloody butcher's axe!
           There is a conspiracy of shadows
           Plotting against the moon!
           Send a warning through
           The customary channels!
           Notify all cadres that
           Winter will not end this year.

Music, harsh and discordant. From out of the shadows behind the cage appear two men and a woman dancing in the rhythm of a slow march. Behind them appears a fourth dancer whose movements are more violent than the others. He attempts to confront the prisoner to whom he bears a strong resemblance, but is prevented by the trio. This sequence should have the quality of a dream, which indeed it is, the dancers being merely the creations of the prisoner's delirium. The fourth dancer, to whom, for the purpose of clarification we shall refer as Robert, is Hanau's projection of himself. The music ceases abruptly, leaving the dancers grouped in attitudes of antagonism to Robert, who makes a grotesque and mocking bow to the prisoner.

Maria!

The woman slowly turns to him without speaking.

No word of greeting?
Anderson? Rolf?

The two men turn and face him.

They said that you were dead!

Maria.   They say that you are damned!

Rolf.   Broken to the bit of treachery!

Anderson.
          They say that from now on you'll tread
          Only the beaten track, where you will stand,
          Bareheaded,
          With a yellow permit in your hand.

Rolf.   One of the patient ranks
          Of those who sell themselves
          For the bare expenses
          Of a counterfeit existence.

Hanau.   Who says such things?

Anderson.
          Voices in every street.

Rolf.   The sentries who guard the ultimate defences.

Maria.   Whispers resound like tolling bells
          In every channel of the underground.

Hanau.   No!

Maria.   Is it true?

Hanau.   Maria, you knew me well,
          We were together in the March days
          When the deluge was unleashed
          And all our world was covered
          By its foul waters.

Anderson.
Rolf (*together*)
          Is it true?

Hanau.   No! No!
          Am I to be murdered in duplicate,
          Once by my enemies and once by you?
          Here are voices that will speak for me,
          Mouths that will testify on my behalf.

He tears open his prison jacket, exposing wounds and burns upon his body.

          Tell those who whisper my damnation
          That you heard my flesh scream 'Liars! Liars!'
          Tell them I am an exposed nerve
          Throbbing in the world's teeth,
          That my body is a field of flowering wounds
          Or a tree that's twisted to a crooked cross
          On which my dreams are crucified.
          The croaking voices of my wounds
          Have begged for nothing except nothingness

> And in my extremity, my friends
> Have handed me the sponge of slander.
> Tell them I am no longer human
> But a void, a loathsome pit
> Where agony ferments
> And poisons every heart-beat
> With its rank exhalations.

Robert. Have you said everything?

Hanau. Is he another of my accusers?

Robert. I am an old friend of ours.

Hanau. (*To the others*) Do you know him?

Maria, Rolf and Anderson shake their heads.

> Why are you here?

Robert. Exile has been tedious.
It was time that I came home.

Hanau. Riddles!

Robert. To which you know the answers.

He addresses the others.

> I, too, have a message to deliver;
> Tell them that two of us are here,
> Hanau and Hanau's prisoner,
> And that salvation is in short supply.
> Say that there's only enough for one of us
> And that the one who wins it, wins it all
> And shifts the whole burden of damnation
> On to the other's shoulders.
> Tell them that!

The others slowly turn and begin to move towards the shadows from whence they came.

Hanau. Don't go! Maria! My friends!
There is no message but the one I gave you!

They look back and raise their arms in a sorrowful farewell.

Hanau. Stay, just a little! Wait!
This creature is no prisoner.
Look at his face!
His trade is written there on every feature.
He's an informer, a tame crow
That wears the stool bird's plumage.

They go; very softly, like a faint echo, is heard the noise of tapping and the prison's voice. 'Hold out! We are with you!'

Robert. No, Hanau!
They are not with us.
No one can follow us
Along the spiral staircase
Of our soul.

Hanau. Who sent you here?
Answer me!
Where are you from?

Robert. From the frontier
Which you dare not pass.

Hanau. I have crossed all the frontiers.

Robert. Think!

Hanau. I know them all.
May is the first frontier
With its banners of spring
And eager faces, and after May
July – the armoured wall
Which guards the boulevards
And the clearing-house in Père-Lachaise.

Robert. And beyond July?

Hanau. The eastward journey
To the last frontier,
October.

Robert. And there,
Each honest traveller
Renews his passport.
Looks around and checks
The details of his own identity.
Have you done that?

Hanau. I've paid full fare
For every mile I've travelled,
That is enough! The worms
Which guard the terminus
Will need no affidavits
To prove that I am theirs.

Robert. The terminus was not our destination.

Hanau. Our destination! Ours!

Robert. Ours! Yours and mine.

Hanau. So this is the line of attack
Decided on by Graubard!
I'm to have a fellow-traveller,

The Doctor's own creation,
One of his spare eyes,
An honest tradesman
Who, for a living wage,
Will undertake to make
A corpse yield information.
Tell me, does Graubard instruct all his spies
In metaphysics, or did you specialise,
Graduating first in simple murder?

Robert.   Why are you so afraid?

Hanau.   Afraid? Of what? Of you?

Robert.   Yes, of me.
Not of what you wish to think I am
But rather of who I am.

Hanau.   I am past all fear
Except the fear of fearing.

Robert.   You are afraid of silence
Because the voice of silence
Constantly repeats a fundamental question
Which, if your life and death are to achieve
Even a momentary significance,
Demands a truthful answer.
And in the course of answering
You may be forced to deal
The death-blow at your dreams
And see yourself completely stripped
Of all illusions, all supports, to find
That you are just a hollow shell
Left in the wake of an incurious wave
Upon a rotting beach.
It is because you are afraid
That you attempt to fill the void
With noisy speech and clamour,
For silence may bring sudden recognition
And the discovery of my identity
Would raise the question of your own,
Of proving that you are yourself
And not just one who's taken refuge
In a crowded fantasy because
He was constitutionally unfitted
To live at the same time as himself.

Hanau.   Who are you?

Robert.   My name is Hanau, Robert Hanau!
I am yourself.

Phrase of music. Hanau begins to laugh. The tapping on the pipes is heard.
Suddenly, Hanau stops laughing and begins to talk with exaggerated calm.

Hanau.   This is a dream, a crazy dream,
          The product of the madness prison breeds.
          Dreams grow like fungi in the dark,
          Needing no special season for their seeds.
          You are myself, it's true, for I created you
          And I can banish you again as easily.
          I am myself and master of myself;
          If I exert my reason, swim against the stream
          Of my delirium, you'll disappear.

Robert.   Fear is your stimulus, not reason.

Hanau.   Would I myself preach treason to myself?
          You are a symptom of confinement
          Like sleeplessness or loss of appetite,
          No more significant than that
          Grey pallor which is common to us all.

Robert.   There is a difference:
          I have the power of speech.

Hanau.   This is a world of voices,
          Every minute is articulate,
          Every shadow has its blabbing tongue,
          Even the bars have mouths.
          Since the first day I was buried here
          I have kept a careful check upon the signs
          Which mark the progress of decay.
          At first there was the voice, sudden, remote,
          Ceasing abruptly on the unformed word,
          Leaving a hollow where the silence swirled
          And eddied, drowning me, causing me to panic
          In the unclean flux of fear and doubt,
          A doubt inhibiting all other thought;
          But I fought the doubt with reason,
          Argued that speech is a necessary habit,
          Part of the complex process
          Of the mind's co-ordination;
          And rationalisation of my doubt
          Destroyed my fear. For if a man here
          Continues to explain the causes
          Of his minor aberrations,
          Then that man's sanity is sound.
          You are an aberration,
          A phantom, inhabiting my brain,

Whose function is to play companion
On the journey out of pain
Which follows each interrogation.
It always happens.
It's a form of compensation,
An aspect of the subtle defence-mechanism
With which the mind protects itself
From what the body must endure.
Once, as they beat me on the genitals,
I found myself preoccupied with time,
Worried because I'd lost count of the days,
Obsessed with the thought that I couldn't be sure
Whether the day was Saturday or not.
As if it mattered! For pain is timeless.

He laughs and then continues.

It is all time
But not all space.
That is what they cannot realise.
For when my body lies broken in their hands
My mind escapes the foul abyss of pain
And stands and watches.
Even when my ears are full of screams
And each small cell erupts in agony
There is part of me which stands outside
And reasons . . . reasons! . . . reasons!

Robert. I am that part,
The divided self.

Hanau. You are a dream.
I am reality.

Robert. Where did you acquire the habit
Of making such fine distinctions?
Reality is what is,
Not just what we accept.
If I'm unreal because I am a dream
Then all your thinking is unreal too,
For dreams are just as real as thoughts
Conceived as they are in the same womb
And fathered by the same experience.

Hanau. Leave me! I am exhausted.
I can talk no more.

Robert. Then I will talk and you can listen.

Hanau. Why do you torture me?

Robert. Why have you condemned us both to death?

Hanau. The decision was not mine.

Robert. They offered an alternative.

Hanau. To live on their terms
Would be less than life
And more than death.
Every breath would be a knife
Hacking at my self-respect.
Better to die once and be forgotten
Than to die a thousand times a day,
Murdered by memories, perpetually
Wounded by men's eyes, a symbol
Of contempt and lies, a rank, dead weed
Whose dry, marcescent leaves deceived no one
But reminded all of how the root was poisoned.

Robert. My question is unanswered:
Why are we to die?
For what reason?

Hanau. Because of my belief in truth.

Robert. Men have been known to die
For faith even when the basis
Of faith had crumbled
And disappeared.
Such men are like snakes
That cannot shed their skin.
Belief is sometimes the result
Of empirical knowledge but often
It is a sign of mental cowardice
Or self-inflicted blindness.

Hanau. And yet men die for it.

Robert. Men die for many reasons,
Few of which are laudable.
They die for words – or rather for
The sound of words – hypnotic
Echoes of the voices of the dead
Which fill their ears with loud commands
To come and join the band.
Some die of laziness;
Living demands much effort and much skill;

It is easier to die, to kill and be killed,
Less painful than facing the final truth
About themselves. Vanity also
Claims a high percentage of the martyrs,
Those who sell their lives for approbation
And die because their friends expect them to,
Lacking the strength of mind to oppose
The wishes of the most casual acquaintance.

Hanau. Your wish to live at any cost
Makes you contemptible.
You would reduce all life
To such a mediocre level
That by comparison
The instinct to survive
Would assume the proportions
Of an act of heroism.

Robert. Is it less heroic than
The instinct to escape from life through death?

Hanau. Yes! Yes!

Robert. And that is the fine belief we die for!

Hanau. I believe in life.

Robert. Only when it's tamed and wearing harness.

Hanau. I believe in man.

Robert. But not in men.

Hanau. I believe in the free mind
With its infinite capacity
For extending life,
In the flowering consciousness
Which can encompass all reality.

Robert. The mind which puts your body in a cage?

Hanau. The mind which holds the seed
Of all potential energy;
The starting-point and field
Of endless chain-reactions which can make
All things possible, even rejection
Of a familiar world of social anarchy
For an unknown universe
Where the mind will have to leap
Instead of crawling as it now does.
I believe in man's ability
And his intention to create

A social mechanism which will be
So perfect and so unobtrusive that
Man will have time to achieve humanity;
And living will assume such complex and
Such varied forms that men who look back
Will see us as symbols of abortive growth,
Crude products of a crude machine.

Robert. That *was* your creed.

Hanau. That *is* my creed.

Robert.   And has your life run parallel
To your beliefs?
Suppose, for the sake of argument,
Your death should merely contribute
To that appalling waste of life
To which you are opposed. Suppose
Your dreams were merely symptoms of
A terrible neurosis which
Produced an epinastic growth,
Distorting life. Suppose that those
Whom you describe as enemies
Were really the only healthy ones
And that the host was sick because
Bacteria was waging war
Within the blood. Can you be sure
That your refusal to accept
Life as it is is not a proof
Of some deficiency in you?

Hanau.   The words are yours,
The arguments are Graubard's.

Robert.   What difference does it make?
Is your acceptance of a truth
Conditioned by who speaks it?

Hanau.   These apologetics are not truth.

Robert.   Have you never felt doubts
Or questioned your beliefs,
Weighed your illusion on the scales,
Or measured faith against experience?
Fear of doubt is doubt
In its acutest form.
It cripples the mind,
Burdens it with guilt,
Implies that the fabric of belief
Has worn too thin to bear the weight of truth.

Hanau. I have settled with my doubts.
In the light of analysis they disappear.

Robert. And yet there are men of judgement,
Men of undisputed courage
Who, on looking inward, saw
Their solid faith evaporate
Like so much mist. They were your friends
And suffered what you suffered,
Fought where you fought, starved,
Knew exile, poverty, humiliation;
But now they stand opposed, hostile
To the cause for which they sacrificed.
Can you explain the reason?

Hanau. Every battle has its casualties.
Only the strongest can survive.

Robert. Oh, let us finish with these platitudes!
Can you not see that the battle is lost,
That it is always lost, that defeat is implicit
In the nature of the dream? Admit it, man!
Your dream is broken by reality,
Consign the fragments to the attic
Where they can lie forgotten,
Toys to instruct a childish fantasy.
Remove the bandage from your eyes,
Scrutinise your cause,
Look revolution in the face.
Is its beauty unimpaired?
Is that the same fair mistress
That seduced your youth?
Is what you see the subtle instrument
Of history, the alchemical device
For changing dreams into reality?
Or is it a primitive machine
Which dominates its engineers?
Yours is not the only cause
That men have died for,
And gone on dying for,
Long after the cause had lost its meaning.
Each age imagines that it has produced
The perfect solution of all the problems.
And yet life doesn't change,
In its essentials it remains the same.
The seasons come and go,
With a show of flowers and snow
And beneficial rains.
The seas accept the gifts

That rivers bring from plains
And dying mountains.
Nothing is changed.
Men live and procreate
And the wise ones take
The kisses which life offers
Without requiring proofs
Of her virginity.
Hanau, it's not too late
For us to salvage what remains
Of time and life.
One word to Graubard . . .

Hanau. No!
The price is too high.

Robert. The price of freedom cannot be too high.

Hanau. Freedom!

Robert. Yes, freedom! Not the illusion
But the thing itself.

Hanau. Freedom from what? From self-respect?

Robert. From all unnecessary thought,
From dogmas, duties, rules,
From self-imposed responsibility.
Just let the mind be free of such restraint
And it becomes as buoyant as a bird,
Choosing its element to suit its mood.

Hanau. More like a carrion crow that picks the eyes
Out of a murdered conscience.

Robert. All my life I have been led
By that relentless part of you
Which dreams an iron dream.
Now I am asking for my liberty.

Hanau. I am weary of this argument.

Robert. Do not cover your face with the shroud,
Nor close your eyes,
Nor seek the company of shadows.
We can trample upon death
As the swan tramples upon the water
Or the horse upon the plain.
I want to show you a life like a swallow's flight,
Effortless, full of grace.
There is no virtue in the renunciation
Of life and the taste of her mouth.
Help me to escape the heavy burden

> Which you have put upon me
> And my freedom will win peace for both of us.

Hanau. Why do I listen to this voice?
And yet – what if the dream were false?

Faint music.

Robert. (*Ecstatically*) Listen! (*He stands tense and expectant.*)

The earth sings.

The music becomes fuller.

> Keen blade of music swings through silence.
> The sleeping spring awakes,
> Opens the shutters of the darkness,
> Breaks the long winter.
> This is resurrection!

Percussion, loud and triumphant. The light in the cage lessens. Pools of coloured light form in the region outside the cage. Three girls leap from behind the rim of the darkness. One wears a dress of white, another a green dress and the third a dress of crimson. Robert leaps towards them and dances from one to the other. The music changes, becomes lyrical. The Moon enters dancing, a flaxen-haired girl in a silver dress, a blue hyacinth in her hand. On seeing her, Robert becomes perfectly still. The stage is suffused with blue light.

Robert. She has broken the cloud's net.
My heart sings after her,
Not the brown gull is she,
Not the blue tern
But the white seal on the black wave.

He attempts to approach her but constantly finds himself confronted by the other dancers.

White Girl. (*Confronting him*)
She is not the glad song
Nor the heart's music,
But the lost echo of a dead voice.

They dance.

Green Girl. (*Confronting him*)
She is not the rose,
Nor the carnation,
But the wax-lily without odour.

They dance.

Crimson Girl. (*Confronting him*)
She is not the warm flesh,
Nor the quick blood,
But the bone the wind polished.

Robert. Let me pass!

He reaches her and they dance together, but without touching, in rapt concentration. The other three come together and dance as a group on a fixed spot, following the rhythm with the upper halves of their bodies.

Robert. What lies beyond the horizons of your eyes?

Chorus. No fire,
No gift,
No final landscape.
Only ashes,
And the promise unfulfilled,
Only the desolate night.

Robert. Teach me the words of the song you sing
When the year trembles on the edge of spring.

Chorus. No song,
No voice,
No whispered answer.
Only echoes
And the silence after
The last reverberation;
Only the question.

Robert. Must I go on alone upon the quest
Never knowing the taste of your mouth,
Forgetting the lustre of your hair,
And the milky cluster shining there,
And the jewel of Sirius lying on your breast?

Chorus. The quest is a journey between heart-beats,
A voyage on the river of the blood.
There is no goal, only the journey,
There is no end, only the means.
There is no answer, only perpetual renewal
Of the question and the one who questions.

Robert attempts to embrace the Moon but she eludes him.

Robert. Go then! Be chaste and barren.
No, not chaste! Merely indifferent.
I have regained my sight!
I see you clearly now, a white-faced whore
Who walks the beat of darkness
Soliciting men's dreams,
Sowing infection in the crystal night.
Leave me! I'll sleep no more,
Nor strive to scale the rock of shadows
With its inaccessible pinnacle of dream.

The Moon glides off and the light fades.

The time of preparation is behind me.

The music changes. A simple, childish theme is introduced but still in dance tempo, rather like the 'Henry Martin' theme in Mahler's First Symphony. The three girls dance towards Robert. He seizes the girl in white and dances with her.

Can you answer riddles?

White Girl. I can only ask them.

Robert. Tell me your name.

White Girl. I have no name.

Robert. What are you then?

White Girl. A voyager on the wave's crest.

Robert. You too?
Would my hands falter in their praise
If I touched your sleeping breasts?

White Girl. The web of your hands would bruise my heart.

Robert. You are trembling.

White Girl.
With joy, with fear!
Oh, what is this I feel?

Robert. Time vibrates like a plucked string.

White Girl.
It is shrill in the ears.

Robert. The earth opens.
Jump!

White Girl.
Not yet!
Let me sleep a little longer.
Your quest has just begun.

Robert. The quest!
You know about the quest?
Who told you?

White Girl.
I read it in your eyes.

Robert. And what is the object of my quest?

White Girl.
The song unsung,
The rose unopened.

Robert. Who am I? Can you tell me that?

White Girl.
> The welcome thief,
> The destroyer who heals by wounding.
> You are the dream who comes when he is beckoned.

Robert suddenly backs away from her.

Robert. A dream?

White Girl. Yes?

Robert. Your dream?

White Girl. My dream, the prisoner of my sleep.

Robert. You're lying!
> I have turned my back on sleep.
> You are the thief, not I!
> I am myself and master of myself!

Hanau laughs in delirium.

Hanau. Four paces and the bars.
> Four paces and the cage
> And between each pace the heartbeat.

He laughs again but the music swells up and covers the sound. The girl in white dances away from Robert. The other two dancers move towards him. He dances with the girl in green.

Robert. Who are you?

Green Girl. One who waits at the crossroads.

Robert. Why do you wait?

Green Girl. For a stranger who will pass this way.

Robert. Are you sure he will pass?

Green Girl. There is no other way.

Robert. What is your name?

Green Girl. Until the stranger comes I have no name. When he has passed, a child will christen me.

Robert. When will he come?

Green Girl. In the spring, when death renews itself.

Robert. And how will you recognise this stranger?

Green Girl. He will come bowed under a great burden.

Robert. I wonder if his burden will be as heavy as mine.

Green Girl. It is my burden, not his. He only carries it until I'm ready. I am ready now.

Robert. And you will carry it alone?

Green Girl. Life is too heavy to be borne alone.

Robert. And yet it must be borne.

Green Girl. But not by us, always by the one who comes after – always by him.

Robert stands silent for a moment, facing the girl.

Robert. Do you know who I am?

Green Girl. Yes, I know.

Robert. Who?

Green Girl. You are the father of my unborn child.

Robert thrusts her away from him.

Robert. No! I'll not relinquish my identity. Was I born to play porter to your needs?

Green Girl. You can be rid of the burden, you can rest.

Robert. So I'm to lie in your body's tomb and wait for death! I'm to abandon the quest before it has begun!

Green Girl. My body is the guarantee of the quest's continuity.

Robert. But I am more than your body's instrument. I am a man, not an abstraction – neither a young girl's dream nor a woman's appetite. I am a free traveller and my burden is my own.

Music. The girl in green retreats. The crimson girl comes forward and dances alone. Robert attempts to escape but is always drawn back to her, like a moth drawn to a candle's flame.

Robert.
>Red is the colour of hunger.

Crimson Girl.
>Red is the colour of the harvest moon.

Robert.
>My hunger was born in the moon of mists,
>The white moon of March put an edge on it,
>Fashioned it into a keen, cold blade.

Crimson Girl.
>Dead is the blade without blood on it.
>Put a handle on the blade of hunger,
>Let it swing through the corn.

Robert. Why?

Crimson Girl. I like to hear it sing.

They dance together. The white girl and the green girl dance on a fixed spot and speak in chorus.

Chorus. She will have flesh.
In the morning,
At noon,
In the whispered night.
The delicate loin,
The tender undercut
The bishop in the blue mitre.
She will have that.
She will have that.

Robert and the girl in the crimson dress dance off. The light outside the cage fades. The two remaining girls retreat into the shadows. Hanau groans and the interior of the cage is illuminated again. Very softly, at first, the metallic tapping begins, grows louder. Voices are heard, filling the world of Hanau's nightmare.

Voice of the Prison.
Hold out! Hold out!
You are sick but the night is dying.
Hold out! Hold out!

Music.

Can you hear? Can you hear?
It is the song of the wall
And the voice is the voice of history.

Hanau. History has no voice,
No eyes, no ears,
No memory,
No anything.
Only prisons and prisons and prisons
Without end.

Voice of the Prison.
Do not break
Nor reject the prize,
Nor forsake the ranks
Of those who walk behind us
With the sunlight in their eyes.

Hanau. (*Shrieking*) Hanau is dead!
They murdered him with voices!

Music.

Voice of the Prison.
Earth stirs and the wind sings.
Roses bloom in the barrels of the guns.

The faint sound of marching feet is heard behind the music.

Hanau. Stragglers stumble, fall –
    The moving columns cannot wait.
    I have fallen to the wolves.

Voice of the Prison.
    Your body is theirs.
    Your death belongs to us.

Hanau. Robert? Robert?
    You dead man's shadow!
    Why did I learn your language of the blood?

The metallic tapping fades out. The music changes. Simultaneously the light inside the cage is dimmed and the curtain concealing the raised plane on stage-right is drawn. Almost the entire area of the plane is occupied by a great bed over which is spread a shimmering black coverlet. The girl in crimson is discovered asleep, her arms outstretched. Robert stands by the bed looking down at her. When he moves it is with the slowness of a man in a dream. Far away, in the distance, a trumpet sounds. Robert raises his head and listens.

Robert. It has a familiar sound.

The trumpet sounds again, slightly nearer. Robert takes a step away from the bed and then stops.

No, I will not leave this room. The journey is finished . . . finished. Here, in a moment of forgetfulness, I found myself, knew, for one brief instant, death and immortality and the sweet pain of birth.

He looks at his hands as if seeing them for the first time.

Skin instead of feathers, flesh where there was light . . . and yet I learned to fly like any bird across a night of immeasurable distance. How pale and cold the sun is compared with the fiery beacon of the body's joy.

He approaches the sleeping girl.

Sleep robs me of her love – or is it my wakefulness that makes her so inaccesible?

He kisses her lightly.

My love.

Crimson Girl. The tide will carry us.

Robert. Open your eyes.

Crimson Girl. Yes . . .

Robert. It's morning.

Crimson Girl. Oh, not yet.

Robert. It scrapes at the window like a hungry cat.

Crimson Girl. Send it away.

Robert. Do you remember . . .

Crimson Girl. Put your arms round me.

The trumpet sounds again, nearer.

Robert. There it is again. Did you hear it?

Crimson Girl. I didn't hear anything.

Robert. A sound like a knife tearing through the fabric of a dream.

Crimson Girl. You imagined it. Come, lie by my side. Sleep. Rest.

Robert. Yes . . . yes . . . to sleep enfolded in your body's warmth. Only that is real. And yet . . .

Crimson Girl. You are troubled.

Robert. I feel as if there were a bird imprisoned in my breast and it was trying to escape. The beating of its wings is shaking me.

Crimson Girl. I will open the door of the cage.

Robert draws back quickly.

Robert. What did you say?

Crimson Girl. Love, what is it?

Robert. I thought . . .

Crimson Girl. You have awakened too early.

She kisses him.

Robert. If only . . .

Crimson Girl. If only what?

Robert. Tell me who you are.

Crimson Girl. But you know.

Robert. Last night I knew – or thought I knew – but now . . . Your beauty is a secret thing – it places you beyond my reach, makes you so complete, so perfect, so unapproachable.

Crimson Girl. Unapproachable? I?

Robert. If only I could see beyond the barrier of skin and flesh and tissue. No, to see is not enough. I want to be that little pulse which trembles in your throat.

Crimson Girl. Oh, my love!

Robert. Will the moment of recognition ever come again?

Crimson Girl. It is ours forever.

Robert. No, it comes like a flash of lightning, then it's gone. It passes on a tide of sleep. Oh, it was criminal to sleep.

Crimson Girl. It was beautiful, warm . . .

Robert. It's strange that you didn't ask my name.

Crimson Girl. There was no need to ask. The moment I saw you I recognised you.

Robert. You did?

Crimson Girl. Of course.

Robert. Why 'of course'?

Crimson Girl. I had been waiting for you.

Robert. Waiting for me? But . . . tell me, who do you think I am?

Crimson Girl. I don't think – I know.

Robert. Who am I?

Crimson Girl. You are mine.

Robert thrusts her from him.

Robert. No! You fool! You fool!

Crimson Girl. Oh, love . . .

Robert. You have murdered love! I belong to no one but myself.

Crimson Girl. But I only wanted . . .

Robert. You wanted to take me prisoner, put out my eyes and have me live in a cage. You wanted a tame bird who would sing at your command. But you've failed! The snare is empty. I am still free!

Crimson Girl. Oh, do not leave me!

The trumpet sounds, loud and clear.

Robert. I remember now! The quest!

Crimson Girl. Stay a little longer!

Robert. And lose my inheritance?

He leaps off the raised plane on to the stage. Music. The light fades on the crimson girl. The curtain falls across the plane. The Moon, the girl in white and the girl in green appear out of the shadows. They dance round Robert, hemming him in. This episode should have the quality of a children's singing game.

Chorus.   You cannot escape.
                The quest is a stage
                In the journey between
                The bars of the cage.

Music.

> Twist and turn,
> Round about,
> The cage is sealed
> You can't get out.

Music.

> Twist and turn
> Turn and spin,
> The bars are strong
> And you are in.

Music.

> Spin and twist
> Twist and turn,
> Go from us
> But you'll return.

The music which accompanies the above sequence cross-fades with a slow theme. The crimson girl enters dancing with Graubard. She is heavy with child. The chorus fall away from Robert and breathe a great sigh.

> Aa . . . a . . . a . . . ah . . .
> Our sister has crossed tomorrow morning.
> Aa . . . a . . . a . . . ah.

Robert take a step towards the dancers, then recoils.

Robert. Ho! my bloodied mare of night,
> Who rides thee now?
> Who makes thee prance across the water?
> Who touches thy flanks with spurs of ivory?
> Who bridles thee with diamond bit?
> Ho! my chestnut mare,
> You carry a dead man in the saddle,
> A bladder of wind.

Crimson Girl.
> It could have been your child.

Graubard.
> Come!

They dance off.

Robert. Does life consist of nothing but a choice between different forms of bondage? What am I searching for?

Chorus. For rest,
> For peace,
> Escape from the ceaseless quest.

Robert. Is there no blessed regime,
No fertile valley,
No green oasis,
Lying between
The stony ridge of living
And the gulf of sleep?

Chorus. There is a valley between the breasts
Where bliss is.
There is a healing well of kisses,
In the loved one's eyes
A blessed region lies,
In the arms' embraces
In the green oasis.

They approach him with gestures of supplication.

Robert. You sing with the voices of nightingales but your dreams are ravens on the wing for carrion.

White Girl. My lips are a cure for thirst.

Robert. They are camouflage for teeth: white, sharp teeth that would gnaw my soul to shreds.

Green Girl. My hands could teach your body how to sing.

Robert. They are tipped with iron claws.

The trumpet sounds, far away.

Chorus. Words bruise,
Love sighs,
The mind is blind,
The blood is wise.
Sleep is kind,
The spirit tries
In vain to gain
The world which lies
Beyond the bars.
The stars are far away
But love is near.

The music reaches a climax. Robert, retreating before the advancing chorus, finds himself against the cage. He covers his ears with his hands to shut out the intolerable sound of the shrill violins. The trumpet sounds again, nearer. Hanau begins to laugh. The music fades. The chorus avert their faces from the cage and slowly leave the stage.

Robert. Hanau!

The laughter ceases abruptly.

Hanau!

Hanau draws himself up into a sitting position.

Hanau. You!

Robert. Yes.

Hanau. Well?

Robert. You were laughing in your sleep.

Hanau. I was dreaming,
I thought that I was free
And you were in this cage.

Robert. A strange dream.

Hanau. Why have you returned?

Robert. To rest a little.

Hanau. Have you tired of freedom then?

Robert. I am tired of chasing its shadow.
I am sick of the weight of my body.

Hanau. This is rank blasphemy from you.

Robert. My body is a tethered goat,
An appetite with horns,
A slave condemned to tread
The dwindling circle of its own hot lust.
Round and round it goes
Until it stands, helpless at last,
Held fast against the post,
Incapable of any movement
Except the awkward turn
Which marks the repetition
Of the senseless journey.

Hanau laughs.

Hanau. And this is your great discovery!
You can trample upon death
As the swan tramples upon the water!
Or so you said, but instead
You have trampled upon life
And made as much impression
As the snail which tramples the bare stone.
You wanted freedom!
Not the illusion but the thing itself;
Freedom from dreams, from rules,
From self-imposed responsibility.

Robert. The quintessence of freedom.

Hanau. The quintessence of death.

Robert. I will find it yet.

Hanau. Only in the grave.

Robert. I will discard my body,
Forswear all action,
Except the action of the mind,
For the mind has neither weight nor mass,
Only motion.
I will go among the mountain peaks
Where the air is rarefied
And the blind lichens feed on time.
I will climb a pinnacle of abstract thought
And there on the summit
Build a laboratory where
I will distil pure Knowledge,
Reducing it until I find
A perfect crystal of reality.

Hanau. And how will you use this knowledge?

Robert. Use it? Why should I use it?
To possess it is enough.

Hanau. In isolation?

Robert. Why should I force a vintage wine
On men who are satisfied with water?

The trumpet sounds.

Hanau. There is not much time left.

Robert. Are you sending me away?

Hanau. Yes . . . yes . . .
There are doubts to be resolved,
Questions to be answered . . .
Is there another way out of the night . . .

His voice is drowned in a great surge of music. The curtain, concealing the raised plane stage-left of the cage is drawn, revealing Graubard seated on a glass throne. He wears white overalls patterned with eyes. In his right hand he holds a human skull and in the other a large hypodermic syringe. At his feet kneels a girl in the uniform of a nurse. The insane enter, dancing on the stage below. There are four men and two women and they wear grey, loosely fitting shirts and grey trousers or skirts. Their number includes an architect with delusions of grandeur, a young labourer with persecution mania, an old man with catatonic schizophrenia, an old woman with euphoria and a young woman with peace-mania. Suddenly, Graubard raps on the skull. The dancers freeze. He touches the nurse's head with the syringe as though knighting her.

Graubard. Arise, our best-beloved subject. Serve us well and see that none disturb the peace and quiet of our realm.

Nurse. Amen. (*She takes the syringe.*)

Graubard.
Bid the dawn approach.
We are ready to assume
The cares and burdens
Of our daily office.

Fanfare of trumpets.

Nurse. Yes, my lord.

Graubard. And the doors?

Nurse. All bolted, my lord.

Graubard (*To the architect*) Hey! Caitiff, varlet, rogue, vassel, serf, wretch, miscreant, scullion, rascal!

Architect. Who, me?

Graubard.
Aye, thee!
Hast had any dreams of late?

Architect.
Last night I dreamt the past was dead
And all the people of the world
Had gathered to attend the funeral.

Graubard. (*To the nurse*)
Be thou my scribe, my cunny thou,
And let the purport of the prisoner's words
Be taken down and used as evidence.

He hands her a notebook. Meanwhile the young labourer has begun to sway backwards and forwards like a man wrestling with invisible chains. Suddenly he takes a tremendous leap into the air.

Labourer. (*Triumphantly*) Pawn to King's square.

The nurse directs the nozzle of the syringe at him and sprays him with water. The tension leaves his body, he slowly sinks to the ground and assumes the foetal position. Graubard leaps to his feet and begins to rant like a barker in a side-show.

Graubard. A prize for the little lady! 'Ere y' are! 'Ere y' are! Four for six! Four for six! Hit 'em on the top to win. You can't afford to miss! (*He sits down again and addresses the architect.*) Dids't say a funeral?

Architect. A funeral.

Graubard. Thou art morbid.

Architect.
> It was no melancholy spectacle:
> Men sang for joy and women danced
> As they accompanied the corpse
> On its last journey through the streets
> Of the perfect town which I had built.

Young Woman.
> If it is lost forever,
> Then I am lost.

She approaches the old man, who stands perfectly still, looking at the ground.

> What have they done with peace?
> Where have they hidden it?
> You are old and must know many things.

Graubard.
> Quiet, wench! Restrain thyself!
> Curb thy depraved appetite.
> Wouldst have bismuth?
> Wouldst have insulin?

Young Woman. No . . . no . . . no . . .

She cowers away from the old man.

Graubard. (*To the architect*) Proceed!

Architect.
> At last the cortège reached the city walls
> Where, ready to receive the grisly corpse,
> A tall, unfinished campanile stood
> Still wrapped in scaffolding. And there
> A score or so of masons were engaged
> In carving figurines and bas-relief
> To decorate the raised entablature.
> An artist more proficient than the rest,
> An old man, sick with memory, in whom
> Imagination had become diseased
> Fashioned a mask, the image of your face
> To be the centre of a monstrous group
> Of gargoyles.
> But scarcely had he finished carving it
> When the stone was seized with sudden nausea,
> The walls began to vomit powdered quartz,
> A spasm of convulsions rocked the tower
> Which tossed upon the writhing pilasters,
> The bending transoms parted from the walls,
> Leapt into the air and in an instant
> Nothing remained of the great catafalque
> Except a heap of dust and rubble,

Which soon was scattered by the cleansing wind.
The past was dead and memory was dead
And in that moment, time was born again.

Graubard. By St Freud! Thou art a pert, persistent paranoic. But I'll cure thee yet! We are inured to men's ingratitude and heed it not.

Architect. Ingratitude? Why should I be grateful?

Graubard. Did we not offer sanctuary to thee when thou wast sore beset by cares and troubles? Did we not offer thee a quiet retreat from the clash and turmoil of an embattled world? Look around thee, caitiff, and see if thou wantest aught. Dost want for food or raiment, a bed to sleep in or a roof to shelter thee? Nay! Thou hast everything that most men toil for. Ay, and time to think, to ponder life's incalculable problems. Here, we have built for thee a private world with all the civilised amenities and none of life's responsibilities. Here thou canst live in idleness tended by fair damsels in a world without collision. And still thou art not satisfied. Thou needs must dream and share thy dreams.

Robert slowly approaches Graubard.

Robert. Excuse me . . .

The insane advance upon him eagerly.

Insane. What news? What news? What news?

Architect. Has the edifice collapsed?

Young Woman. What have they done with peace?

Labourer. Are the pieces threatened?

Old Man. What is the meaning of meaning?

Insane. What news of the sleepers?

Graubard. (*Jumping to his feet*) Avaunt! Avaunt, thou carrion, or by the blood of St Adler I'll stop thy sweet pudding at lunch.

The insane fall away from Robert, whimpering.

Now, sirrah, speak! What meanest thou by intruding on us thus?

Robert. I am looking for a refuge, A sanctuary for meditation.

Graubard. Art a sage? Art a philosophical fellow? Dost dream?

Robert. No, I have turned my back on dreams.

Graubard. Then this is no place for thee. None but dreamers are accommodated here. Thy place is in the city of the plain.

Robert. I have searched there
And all I found was shadows.

Graubard. What art thou searching for?

Robert. For freedom, truth.

Graubard. Freedom? Truth? Thou art obsessed. Oh, thou art sick . . . Dost alternate between despair and ecstasy?

Robert. I have known both.

Graubard. A schizophrenic! I'll take my oath on't! He hath a pale and hungry look. He feels too much. Such men are dangerous.

Nurse. My lord, we have expected the arrival of this man.

Robert. Expected me? Impossible!

Nurse. I have his case-history here.

Graubard. Read it.

The nurse reads from the notebook.

Nurse. Name: Robert Hanau. Sex: male. Profession: man. Condition: malcontent. Description: Head, one; torso, one; limbs, four. Blood, skin, bone-tissue, nervous system central, nervous system sympathetic, endocrine system, etcetera. Distinguishing marks: acromegalous reasoning powers. Prognosis: sudden death. Diagnosis: fragmented mind, schizophrenia, hebephrenia, psycho-neurosis, psychopathic condition, paranoia, erotomania, etcetera. Symptoms: mania, phobia, delusional, confusional, obsessional, hallucinate. Tendency towards violence. Very dangerous.

Graubard. Dost thou admit the charges?

Robert. I admit nothing.

Graubard. Put him to the question! Pentethol!

He claps his hands. The other patients leap upon Robert and drag him towards Graubard.

Insane. Forgive us. We know not what we do.

The nurse sprays Robert with the syringe. The insane fall away from him. Music. The light changes, becomes dimmer. Robert staggers about the stage. The insane huddle together and speak in chorus in rhythm with his footsteps.

> One, two, three, four,
> Four paces and the bars.
> One, two, three, four,
> Four paces and the cage.
> One pace, one heartbeat,
> One pace, one heartbeat,
> One pace, one heartbeat.
> Four paces, one breath,
> Four paces, one breath,
> Four paces, one breath.

One breath, one life.
One cage, one life,
One cage, one death.
One breath, one life,
One cage, one death.

Hanau. (*Screaming*) Robert!

The music stops. Robert comes to a halt and stands facing Graubard. The light has faded so that now only Robert and the skull in Graubard's hand are illuminated. The rest are just amorphous clots of shadows. A drum begins to beat in a slow, steady rhythm.

Nurse. Take a deep breath. Relax. This won't hurt.

Mic. Voice.
Deep breath. Deep breath. Deep breath. Deep breath.

Nurse. Aina, peina, para, peddera, pimp, ithy, mithy, owera, lowera, dig, ain-a-dig, pein-a-dig, par-a-dig, peddera-dig, bumfit, ain-a-bumfit, pein-a-bumfit, par-a-bumfit, peddera-bumfit, giggy . . . out.

Mic. Chorus. You're out! You're out! You're out. Out! Out! Out! Out! Out! Out! Out!

The insane hiss. Graubard raps on the skull.

Graubard. Wilt swore to spike the ruth, the bold ruth and butting but the ruth?

Robert. I will.

Graubard. Twelfth man and true-blue are near to steer the dead events.

Insane. Now is the tomb of all dead men so run to the blade of the party.

Graubard. Violence in port!

Mic. Chorus. Tick-tock! Tick-tock! Tick-tock! Tick-tock!

Graubard. Thou are abused of being a devoded man, of soaking to effect undesirable and fundamenial changes inter social larder. Beerover thoo hast pants-pressed the litter of the Beaverly lore which sues a subject of the state cannote fush for thrut in Static waters widoubt a spermit, farm, herstiffibate or lessence. Aleso, yow hast with Alice, a whore bought, maid sindray efforts to Walter the moaning of ruality. Dost oddman the charges?

Robert. I do.

Graubard. Hast anything to pay differ I pronoun syntax against thee?

Robert. Nothing.

Graubard. Then thou art conflicted and condamned. I phoned thee guilty, double one double one.

Nurse. Allelulia!

The insane clap their hands three times. The light changes.

Graubard. Thou art now officially enrolled as a citizen of this secluded realm and here thou wilt reside until successive insulin assaults have breached thy madness.

Robert. I am not mad.

Insane. We are not mad.

Graubard. Oh, but thou *art*, infectiously and dangerously mad. All thought pursued beyond a certain limit is a form of madness. If thought were naught but what it seems, then it were nothing. If it were self-sufficient then 'twould be a toy to while away an idle hour, but no! Thought must needs extend itself in action and therefore must be dammed up at the source. Look round upon thy fellows and see if they are not mad. Observe that withered crone who stands behind thee. See how she smiles and smiles and smiles, her gaze intent upon her secret thoughts. What is it makes her smile? Some meditated crime against the state, some flaw in man that only she can see? I tell thee, whatsoever be the cause of her euphoria, the effect is dangerous, for that perpetual, mocking smile would destroy the basic *fear* on which all laws and institutions here are founded.

The young labourer leaps into the centre of the stage.

Labourer. The Knight is finished, taken en-passant!

Insane. Ah!

Graubard. This wretch hath persecution mania. He doth imagine he is a pawn and that I, his benefactor, have ordained that he should occupy an unimportant square upon the board. If this were the full extent of his strange malady, he would be harmless, but he must constantly incite the other pawns to clear the board of more important pieces.

The young labourer begins to march and countermarch across the stage.

Insane. One, two, three, four,
King's Pawn to King four.

Labourer. Advance, pawns! Double file!

Insane. Five, six, seven, eight,
Pawn queens. Checkmate!

The labourer jumps on to Graubard's plane. The nurse sprays him with water and he falls on to the stage.

Graubard. Could he but learn the rules of the game, he would be cured, just as yonder wench there would be cured if she'd accept her biological responsibilities. Hey, wench, approach and be acquainted with a friend!

The young woman backs away from Robert.

Young Woman.
>I will not bear your child,
>Nor any man's.
>I will not carry the seed of death.
>What have they done with peace?
>Where have they hidden it?

She moves around, peering into the shadows.

>So many dead in the world,
>So many dying . . .
>I'll breed no more,
>My body is sealed.

Robert steps towards her.

>No, do not touch me!
>It is the sowing time
>And I am fertile.
>If you touch me
>I will conceive murders,
>Bear a litter of skulls.

Architect.
>Golgotha was built of skulls,
>Paris and Byzantium.
>Colchis was built on a fever-swamp
>And Nineveh was plagued by flies
>That swarmed in Tigris River.
>Bone and blood built Troy town,
>But the blood was green
>And men were poisoned
>By the sewers of Babylon.
>Give me a plot of ground,
>A river and two hills
>And a tenth part of the energy
>Which is dissipated in a day of war
>And I will build a city
>Like a song. A place
>Where nothing will offend the eye
>And nothing will be hidden.

Graubard. Thou art dreaming again.

Architect.
>If I cannot build a dream
>Then I'll not repair a nightmare.
>I will sit on my hands and listen.
>I will hear it soon.

Robert. Hear what?

Architect.
>The crack of doom,
>The rumble of collapse
>The world is breaking up
>Like sheet-ice in the spring.

Insane. Crack! Crack! Crack!

Graubard groans.

Nurse. My lord, what is it?

Graubard.
>Our belly doth complain.
>Our privy councillor speaks.

The old man, who until now has stood without moving, suddenly begins to twitch his body. The spasm becomes acute. He takes a few quick steps towards the other patients and then stops.

Old Man. It means . . . it means . . .

Insane. Yes?

Old Man. Take away the stone.

Insane. Lazarus, come forth!

Nurse. My lord, the catatonic symptoms . . .

Graubard. Back, dotard, back! Get thee back into thy rigid self!

Graubard clasps his stomach and groans.

Old Man.
>The trapped thought swings
>In the body's cell,
>Ricochets on taut nerves
>Stretched on hollow worlds,
>Ascends the spiral grooves,
>Beats on a roof of skull.
>Tries to fly beyond
>The wall of muscle,
>Atrophies and falls
>In nothingness.
>Eyes stare inwards,
>Gaze at interior suns,
>Glaze under creeping cataracts.
>Ears fill with wax
>Hear only muffled whispers of the blood.
>Thought dies in this padded world,
>Returns defeated to its source,
>Lives only when the body responds
>To the world beyond the body.

> Where is the world now?
> I will heal it and be healed.

Graubard groans and leaps to his feet.

Graubard. A stool! A stool! My kingdom for a stool!

He runs off, followed by the nurse. Music. The insane begin to dance.

Robert. Wait! There is not much time.

Architect. Time for what?

Robert. Time to revolt!

Insane. No, no! He'll stop the sweet pudding at lunch!

Robert jumps on to the raised plane, the better to address them.

Robert.   They say that we are mad,
           But is it mad to dream
           When dreams are better than reality?

Old Man. What is reality?

Robert.   There are enough of us assembled here
           To overpower the doctor and the nurse.

Insane. It is against the law.

Robert.   The law of the needle!
           Freedom can end that law.
           Freedom lies at your finger-tips!
           Reach out and it's yours.

Architect. Freedom . . .

Robert. With freedom, you can build your perfect town.

Architect. Yes.

Robert. With freedom, the game is ended.

Labourer. Yes.

Robert. With freedom, peace will come again.

Young Woman. Yes.

Robert. With freedom, thought is not fettered in the brain.

Old Man. Yes.

Robert. Freedom is yours if you will take it!

Insane. Yes.

Graubard and the nurse enter.

Graubard. What is this, a mutiny?

Robert. An awakening of the dead.

Graubard. In this, our realm, the dead only awaken at meal-times. (*To the insane*) Hast thou forgotten the terrors of the outside world? Remember how the sane ones hunted thee like dogs?

Robert. Would you have freedom?

Graubard. Wouldst miss thy lunch?

Insane. No . . . no . . .

Robert. Remember your dreams.

Graubard. (*To the nurse*) Fetch thou some warmer raiment for our friend.

Exit nurse.

What, dost desert thy deliverer already?

The insane cower back.

It is well. It is a sign that thou all art cured. Thou, master architect, wilt be released this afternoon, and if thy mind hath not lost all its cunning thou shalt proceed upon an undertaking which shall bring thee fame and augmented rations. Tomorrow thou wilt proceed to build an annexe to this place and in return thou shalt have duff for breakfast, lunch and dinner every day. Art satisfied?

Architect. Yes.

Old Man. A sweet at every meal?

Graubard. At every meal, and thou shalt have it, too. For thou shalt teach the young how to sterilize thought.

Old Man. Yes.

Graubard. As for thee, my good Pawn, thou shalt become a Pawn of substance and teach the other Pawns the rules of our game.

Labourer. Yes.

Young Woman. And what of me?

Graubard. The seed will flourish in thy womb and in the time of harvest thou wilt bear fruit for thine own sustenance.

Young Woman. Yes.

Graubard. This is farewell. Go forth and multiply, and dream no more.

Insane. Yes.

They turn and file out like sleep-walkers. The nurse enters, carrying a strait-jacket.

Robert. No! No! It must not end like this!

The nurse and Graubard fall upon him and force him into the strait-jacket.

Graubard. This is for thine own safety.

Robert. Let me go!

The trumpet sounds.

Graubard. 'Tis time for lunch. Come.

He goes off, followed by the nurse. Robert stares at the strait-jacket in stunned bewilderment.

Hanau. Robert!

Robert's mouth moves spasmodically, but no words come.

Robert!

The metallic tapping is heard, grows in intensity.

Voice of the Prison. Are you all right? Are you all right?

Robert. There is no road back! We are lost . . . lost . . . lost . . .

The tapping reaches a peak of unendurable intensity. Music swells up, harsh and dissonant. The curtain falls   *[End of Part One]*

[**PART TWO**] *An hour has elapsed. The cage apears to have increased its floor area and the shadows cast by the bars radiate over the stage like a great spider's web. To the left of the cage is a raised platform on which is built the interior of a railway carriage with a door at the back leading into a corridor. Hanau is seated in the cage staring straight in front of him. Robert, outside, leans against the bars, his back towards Hanau. Music is heard in the background, the slow march of an earlier sequence. A steel door clangs and the music stops.*

Hanau. And there is no retreat.

Robert. None.

Hanau. Nothing to do but wait.

Robert. Nothing.

Hanau. No manumission that would leave us whole.

Robert. No.

Hanau. No life without stigmata.

Robert. No.

Hanau. Only bars and silence.

Robert. Death and silence.

Hanau. The future and silence.

Robert. Yes.

Hanau. No company but the dying.

Robert. And the dead.

Hanau.   Only brittle words,
          Voices of hands on metal pipes.

Robert. Only that.

Hanau. We have come full circle.

Robert. Yes.

Hanau. You said . . .

Robert. I said what I was told to say.

Hanau. By whom?

Robert. By you.

Hanau. If you had been less inconsistent . . .

Robert. That was how you created me.

Hanau. Yes . . . in my own image . . .

Robert. Yes.

They are silent for a moment.

Hanau. Well?

Robert. (*Turning to him*) Well?

Hanau. Has anything been left unsaid?

Robert shakes his head.

We have lived dangerously.

Robert. We have lived.

Hanau. But to what purpose? If only one could be sure which was the credit side of one's accounts.

Robert. Death will dispose of all our doubts.

Hanau. But not resolve them. Oh, there should be rules for dying!

Robert. There is one rule: death should precede corruption.

Hanau. Yes . . . yes . . . but can a man repudiate his doubts and still be incorruptible?

Robert. What is life but a tight-rope stretched between two doubts? No one ever reaches the other side.

Hanau. And yet if one could see the other side clearly for just an instant, the ultimate fall would lose its terrors. These are difficult days for dying. Life is so confused – such a complex process.

Robert. And such a simple conclusion.

Hanau. Did the others doubt,
          The ones who went before –
          Those who fell at the shooting wall,
          The fustian men in the hulks,
          The dead at the Ebro River?

Robert. Theirs was a simple dream,
          Remote as a star,
          Convenient symbol of unrealised hope.

Hanau. But we have touched our dream,
          Fondled it with bloody hands,
          Lain with it through a long winter,
          Fed it with bitterness and sour despair.
          It was a seedling nurtured in the mind
          But we transplanted it in stony soil.
          Can it survive the climate of reality?

Robert. It has survived.

Hanau. Would the others recognise it now,
          Or would they mourn its metamorphosis?

Robert. We will never know.

Hanau. Why not? You are still free.

The trumpet sounds.

Robert. Am I?

Hanau. It will be the last journey.

The trumpet sounds again.

Robert. What if they deny the dream?

Hanau. Then we die for nothing.

Music. Robert begins to go off.

Robert. I will tell them you are coming.

Exit Robert.

Hanau. They will not hear – or if they hear
          They will not understand.

Music fades out.

>   Death is not curious
>   For it negates all questions
>   And takes, without selection,
>   What life discards,
>   Fragments of dreams,
>   Abandoned hopes
>   And bones of dead desires.

The metallic tapping is heard accompanied by whispering voices.

Voice of the Prison.
>   Do not despair,
>   Night will not last forever.

Hanau.   How can there be night
             When there is no morning?
             Time has stopped!

Voice of the Prison.
             Time stands on the rim of night
             Armed with grenade of sun
             And blade of morning.

   Phrase of music.

             Earth stirs in the trough of sleep.

Mic. Chorus.
             It is the time of decision.

Voice of the Prison.
             Deep fissures rend the darkness.

Mic. Chorus.
             It is the time of decision.

Voice of the Prison.
             Now the moon is struggling in an ambush of cloud.

Mic. Chorus.
             It is the time of decision.

Voice of the Prison.
             The stars open their eyes.

Mic. Chorus.
             It is the time of decision.
             The past dies,
             The minute sings,
             The night is full of wounds,
             The hammer rings on the anvil.
             The dead rise from their tombs.
             The night is torn
             On the rock of dawn.
             Hope is born
             In the disinherited.
             Now is the time,
             The reaping time,
             For all good men,
             When once again,
             Then all good men –
             Now is the time,
             Now is the time,
             Now is the time . . .

*Behind the above chorus the sound of a railway train is heard, synchronising
with the voices. It grows louder until the voices are no longer audible. The light*

in the cage is faded down and simultaneously the railway carriage is illuminated. Robert is discovered seated.

Hanau. Ask them how long the night will last.

The train gathers speed, the rattle of the wheels becomes louder.

Voice of the Prison.
    Wind howls
    And the wheels flash
    On the strip of hypnotic parallel.
    Plumes of sparks
    Bloom for an instant's season.
    Cities pass and seas and mountains
    Centuries and dreams are left behind.
    It's the Express History,
    The dark comet across the universe!

From the corridor a man enters the railway carriage. He wears the semi-uniform of a Spanish dynamitero.

Mic. Voice. Francisco Piera, coal-miner: died in the siege of Oviedo, nineteen-thirty-seven.

Piera sits facing Robert. A woman enters. She is dressed in the costume of the National Guard adopted by the citizens of the Faubourg Montmartre in the Paris of 1871.

Mic. Voice. Clémence Gaudry: died in the commune of Paris, eighteen-seventy-one.

She sits facing Robert. A man enters wearing worker's attire of the period of 1840.

Mic. Voice. James Guthrie, weaver: died in the struggle for the Charter, eighteen-hundred-and-forty.

He sits facing Robert. The sound of the train is held at peak for a moment then faded down until it is scarcely audible.

Piera. Well?

Robert. Forgive me if I have disturbed your peace.

Gaudry. Is the struggle ended then?

Robert. It grows fiercer every day.

Gaudry. Then how can we know peace?

Robert. But surely for the dead . . .

Gaudry. Yes, we are dead,
    Our bodies are broken.
    The winds and rains have scattered us,
    Washed us into the earth's mouth,

Left no residue of bone or hair.
We have fed woundwort and willow-herb,

Guthrie. An' the muckle fishes.

Piera. Yes, we are dead,
And yet we are more a part of life
Than the sleek-haired pistoleros
Who walk across our graves
Carrying death in their portfolios.

Gaudry. Our wounds are banners.

Guthrie. Our deiths are sangs.

Piera. And our deeds are dynamite,
Exploding in the living memory.

Robert. Yours was a time of hope –
You died whole.

Gaudry. I died on a grey morning
While the smoke erected twisted columns
Above the ruins of Belleville
And wrote the Commune's epitaph
In dirty smears across the sky.
You talk of hope!
But hope was murdered,
Butchered by the Versaillese.
It died a thousand deaths on every street,
And left its corpse at every barricade.
We who had lost a thousand battles
And survived to fight among the graves
In Père Lachaise and die before the wall
Were not sustained by hope but by despair.

Robert. You had grown accustomed to defeat,
Learned to embellish death with words,
Like 'justice', 'freedom', 'human dignity'.

Gaudry. And are the words forgotten?

Robert. Time has blurred their meaning.
They are like old shoes
Which anyone can wear.

Guthrie. The words were bleezin' suns
That lichtit the blackest corners
O' oor makeshift world.

Robert. But nothing has changed.

Guthrie. Ay, we were changed,
For we kent then wha we were
An' whit we were and whit we could become.

Robert. All because of a few tattered phrases?

Guthrie. We made the words oor ain
              An' sent them singin' doon the sunless roads,
              Whaur the shilpit collier-bairns crooched agin the rock.
              They ris abune the stramach o' the looms
              An' folk wha stuid perpetually stoopit
              Straightened their shoulder an' minded they were men.

Robert. The words were abstractions!
              What could they mean to you?

Guthrie. They pit a limit tae the time o' skaith.
              They were comets i' the nicht
              An' by their licht I fund a path
              Which sprauchled heigh abune the wa's o' darkness.
              The words were blyth an' but for them
              Ma life had a' been mirk . . .
              The weirdless agony o' birth,
              The blin' years tint i' the mill stour,
              An' deith claumin' at ma thrapple
              I' the ugsome hold o' a transportation hulk.

Robert. Yes, it was different for you.

Gaudry. How was it different?

Robert. You never had to bear the burden of a victory.
              You minted deathless phrases out of dreams.
              Ours is the heavier task: we build a world.

Gaudry. It is a task for heroes.

Robert. The junk and debris of the ages
              Is our inheritance.
              We carry it upon our backs.

Gaudry. But you are strong.

Robert. There are times when even the strongest men
              Are overcome with weariness and yearn
              To bed down in the rubble of the world
              And sleep . . . and sleep . . . and sleep.

Piera. We have slept too long.
              The time of awakening is overdue.

Robert. Have you never doubted the moment of awakening?

Piera. We have doubted it and feared it,
              For who is not vulnerable in sleep?
              And yet on that brittle noon,
              When the smoking guns
              Were stuttering calumnies

Against tomorrow
And death ran howling
Through Oviedo's streets,
I knew a moment of reality
When history spoke,
Delivered its ultimatum:
Awake or perish!
And even as the sleepers murdered us,
I knew they were condemned,
For they were deaf and did not hear the voice.
And they were blind
And thought their dunghill was a mountain peak
Comparable with the highest ranges of tomorrow.

Robert. No one has seen tomorrow's peaks.

Piera.   But we have seen the dunghill
And watched life decay.
If, out of all the riches of the earth
We cannot create conditions for survival
Then it is time that man was written off
As one of evolution's failures.

Gaudry. Ours was a time of hope, you said,
But yours is the time of labour;
History is brought to bed with child,
A new world struggles in the womb.

Robert. Suppose the child is born deformed?

Gaudry. Then you will know that history
Has done the act of darkness with the past.

There is a roar of wheels as the train enters a tunnel. The carriage is plunged in
darkness. Hanau shrieks in delirium.

Hanau. Robert! Robert!

Voice of the Prison.
The lines branch
Left and right,
Route to the sun,
Road to the night.
There are no brakes,
There's a world behind,
Signals flash,
But the driver's blind.
Hands on levers,
Fumble, grope,
Without skill,
Without hope.

The train gathers speed. Suddenly it emerges from the tunnel. The carriage is illuminated again but Guthrie, Gaudry and Piera have disappeared and in their places sit three other passengers: Graubard, balancing a brief-case on his knees and looking like a prosperous man of business; the commercial traveller asleep in a corner; and the brave little woman asleep in the other corner. The sound of the wheels fades.

Robert. Where are they?

Graubard. I beg your pardon?

Robert. My friends . . . they've disappeared!

Graubard. Really!

Robert. They were dead.

Graubard. Ah! You were dreaming.

Robert. Was I? Then what am I doing here?

Graubard. You are travelling.

Robert. Yes, but where to? Where is this train going?

Graubard. Does it matter? Surely one should travel for the sake of travelling. Travel broadens the mind.

Robert. Your face . . . it seems familiar. I'm sure I've seen you somewhere.

Graubard. One of my many brothers, perhaps, or a distant cousin. We are a large family.

Robert peers through the window.

Robert. Darkness, nothing but darkness and a trail of sparks.

Graubard. One can easily dispose of the night.

He draws the blind down.

You see, it's very simple.

Robert. I've forgotten something . . . I have an appointment and yet I'm sure I shouldn't be here. Isn't there some way of stopping the train? I must get out of here! I can't breathe!

Graubard. Please! . . . please! You'll wake the other passengers. Why not try to sleep? Sleep is a wonderful thing.

The train rocks violently. Robert is thrown off balance. The sound of the wheels is heard for a moment as the train gathers speed.

Robert. Why are we travelling so fast if we aren't going anywhere?

Graubard. We are going downhill.

The sound of the train is faded up again, travelling still faster. Robert stands up in sudden panic.

Robert. There's something wrong. I feel it. We are leaving the rails.

Graubard. Nerves! Just nerves!

Robert. I tell you, this train is out of control. There's something wrong. Perhaps the engineer is ill!

Graubard. There is no engineer on this line.

Robert. No engineer? Then who drives the train?

Graubard. It drives itself.

Robert. But the risk!

Graubard. Exactly. That is what makes travel so fascinating.

Robert. But surely the passengers . . .

Graubard. The passengers have not complained about our administration.

Robert. Your administration!

Graubard. I am a director of the company which operates this line.

Robert. And yet you don't know where we're going?

Graubard. I do not.

Robert. But it's criminal!

Robert shakes the other two passengers.

Wake up! Wake up!

Commercial Traveller. Eh! Eh! What is it?

Robert. We're in danger. The engine's out of control.

Commercial Traveller. Out of control?

Robert. There's no driver on the train.

Commercial Traveller. Well, what do you expect me to do?

Robert. But we can't just sit here and wait for it to crash!

Commercial Traveller. Driving a train isn't in my line of business.

Graubard. As a director of the railway company . . .

Commercial Traveller. A director? Really, sir!

Graubard. Actually, I'm the managing director.

Commercial Traveller. Now, that's very interesting. I wonder if I can interest you in a little business proposition?

Robert. Are you crazy? We are all in peril!

Graubard. Please! May I ask, Mr . . . er . . .

Commercial Traveller. Christie's the name.

Graubard. What is your line of business?

Commercial Traveller. Loaves and fishes, sir, loaves and fishes.

He rises to his feet and opens his sample case.

Now here are one or two samples which may interest you.

He hands several small loaves and fishes around the carriage.

Food for the multitude. The staff of life. At the present market price and allowing for fluctuations due to wars, floods, earthquakes and political crises . . .

Robert. This is monstrous! The loaves are rotten, full of worms. Do you expect people to eat such filth?

Commercial Traveller. Eat them? You don't eat them! You sell them.

The sound of the wheels is heard again, the speed increasing.

Robert. It's going faster . . . faster . . . Lady, we're travelling with lunatics.

Brave Little Woman. Oh, surely not.

Robert. The train is heading for destruction.

Brave Little Woman. You must be mistaken. I've been travelling on this line for years.

Robert. But look out of the window!

Brave Little Woman. I'll do no such thing. I'm quite comfortable where I am. My father worked all his life for the railway company and when he was killed, the company paid the funeral expenses and sent a wreath of daffodils. They were so kind. It's the little kindnesses that count.

Graubard. Quite!

Brave Little Woman. I believe in minding my own business. No good comes of interfering in things which don't concern us.

Robert. Doesn't your life concern you?

Brave Little Woman. Life has given me everything I've asked for. I'm quite content to sit in my little corner and dream. George – that's my husband – I have his picture here . . .

She produces several snapshots.

Graubard. Hmm!

Brave Little Woman. We've only a little camera. That's my little boy and that's my little house standing in my little garden. The gladioli won a prize this year, a little silver cup . . .

Robert. Will nothing wake you up?

Commercial Traveller. Be quiet!

Robert. If you won't do something then I must try alone.

Graubard. Can you drive a train?

Robert. I can try – and that's better than sitting here waiting to be killed.

He makes for the door leading into the corridor.

Graubard. One moment!

He produces a pistol from his brief-case.

I must ask you not to interfere in the company's affairs.

Robert. My life is my affair.

Graubard. Not while you travel on this line.

Robert. I am going to stop this train or learn to drive it.

Graubard. I'm sorry, but it's against the regulations.

Robert. Then damn the regulations!

He opens the door.

Graubard. You leave me no alternative.

He shoots Robert.

Your pardon, madam.

The brave little woman, however, is asleep.

These little contretemps occur from time to time.

Commercial Traveller. About my proposition . . .

Graubard. Later. Some other time.

Commercial Traveller. Later, then. I think I'll have a nap.

He sleeps. Graubard stands up.

Graubard. Yes, sleep. It passes the time. Perhaps there is an element of danger. Fortunately the company provides an armoured coach for its directors. Good-bye, young man. If you had learned to sleep on journeys, this would never have happened.

Exits via the corridor. The sound of the train fades up, a deafening clatter. There is a loud explosion and a blinding flash. Robert is hurled towards the cage and the railway carriage is blacked out. The light in the cage increases.

Hanau. Always the same ending.

Robert rises to his feet.

Robert. And what now?

Hanau. We will wait for the morning
             To lend a little light for death.
             We will look her in the eyes.

Robert. The sun cannot penetrate
These barriers of darkness.

Hanau. It can and will.
Soon it will climb to its meridian.

Robert. Strange to think the sun still shines.

Hanau. We have lived through a long night
But now the sun stands poised and ready
On the furthest ridge of Capricorn.

Robert. Then we can rest.

Hanau. Yes.
It has been an uncomfortable journey.
And we have not slept.

Robert. Have we accomplished anything?

Hanau. We have travelled.
We have looked over the horizon.

Robert. And the body pays for the mind's excursion.

Hanau. It is a fair exchange.

Robert. And doubt?

Hanau. Our doubts are growing pains,
Symptoms of the nascent mind
Extending its sphere of operations.
We doubt tomorrow only because
We have not escaped from yesterday.

Robert. So the journey is ended!

Hanau. Our journey is ended,
But there are other travellers.

*Music, quiet and intimate, in which a cello takes the solo part, singing of man's
hope. Suddenly the mood is broken by a distant pistol shot. The music stops.
More pistol shots are heard. The metallic tapping begins.*

Voice of the Prison. Number Three! Number Three! Can you hear? Answer,
Number Three! Can you hear? Number Three! They are coming!
Number . . .

There is a shot, loud and hollow, then silence.

Hanau. The journey is ended.

Robert slowly backs away from the cage, moving towards the shadows beyond.

Robert!

Robert. The shadows beckon.

Hanau. Do not go yet.
      Share this long night-watch.

Robert. The night is spent.

Hanau. Your image slips away, dissolves
      Into the cloudy mirror of the darkness.
      Face blurrs, featureless.
      Body thins to shadow
      Without edge or substance.
      Circumference of life contracts.
      Too far to see, to concentrate . . .
      Remember feeling often known,
      Room full of shadows,
      Discreet agony of darkness.
      Stay! Stay!
      Will not resolve itself
      Until the cold sweat of dawn.

*Graubard has entered. He is dressed as on his first appearance and is slightly
drunk. Robert stands back in the shadows unseen by Graubard.*

Graubard.
      Still fighting shadows?
      Not at the frontier yet?

Hanau. (*To Robert*) Stay and we will talk about the morning.

Graubard.
      Do they leave you, then?
      Have they deserted you?
      Dreams are poor companions.

Hanau. Come, there is a song . . .
      We will forget our wounds.

Graubard.
      There is a long forgetfulness.
      It will soon be yours.

Hanau. That bleary eye of light
      Is not the sun.
      What have they done to my hands?

Graubard. Hanau! Hanau!

Hanau. (*Slowly turns his head*) Yes.

Graubard. So you can hear?

Hanau. Yes.

Graubard. Do you recognise me?

Hanau. You are death.

Graubard.
> No, my friend, not death,
> Merely a humble employee.

Hanau. There is a void behind your eyes.

Graubard.
> A slight myopia, that's all.
> We had an appointment.
> You and I. Remember?

Hanau. Will you teach me the language of the worms?

Graubard. You will learn it soon enough.

Hanau. I remember now. Graubard . . .

Graubard.
> I would have joined you earlier
> But I was detained.
> The Commandant was big with speech
> And needed a midwife for his wind.
> His relations with the spoken word
> Are most unsatisfactory.
> Fortunately, he provides
> His audience with brandy.
> Do you remember the taste of brandy,
> The way it evaporates upon the tongue
> And tenderly ascends into the brain
> In warm caressing spirals?
> But how could you?
> You have forgotten everything except a dream
> And soon you will have forgotten that.

There is a distant volley of shots.

> Do you hear, Hanau?
> Spring cleaning has begun.
> Your friends are being moved
> Into a permanent habitation
> And when we leave . . .

Hanau. Leave?

Graubard.
> Of course, you didn't know.
> We're abandoning the camp.

The sound of firing is heard, nearer.

> There's not much time, Hanau,
> If you would save yourself.
> A few words on the radio,
> An announcement to your followers
> That you accept the inevitable.

Hanau. I do accept the inevitable,
That is why I'm here.

Graubard.

What is it makes you take upon yourself
The burdens of this shoddy world?
Don't tell me that you still believe in man,
In the inherent goodness of the species.
Surely you are cured of that illusion!
They are louts, Hanau, louts!
When they're not stupefied with fear
They're drunk with ignorance.
Examine them under the microscope
And beneath the accretions of the ages
You will find a clumsy ape
Who dreams of nothing but his past.
And you would make him dream about his future!
I tell you, he has no future!
One or two individuals have a future,
Those who can see themselves objectively,
The deviations from the type;
The rest are quite content to move
Backwards and forwards, emulating
The shuttle in its groove.
Man is content if he acquires
His little stock of superstitions
And his book of rules.
Examine him coldly, without sentiment
And tell me honestly if what you see
Is worth the expenditure of a single thought.
How does he differ from his ancestors,
This snivelling, shiftless clown?
He has less hair, it's true, and smaller teeth;
His patella is more flexible and compensates
For the loss of that shambling stoop
By allowing him to assume
The posture of permanent genuflexion.
He doesn't want your future, or your dreams.
He'd rather wallow in his filthy rut,
Lost in a state of fugue.
For him the highest point of life is reached
When some hungry female of his kind
Offers the sweaty pit of her body
For his immolation.
And you would die for him!
Why? Why? What is this quality
Which defies my understanding
And eludes all definition?

Hanau. The quality of life, Graubard.

Graubard.
>Do you talk of life to me,
>You who have lived with death these last three years?
>I have looked life squarely in the face,
>Accepted it for what it is,
>As one accepts a woman for one's pleasure.

Hanau. You have looked in a sewer
>And seen your own reflection.
>The image has aborted thought.
>Your eyes are clouded over
>With the malice of emasculation.

Graubard. I am drunk and therefore tolerant.
>Believe me, Hanau, if I envied you
>Or coveted your precious fantasy
>I'd tear it out of you as easily
>As one removes the filling
>From a dead man's tooth.

Hanau. Once, Graubard, I thought that you,
>And what you represent, might dam the course
>Of history for a thousand years.
>That was before I knew you,
>Before I realised that your hatred
>Of all life developed beyond the termite stage
>Springs from a terrible fear.
>Your mind is crippled, twisted horribly;
>It approaches life with a clumsy, crab-like gait
>And looks at everything through bloodshot eyes.

Graubard. Have you finished?

Hanau. You hate us because you envy us,
>You envy us because we walk upright
>And constantly remind you
>Of your own mis-shapenness.
>How does it feel to know
>That life has cast you off?

Graubard. You have too much breath, Hanau.

He produces a pistol from his pocket.

>I will give you an injection
>Which will make you sleep.

Hanau. Your contribution to social medicine.

Graubard. An instrument to rid you of delusions.

Hanau. Will it cure your deformity?

Graubard. Stand up!

Hanau. What, are we to stand on ceremony?

Graubard. I want to see you fall.

Hanau. Must I teach you to die?

Graubard. Get up!

Hanau pulls himself up. Music fades up. Hanau turns, listening intently.

What is it now?

Hanau. Music. I can hear music.

Graubard.
>A choir of worms, most likely,
>Singing for their supper.

Robert slowly advances to the cage.

Hanau. Yes, it's time that we were joined.
We will die whole.

Robert slips between the bars into the cage.

>We will trample upon death
>As the swan tramples upon the water,
>Or the horse upon the plain.

Graubard.
>Hanau, come back!
>You cannot escape again!

Hanau. I can smell the dawn, Robert.

Maria enters behind Graubard and stands in the shadows.

Hanau. Maria!
Did you tell them?

She nods in the affirmative.

Graubard.
>No, I'll not shoot
>While you're anaesthetised with dreams.
>You must be lucid
>For that final interview.
>When death comes
>I want to look into your eyes
>And see the endless vista of despair.
>I want you to be conscious of
>The full extent of your defeat.

Piera and Anderson enter and stand in the shadows.

Hanau. Guthrie.

Graubard. More phantoms?

Hanau.   The spectres that haunt Europe,
              Those who call from the high hills
              Across the arid years. The deathless ones
              Who cannot be silenced.
              These are your judges, Graubard.
              And all your loud-mouthed threats,
              Your thunderous denunciations,
              Your chorus of sonorous guns
              With their emphatic statements of defence,
              Cannot delay the verdict
              Nor postpone your execution.
              Your world is dying, Graubard.
              It totters in the final stages of decrepitude.
              It is incapable of all activity
              Except the activity of decay.
              Do you think you can outlive it
              Or halt the process of senility
              By prescribing a diet of blood?
              Can you disguise its atrabilious stench?
              The sulphurous reek of cannon,
              The acrid stink of fire-raped towns,
              The flowers of infamous harvest
              And all the perfumes of synthetic victory
              Will not eradicate
              The hellish odour of putrefaction.

Graubard. My world will survive you, Hanau.

Hanau.   Yes, but it will not survive
              The new world that is being born.

Graubard.
              And who will sire this precious infant?
              Not you, my friend! Who, then?
              One of the barren shadows of the dead?

   Music which dies away on a flourish of trumpets.

              What was that?

Hanau. The cock crew.

Graubard. Nonsense! It isn't morning yet.

Hanau. And yet the cock crew.

Graubard.
              Strange! I could have sworn there were two of you.
              Stand still. Stand still!
              What! Have you multiplied?
              The atmosphere of your apartment

> Combining with the Commandant's liquor
> Has given me the doubtful pleasure
> Of seeing you in duplicate.
> I have four eyes with which to watch you die
> And by killing both of you
> I'll double the measure of my satisfaction.

The trumpet sounds again.

> There it is again.

Hanau. The second summons.

Graubard.
> Some cock with a full crop
> Impatient for the tread.

Robert. It stands on the roof of night.

Hanau. It sees the dawn.

Chorus of the dead. Tick-tock, tock-tock.

Robert. The minutes fall like dead leaves.

Chorus of the dead. Tick-tock, tick-tock.

Hanau. The world dies in a bed of mould.

Chorus of the dead. Tick-tock, tick-tock, tick-tock, tick-tock.

Graubard.
> My ears are practising an imposture
> Upon my reason.
> There's no clock here, no voices,
> Only the dry scampering of rat's feet.

Robert. And the heart tolling its own funeral.

Chorus of the dead.
> Tick-tock, tick-tock,
> Another beat nearer death,
> Tick-tock, tick-tock,
> A minute lost, a lost breath.
> Tick-tock, tick-tock, tick-tock, tick-tock.

Graubard. Stop!

Voice of the prison. Stop! Stop! Stop!

Graubard. Sleep too little . . . can't sleep . . .

Voice of the prison. Can't sleep. Can't sleep. Can't sleep.

Graubard.
> Thoughts go on echoing inside my skull
> Long after formulation.
> Am I breaking up?

Voice of the prison. Breaking up!

Graubard. Something moved in the shadows!

Hanau
Robert. (*together*) Look round, Graubard!

Voice of the prison. Look round!

Chorus of the dead. Look round!

Graubard. What is there to see but shadows?

Chorus of the dead.
>   The shadows fly before the rush of light.
>   The sun destroys the ambush of the night.

Voice of the prison.
>   The past dies, the minute sings.
>   The dead arise, the earth swings
>   Into a new constellation.

Graubard.
>   Delirium is not infectious
>   And yet in some strange way . . .
>   No, that's impossible!
>   I need rest, that's all, rest!

Chorus of the dead.
>   You cannot hide from tomorrow's eye,
>   You cannot escape a universal dream
>   Or silence tomorrow's hope.

Graubard.
>   I have an antidote for dreams,
>   A prophylactic against hope.
>   Here, Hanau, take it!

He shoots Hanau, who, for a moment, stands swaying against the bars and then slowly sinks to the ground. Music in the rhythm of a slow march. Enter Death as an old woman and the Morning as a girl in a gold dress patterned with red suns. They dance towards the cage. From out of the shadows behind the cage appear Gaudry and the dead Chartist.

>   Now the stillness moves.
>   The cock grows in my head.
>   Oh, I am sick! sick!

Robert. You are dying.

Graubard. What, do you still stand?

He shoots at Robert. The music stops. The air is full of whispers.

Robert. You have planted banners in the hungry soil.

Chorus of the Dead.
> Red like anger
> Like the disc of sun in the mist of morning.

Graubard. This place is full of echoes.

Voice of the Prison. His voice is an infinity of echoes.

Graubard.
> His voice is lost in silence,
> Withered away.

The Morning. It is time.

Music. Robert slips out of the cage and dances off with the Morning. Graubard attempts to follow but is restrained by Death.

Death. You cannot go after him.

Graubard. You have not paid me for your lodging, Hanau!

Death. I will pay you, son.

Graubard.
> The light behind your eyes was mine.
> The instrument which made that fine-spun dream
> Is my inheritance. Where has it gone?
> Is this unyielding clay, this grey silence
> The sum and total of my legacy?
> You have left me nothing, Hanau,
> But a worn-out body and a cage.

Voice of the Prison.
> Five paces and the bars,
> Five paces and the cage.

The Dead begin to advance slowly upon Graubard. The light on the stage lessens.

Graubard. I am beset by hostile shadows.

Death. Come to me, my son. Come home.

Graubard. Back, old woman.

Death. Do not shrink from your mother, child.

Graubard. Where has Hanau gone?

Death. He is there, son.

Graubard. That is not Hanau. What am I doing in this cage?

He rattles the bars furiously.

Hanau! Hanau! Let me out! Let me out, Hanau!

There is a great crescendo of music. Graubard continues to shout as the curtain falls.					*[The End]*

Epilogue

Though all theatre is, in a broad sense 'political', the term 'political theatre' has been accepted as defining a left-wing theatre, critical of the capitalist system and expressing in its work the need for radical change.

The first organised political theatre in this country was the Workers' Theatre Movement, which spanned the period from 1928 to 1938. 1968 saw the upsurge of Alternative Theatre and the formation of several socialist theatre groups. Linking these two movements was the pre-war work of Theatre Union in Manchester and the post-war work of Theatre Workshop.

The Workers' Theatre Movement of the thirties, as important a cultural and political manifestation in its own time as the Alternative movement of the seventies, has been almost completely ignored in the main stream of writing on theatre history, and such information as is available is limited, in the main, to specialist journals such as *History Workshop*.

The third edition of the *Oxford Companion to the Theatre*, though it claims 'an effort has been made to provide information on every aspect of the theatre up to the end of 1964' has nothing to say on the subject. *The Illustrated Encyclopedia of World Theatre*, published by Thames and Hudson in 1977, deals solely, in seventy words, with agitational theatre in the U.S.S.R. and Germany before the Second World War, though Theatre Union does get a brief mention under 'Littlewood'. Methuen's *Encyclopedia of World Drama*, published in 1970, and the Penguin *Dictionary of Theatre* have no entry under Street Theatre, Agit-Prop or Political Theatre. Surprisingly, even David Edgar wrote in the *Theatre Quarterly* of winter 1979, 'there are two reasons why 1968 can be taken as the starting date of political theatre in Britain'.

Political theatre goes back even earlier than the start of the Workers' Theatre Movement in 1928, but that year marks the beginning of an attempt to organise left-wing theatre on a comparatively widespread scale. It was directly agitational, rejecting completely all the theatrical conventions of the time, embracing the class-struggle and identifying itself closely with the Communist Party. The revolutionary nature of its work was unable to survive the formation of the Popular Front in 1936 – the alliance between the Communist Party, the I.L.P. and the left wing of the Labour Party. Also, unemployment had declined, industrial strife was easing and progressive forces felt that the urgent need was to unite against what was then seen as the main danger – the rise of Fascism all over Europe. To alert a broader section of the people to this new threat, the direct, simple sketches of street agit-prop had to give way to indoor theatre, full-length plays and, consequently, the need to improve the artistic and technical levels of performance. Joan Littlewood and Ewan MacColl had led the way with Theatre of Action in Manchester as early as 1934, culminating in the production of *Last Edition* in 1940, paving the way for the even more complex requirements of plays like *Uranium 235* in the post-war years.

Though little has been documented of the many groups that made up the Workers' Theatre Movement a great deal is known about the present-day Alternative Theatre. Unlike the Workers' Theatre Movement it is an accepted part of the theatrical scene. Until recently public subsidy has been available to many of them on the basis of their merit. Now, in the political climate of the 1980s, these are being withdrawn from the more radical groups such as 7:84 and they are now fighting for their survival. Many of its writers are established 'names' and their plays are published. Some of these, like John Arden, David Mercer, John McGrath, had been writing since the fifties, but 1968 marked the beginning of the upsurge of left-wing theatre groups in this country, alongside other theatre groups with no specific political commitment.

It is significant that the formation in 1928 of the Workers' Theatre Movement and the rise of political theatre in the late sixties both had, as their springboard, a rejection of orthodox Labour politics and the need to seek out a more radical solution to the injustices of Capitalism though the differences in the economic conditions of the two periods was considerable. 1928 was a time of depression, high unemployment and poverty, and the Workers' Theatre Movement, born out of discontent and struggle, was an integral part of the political movement of the working class. 1968 on the other hand, was a time of comparative prosperity, unemployment was low and the recession had not yet hit the Consumer Society. Nevertheless, the Labour government that had come to power in 1964 had failed to effect any of the expected radical changes. From the resulting disillusionment and the political awareness of students, intellectuals and young theatre workers, some of whom were from the working class, sprang the theatre of protest. Some groups adopted agit-prop techniques, taking their theatre to non-theatrical venues: halls, clubs, pubs, community centres, places of work and out on to the streets, in much the same way as the Workers' Theatre Movement had done.

It may be that Harold Hobson was overstating the case when he said 'I doubt if there would have been any Fringe without Theatre Workshop and Joan Littlewood', but the influence on the work of some of the pioneers of the political theatre in the late sixties has been acknowledged, not least in their appreciation of the need to develop the physical skills of the actors, the value of the use of common speech in the theatre and the advantages resulting from group work. Albert Hunt has said that these were just some of the elements in Theatre Workshop productions he saw over the years that inspired his subsequent work with the Bradford College of Art group. His memorable large-scale piece of street theatre *The Russian Revolution* and drama documentaries like *John Ford's Cuban Missile Crisis* in turn influenced much of the political theatre of the seventies, including the work of groups like General Will and Welfare State. John McGrath has also acknowledged the influence of Theatre Workshop on his work with 7:84 Company and their commitment to create a popular working-class theatre. How this can best be achieved has exercised the minds of everyone engaged in political theatre since the twenties. The agit-prop theatre of those years took their sketches to those directly concerned with specific issues – at their places of work, into clubs or out into the streets; and since the late sixties this form of theatre has been developed by groups like North-West Spanner, Belt and Braces and Red Ladder. Agit-prop certainly ensures that your message gets to the intended audience, and its impact is immediate, but it has obvious limitations. It is unable to cope with the complex historical progression of events, or with rapid transitions of time and place, essential to a play like *Uranium 235*. To effect this and to create the right atmosphere for each scene the help of music and lighting is needed and a flexible form of staging to break up the stage area for the movements of the actors. So a certain amount of technical equipment is necessary, but provided a group is prepared to load and unload this on to a vehicle and rig and de-rig stages, plays of this kind are mobile and can reach working-class audiences in their own clubs and halls.

All this was done in the one-night-stand tours of Theatre Workshop from 1945 to 1952, which included the South Wales mining villages, the miners' halls of the North-East and the Scottish coalfields. We didn't always play to good houses, but we knew that whoever turned up was almost bound to be working class – there were very few others around. A notable success in our search for working-class audiences was the five performances of *Uranium 235* which we played at Butlin's Holiday Camp at Filey in May 1946. Each episode was applauded as though it was an item on a variety bill, and the enthusiasm shown for what must have been, for most of the audience, a novel theatrical experience, confirmed our belief that there was no need to compromise or 'play down' to working people.

There were no recognised venues or touring circuits in the forties and fifties as there are now, and every hall had to be sought out and booked. We were the only political theatre touring at this time. We had no subsidy, and playing six one-night stands a week for months at a time was very hard work. Notable amongst the many groups now touring the country is John McGrath's 7:84 Company, whose work with popular theatre forms, song, dance and documentary drama has attracted new audiences to the theatre in Scotland and England. David Scase, a founder-member of Theatre Workshop, directed *Johnny Noble* for the 7:84 Company in 1983. At the time of writing this company, as might be expected, has lost its subsidy. Perhaps they should follow Lord Gowrie's advice and seek commercial sponsorship!

An important stimulus to this creation of new audiences has been the setting-up of local community theatres all over the country, usually in non-theatre locations – though occasionally conventional theatres have been put to good use. A feature of the work of Peter Cheeseman (who was also influenced by Theatre Workshop), at the Victoria Theatre, Stoke-on-Trent, has been to extend the Living Newspaper form into historical documentaries of local interest, using idiomatic speech and researched by his own group of actors. The Everyman Theatre, Liverpool, also attracted a largely working-class audience, particularly when John McGrath worked there in 1971 and 1972.

Unfortunately much of socialist theatre tends to play to the converted, thereby restricting its audience to the politically aware, and is thus unable to extend the boundaries of theatre to the apolitical majority. The attraction of a ready made, sympathetic response is understandable, but it is the 'unknown quantity' in an audience that provides the challenge to new ideas and stimulating theatre. It also needs to be accessible to working people, which cannot be said of cultural institutions like the National Theatre, the Royal Shakespeare Company or even the Royal Court. That is not to say that socialist writers like Howard Brenton, David Edgar, David Hare, Edward

Bond and others should not be writing for these theatres any more
than that socialist actors shouldn't act there. They have to make a
living, and the mainly middle-class audiences can only benefit from
being exposed to some of the harsher realities of life through some of
the plays of these writers. David Edgar wrote a few years ago: 'the
most potent, rich and in many ways politically acute theatrical
statements of the past ten years have been made in custom-built
buildings patronised almost exclusively by the middle class'. He
quotes scenes from the plays of Edward Bond, Barry Keeffe and
Howard Barker to illustrate this point. Many of those working in
socialist theatre would disagree, but in any case, however exciting
they may be in theatrical terms, the impact of these political
statements is largely negated if they are inaccessible to those most
directly concerned – the working class. David Edgar goes on to assert
that the form and language of these plays requires, for their understanding, a cultural or academic background denied to the vast majority of people, thus rendering them even more inaccessible. It is
possible to write 'up' as well as 'down'! It is a concept of theatre that
differs substantially from that which motivated the work of Theatre
Workshop and the pre-war Manchester groups that preceded it. From
the early thirties political theatre set out to identify, in its work, with
the lives and language of the industrial working class. The aim was for
a theatre that was widely understood while still able to deal with
complex subjects though a wide variety of theatrical styles. This was
epitomised in plays like *Uranium 235* which reached out to a wide
variety of audiences – from the Comedy Theatre in London's West
End to the holiday-makers at Butlin's Camp in Filey.

While plays written for the 'prestige' theatres cannot be said to
contribute to the building of a popular theatre, these writers have of
course also written extensively for socialists groups, and their contri-
bution in this area has been considerable.

My concern is that the theatre should play a part in enriching the
lives of many more people. I believe that the Theatre Workshop
Manifesto of 1945 still holds good as the basic foundation for a
People's Theatre, and that our first production, *Johnny Noble*, embo-
died, to a large extent, our conception of theatre:

> The great theatres of all times have been popular theatres which
> reflected the dreams and struggles of the people. The theatre of Aeschylus
> and Sophocles, of Shakespeare and Ben Jonson, of the Commedia dell'-
> Arte and Molière derived their inspiration, their language, their art from
> the people.
> We want a theatre with a living language, a theatre which is not afraid of

its own voice and which will comment as fearlessly on Society as did Ben Jonson and Aristophanes.

Theatre Workshop is an organisation of artists, technicians and actors who are experimenting in stage-craft. Its purpose is to create a flexible theatre-art, as swift moving and plastic as the cinema, by applying the recent technical advances in light and sound, and introducing music and the 'dance theatre' style of production.

A popular theatre cannot be built solely on the basis of contemporary plays concerned with the political or social ills of our society. The plays inherited from the great theatres of the past, the Greeks, the Elizabethans, the Commedia dell'arte and the Spanish theatre of Lope de Vega, are the heritage of all people and must not remain, as at present, the privilege of the few. These playwrights wrote for a popular theatre of their own time and many of their themes are still relevant today. Who has matched Ben Jonson's exposure of greed and corruption in *Volpone* and *The Alchemist* or the tyranny of power in Lope de Vega's *The Sheepwell*? The Théâtre National Populaire of Roger Planchon and the political theatre of Erwin Piscator in Weimar Germany, both succeeded in creating a popular theatre on the basis of a wide repertoire of plays including the classics. To their names could be added that of Joan Littlewood.

It was no doubt easier in those optimistic days of 1945 to take a long-term view of the function of the theatre and how it could play its full part in the better times we were certain lay ahead. After all, we had a Labour government with a massive majority ready to lead us to the millennium. Our friendship with the Soviet Union had been cemented in war, never to be broken. Fascism had been defeated, a secure future lay ahead for all mankind, and we were determined to build a theatre worthy of that future. It could be said that the political reality turned out to be a lot less worthy than our theatre; and in the 1980's we see MacMillan's phrase 'the unacceptable face of Capitalism' translated into grim reality. The forces of reaction have never been stronger, and the political and industrial strength of the working class is divided and ineffective in the fight against the evils of our society and the ultimate horror – the threat of nuclear extinction. The miners were defeated by the disunity within their own ranks and the lack of organised workers' support rather than by the government and the N.C.B.

The cutting of Arts subsidies following on the abolition of the G.L.C. and the Metropolitan Boroughs threatens the existence of many groups in the Alternative Theatre movement. No effective proposals have been made by Central government to replace the funding previously provided by local government. The disbanding of theatre groups with a social commitment can only be welcomed by a government antagonistic to all progressive institutions. It is part and parcel of the attack on the quality of life and those who strive to enhance it. If we accept that the legacy of man's achievements in our art galleries and museums must be accessible to all, then, equally, the great plays of the past must be made available, not only on paper in libraries but in performance. They are our allies in the struggle for a more civilised society.

The capacity for theatre to stimulate man's critical awareness and question the accepted tenets of our society makes it a danger to conformism. Rather a 'mass' culture based on Bingo, the Generation Game and soap opera, which serves as an opiate, and whose very triviality ensures that it does not impinge on the workings of society or those who live in it. The concept that Art generally, including theatre, exists to enrich our spirit, to inform and extend our horizons is quite alien to those who are content to see it as a form of relaxation for a largely middle-class minority. The Alternative Theatre movement is not only fighting for its own survival but also, hopefully, for this concept of theatre. In the words of Bertold Brecht:

> How can the theatre be entertaining and instructive at the same time? How can it be taken out of the hands of intellectual drug traffic and become a place offering real experiences rather than illusions? How can the unliberated and unknowing man of our century with his thirst for knowledge and freedom, the tortured and heroic, misused and inventive man of our terrible and great century, himself changeable and yet able to change the world, how can he be given a theatre which will help him to be master of his world?

A scene from the ballet sequence, 'Journey into the Senses' in Ewan MacColl's " The Other Animals." In the cage—right, the Prisoner Hanau (Ewan MacColl) and left, His Projection of Himself (David Scase) surrounded by Characters in his Dreams.

Theatre workshop

THE GROUP THEATRE

"The Other Animals"

BY

EWAN MacCOLL

PRODUCED BY JOAN LITTLEWOOD

SEPTEMBER 5th to 10th at 7.30

Programme . 6d.